I0019002

GNU Texinfo 6.0

A catalogue record for this book is available from the Hong Kong Public Libraries.

Published in Hong Kong by Samurai Media Limited.

Email: info@samuraimedia.org

ISBN 978-988-8381-38-8

Copyright 1988, 1990, 1991, 1992, 1993, 1995, 1996, 1997, 1998, 1999, 2001, 2001, 2003, 2004, 2005, 2006, 2007, 2008, 2009, 2010, 2011, 2012, 2013, 2014, 2015 Free Software Foundation, Inc.
Permission is granted to copy, distribute and/or modify this document under the terms of the GNU Free Documentation License, Version 1.3 or any later version published by the Free Software Foundation; with no Invariant Sections, with the Front-Cover Texts being A GNU Manual, and with the Back-Cover Texts as in (a) below. A copy of the license is included in the section entitled GNU Free Documentation License. (a) The FSFs Back-Cover Text is: You have the freedom to copy and modify this GNU manual. Buying copies from the FSF supports it in developing GNU and promoting software freedom.

Minor modifications for publication Copyright 2015 Samurai Media Limited.

Background Cover Image by https://www.flickr.com/people/webtreatsetc/

Short Contents

Table of Contents

22 `texi2any`: The Generic Translator for Texinfo

23 Creating and Installing Info Files

24 Generating HTML

Appendix A @-Command List

Documentation is like sex: when it is good, it is very, very good; and when it is bad, it is better than nothing. —Dick Brandon

Texinfo Copying Conditions

GNU Texinfo is *free software*; this means that everyone is free to use it and free to redistribute it on certain conditions. Texinfo is not in the public domain; it is copyrighted and there are restrictions on its distribution, but these restrictions are designed to permit everything that a good cooperating citizen would want to do. What is not allowed is to try to prevent others from further sharing any version of Texinfo that they might get from you.

Specifically, we want to make sure that you have the right to give away copies of the programs that relate to Texinfo, that you receive source code or else can get it if you want it, that you can change these programs or use pieces of them in new free programs, and that you know you can do these things.

To make sure that everyone has such rights, we have to forbid you to deprive anyone else of these rights. For example, if you distribute copies of the Texinfo related programs, you must give the recipients all the rights that you have. You must make sure that they, too, receive or can get the source code. And you must tell them their rights.

Also, for our own protection, we must make certain that everyone finds out that there is no warranty for the programs that relate to Texinfo. If these programs are modified by someone else and passed on, we want their recipients to know that what they have is not what we distributed, so that any problems introduced by others will not reflect on our reputation.

The precise conditions of the licenses for the programs currently being distributed that relate to Texinfo are found in the General Public Licenses that accompany them. This manual is covered by the GNU Free Documentation License (see Appendix G [GNU Free Documentation License], page 287).

1 Overview of Texinfo

Texinfo is a documentation system that uses a single source file to produce both online information and printed output. This means that instead of writing two different documents, one for the online information and the other for a printed work, you need write only one document. Therefore, when the work is revised, you need revise only that one document.

Texinfo's markup commands are almost entirely *semantic*; that is, they specify the intended meaning of text in the document, rather than physical formatting instructions.

Texinfo was devised for the purpose of writing software documentation and manuals. It is not, and was never intended to be, a general-purpose formatting program. If you need to lay out a newspaper, devise a glossy magazine ad, or follow the exact formatting requirements of a publishing house, Texinfo is not the simplest tool. On the other hand, if you want to write a good manual for your program, Texinfo has many features that will make your job easier. Overall, it's intended to let you concentrate on the content, and thus provides almost no commands for controlling the final formatting.

The first syllable of "Texinfo" is pronounced like "speck", not "hex". This odd pronunciation is derived from, but is not the same as, the pronunciation of TeX. In the word TeX, the 'X' is actually the Greek letter "chi" rather than the English letter "ex". Pronounce TeX as if the 'X' were the last sound in the name 'Bach'; but pronounce Texinfo as if the 'x' were a 'k'. Spell "Texinfo" with a capital "T" and the other letters in lowercase.

Manuals for most GNU packages are written in Texinfo, and available online at `http://www.gnu.org/doc`.

1.1 Reporting Bugs

We welcome bug reports and suggestions for any aspect of the Texinfo system: programs, documentation, installation, etc. Please email them to `bug-texinfo@gnu.org`. You can get the latest version of Texinfo via its home page, `http://www.gnu.org/software/texinfo`.

For bug reports, please include enough information for the maintainers to reproduce the problem. Generally speaking, that means:

- The version number of Texinfo and the program(s) or manual(s) involved.
- The contents of any input files necessary to reproduce the bug.
- Precisely how you ran any program(s) involved.
- A description of the problem and samples of any erroneous output.
- Hardware and operating system names and versions.
- Anything else that you think would be helpful.

When in doubt whether something is needed or not, include it. It's better to include too much than to leave out something important.

It is critical to send an actual input file that reproduces the problem. What's not critical is to "narrow down" the example to the smallest possible input—the actual input with which you discovered the bug will suffice. (Of course, if you do do experiments, the smaller the input file, the better.)

Patches are most welcome; if possible, please make them with '`diff -c`' (see *Comparing and Merging Files*) and include `ChangeLog` entries (see Section "Change Log" in *The GNU Emacs Manual*), and follow the existing coding style.

1.2 Using Texinfo

Using Texinfo, you can create a printed document (via the TEX typesetting system) with the normal features of a book, including chapters, sections, cross references, and indices. From the same Texinfo source file, you can create an Info file with special features to make documentation browsing easy. Also from that same source file, you can create an HTML output file suitable for use with a web browser, a Docbook file, or a transliteration in XML format. See the next section for details and sample commands to generate output from the source (see Section 1.3 [Output Formats], page 4).

TEX works with virtually all printers; Info works with virtually all computer terminals; the HTML output works with virtually all web browsers. Thus Texinfo and its output can be used by almost any computer user.

A Texinfo source file is a plain ASCII file containing text interspersed with @-*commands* (words preceded by an '@') that tell the Texinfo processors what to do. You can edit a Texinfo file with any text editor, but it is especially convenient to use GNU Emacs since that editor has a special mode, called Texinfo mode, that provides various Texinfo-related features. (See Chapter 2 [Texinfo Mode], page 17.)

Texinfo is the official documentation format of the GNU project. More information is available at the GNU documentation web page (`http://www.gnu.org/doc/`).

1.3 Output Formats

Here is a brief overview of the output formats currently supported by Texinfo.

Info   (Generated via `makeinfo`.) Info format is mostly a plain text transliteration of the Texinfo source. It adds a few control characters to separate nodes and provide navigational information for menus, cross references, indices, and so on. The Emacs Info subsystem (see *Info*), and the standalone `info` program (see *GNU Info*), among others, can read these files. See Section 1.6 [Info Files], page 7, and Chapter 23 [Creating and Installing Info Files], page 213.

Plain text   (Generated via `makeinfo --plaintext`.) This is almost the same as Info output with the navigational control characters are omitted.

HTML   (Generated via `makeinfo --html`.) HTML, standing for Hyper Text Markup Language, has become the most commonly used language for writing documents on the World Wide Web. Web browsers, such as Mozilla, Lynx, and Emacs-W3, can render this language online. There are many versions of HTML, both different standards and browser-specific variations. `makeinfo` tries to use a subset of the language that can be interpreted by any common browser, intentionally not using many newer or less widely-supported tags. Although the native output is thus rather plain, it can be customized at various levels, if desired. For details of the HTML language and much related information, see `http://www.w3.org/MarkUp/`. See Chapter 24 [Generating HTML], page 223.

DVI   (Generated via `texi2dvi`.) The DeVIce Independent binary format is output by the TEX typesetting program (`http://tug.org`). This is then read by a DVI 'driver', which knows the actual device-specific commands that can be viewed or printed, notably Dvips for translation to PostScript (see *Dvips*) and Xdvi for viewing on an X display (`http://sourceforge.net/projects/xdvi/`). See Chapter 21 [Hardcopy], page 177. (Be aware that the Texinfo language is very different from and much stricter than TEX's usual languages: plain TEX, LATEX, ConTEXt, etc.)

PostScript (Generated via `texi2dvi --ps`.) PostScript is a page description language that became widely used around 1985 and is still used today. `http://en.wikipedia.org/wiki/PostScript` gives a basic description and more preferences. By default, Texinfo uses the `dvips` program to convert TEX's DVI output to PostScript. See *Dvips*.

PDF (Generated via `texi2dvi --pdf` or `texi2pdf`.) This format was developed by Adobe Systems for portable document interchange, based on their previous PostScript language. It can represent the exact appearance of a document, including fonts and graphics, and supporting arbitrary scaling. It is intended to be platform-independent and easily viewable, among other design goals; `http://en.wikipedia.org/wiki/Portable_Document_Format` and `http://tug.org/TUGboat/tb22-3/tb72beebe-pdf.pdf` have some background. By default, Texinfo uses the `pdftex` program, an extension of TEX, to output PDF; see `http://tug.org/applications/pdftex`. See Section 21.15 [PDF Output], page 187.

Docbook (Generated via `makeinfo --docbook`.) This is an XML-based format developed some years ago, primarily for technical documentation. It therefore bears some resemblance, in broad outline, to Texinfo. See `http://www.docbook.org`. Various converters from Docbook *to* Texinfo have also been developed; see the Texinfo web pages.

XML (Generated via `makeinfo --xml`.) XML is a generic syntax specification usable for any sort of content (a reference is at `http://www.w3.org/XML`). The `makeinfo` XML output, unlike all the other output formats, is a transliteration of the Texinfo source rather than processed output. That is, it translates the Texinfo markup commands into XML syntax, for further processing by XML tools. The details of the output are defined in an XML DTD as usual, which is contained in a file `texinfo.dtd` included in the Texinfo source distribution and available via the Texinfo web pages. The XML contains enough information to recreate the original content, except for syntactic constructs such as Texinfo macros and conditionals. The Texinfo source distribution includes a utility script `txixml2texi` to do that backward transformation.

1.4 Adding Output Formats

The output formats in the previous section handle a wide variety of usage, but of course there is always room for more.

From time to time, proposals are made to generate traditional Unix man pages from Texinfo source. However, because man pages have a strict conventional format, creating a good man page requires a completely different source than the typical Texinfo applications of writing a good user tutorial and/or a good reference manual. This makes generating man pages incompatible with the Texinfo design goal of not having to document the same information in different ways for different output formats. You might as well write the man page directly.

As an alternative way to support man pages, you may find the program `help2man` to be useful. It generates a traditional man page from the '`--help`' output of a program. In fact, the man pages for the programs in the Texinfo distribution are generated with this. It is GNU software written by Brendan O'Dea, available from `http://www.gnu.org/software/help2man`.

If you are a programmer and would like to contribute to the GNU project by implementing additional output formats for Texinfo, that would be excellent. The way to do this that would be most useful is to write a new back-end for `texi2any`, our reference implementation of a Texinfo parser; it creates a tree representation of the Texinfo input that you can use for the conversion. The documentation in the source file `tp/Texinfo/Convert/Converter.pm` is a good place to start. See Chapter 22 [Generic Translator `texi2any`], page 189.

Another viable approach is use the Texinfo XML output from `texi2any` as your input. This XML is an essentially complete representation of the input, but without the Texinfo syntax and option peculiarities, as described above.

If you still cannot resist the temptation of writing a new program that reads Texinfo source directly, let us give some more caveats: please do not underestimate the amount of work required. Texinfo is by no means a simple language to parse correctly, and remains under development, so you would be committing to an ongoing task. At a minimum, please check that the extensive tests of the language that come with `texi2any` give correct results with your new program.

1.5 Texinfo Document Structure

Texinfo documents most usefully have a double structure, reflecting the double purposes of printed and online output. For printed output (DVI, PDF, . . .), with physical pages, there are chapters, sections, subsections, etc. For online output (Info, HTML, . . .), with interactive navigation and no physical pages, there are so-called "nodes".

Typically, the sectioning structure and the node structure are completely parallel, with one node for each chapter, section, etc., and with the nodes following the same hierarchical arrangement as the sectioning. Thus, if a node is at the logical level of a chapter, its child nodes are at the level of sections; similarly, the child nodes of sections are at the level of subsections.

Each *node* has a name, and contains the discussion of one topic. Along with the text for the user to read, each node also has pointers to other nodes, identified in turn by their own names. Info readers display one node at a time, and provide commands for the user to move to related nodes. The HTML output can be similarly navigated.

The names of child nodes are listed in a *menu* within the parent node; for example, a node corresponding to a chapter would have a menu of the sections in that chapter. The menus allow the user to move to the child nodes in a natural way in the online output.

In addition, nodes at the same level are formed into a chain with 'Next' and 'Previous' pointers. As you might imagine, the 'Next' pointer links to the next node (section), and the 'Previous' pointer links to the previous node (section). Thus, for example, all the nodes that are at the level of sections within a chapter are linked together, and the order in this chain is the same as the order of the children in the menu of parent chapter. Each child node records the parent node name as its 'Up' pointer. The last child has no 'Next' pointer, and the first child has the parent both as its 'Previous' and as its 'Up' pointer.

In addition to menus and 'Next', 'Previous', and 'Up' pointers, Texinfo provides pointers of another kind for cross references, that can be sprinkled throughout the text. This is usually the best way to represent links that do not fit a hierarchical structure.

Although it is technically possible to create Texinfo documents with only one structure or the other, or for the two structures not to be parallel, or for either the sectioning or node structure to be abnormally formed, etc., this is *not at all recommended*. To the best of our knowledge, all the Texinfo manuals currently in general use do follow the conventional parallel structure.

1.6 Info Files

As mentioned above, Info format is mostly a plain text transliteration of the Texinfo source, with the addition of a few control characters to separate nodes and provide navigational information, so that Info-reading programs can operate on it.

Info files are nearly always created by processing a Texinfo source document. `makeinfo`, also known as `texi2any`, is the principal command that converts a Texinfo file into an Info file; see Chapter 22 [Generic Translator `texi2any`], page 189.

Generally, you enter an Info file through a node that by convention is named 'Top'. This node normally contains just a brief summary of the file's purpose, and a large menu through which the rest of the file is reached. From this node, you can either traverse the file systematically by going from node to node, or you can go to a specific node listed in the main menu, or you can search the index menus and then go directly to the node that has the information you want. Alternatively, with the standalone Info program, you can specify specific menu items on the command line (see *Info*).

If you want to read through an Info file in sequence, as if it were a printed manual, you can hit SPC repeatedly, or you get the whole file with the advanced Info command *g* *. (See Section "Advanced Info commands" in *Info*.)

The `dir` file in the `info` directory serves as the departure point for the whole Info system. From it, you can reach the 'Top' nodes of each of the documents in a complete Info system.

If you wish to refer to an Info file via a URI, you can use the (unofficial) syntax exemplified by the following. This works with Emacs/W3, for example:

```
info:emacs#Dissociated%20Press
info:///usr/info/emacs#Dissociated%20Press
info://localhost/usr/info/emacs#Dissociated%20Press
```

The `info` program itself does not follow URIs of any kind.

1.7 Printed Books

A Texinfo file can be formatted and typeset as a printed book or manual. To do this, you need TEX, a sophisticated typesetting program written by Donald Knuth of Stanford University.

A Texinfo-based book is similar to any other typeset, printed work: it can have a title page, copyright page, table of contents, and preface, as well as chapters, numbered or unnumbered sections and subsections, page headers, cross references, footnotes, and indices.

TEX is a general purpose typesetting program. Texinfo provides a file `texinfo.tex` that contains information (definitions or *macros*) that TEX uses when it typesets a Texinfo file. (`texinfo.tex` tells TEX how to convert the Texinfo @-commands to TEX commands, which TEX can then process to create the typeset document.) `texinfo.tex` contains the specifications for printing a document. You can get the latest version of `texinfo.tex` from the Texinfo home page, `http://www.gnu.org/software/texinfo/`.

In the United States, documents are most often printed on 8.5 inch by 11 inch pages (216 mm by 280 mm); this is the default size. But you can also print for 7 inch by 9.25 inch pages (178 mm by 235 mm, the `@smallbook` size; or on A4 or A5 size paper (`@afourpaper`, `@afivepaper`). See Section 21.11 [`@smallbook`], page 186, and Section 21.12 [A4 Paper], page 186.

TEX is freely distributable. It is written in a superset of Pascal for literate programming called WEB and can be compiled either in Pascal or (by using a conversion program that comes with the TEX distribution) in C.

TEX is very powerful and has a great many features. Because a Texinfo file must be able to present information both on a character-only terminal in Info form and in a typeset book, the formatting commands that Texinfo supports are necessarily limited.

See Section 21.16 [Obtaining TEX], page 188, for information on acquiring TEX. It is not part of the Texinfo distribution.

1.8 @-commands

In a Texinfo file, the commands you write to describe the contents of the manual are preceded by an '@' character; they are called *@-commands*. For example, `@node` is the command to indicate a node and `@chapter` is the command to indicate the start of a chapter. Almost all @ command names are entirely lowercase.

Texinfo's @-commands are a strictly limited set of constructs. The strict limits are primarily intended to "force" you, the author, to concentrate on the writing and the content of your manual, rather than the details of the formatting.

Depending on what they do or what arguments[1] they take, you need to write @-commands on lines of their own or as part of sentences:

- Some commands are written at the start of a line and the rest of the line comprises the argument text, such as `@chapter` (which creates chapter titles).

- Some commands can appear anywhere, generally within a sentence, and are followed by empty braces, such as `@dots{}` (which creates an ellipsis . . .).

---

[1] The word *argument* comes from the way it is used in mathematics and does not refer to a dispute between two people; it refers to the information presented to the command. According to the *Oxford English Dictionary*, the word derives from the Latin for *to make clear, prove*; thus it came to mean 'the evidence offered as proof', which is to say, 'the information offered', which led to its mathematical meaning. In its other thread of derivation, the word came to mean 'to assert in a manner against which others may make counter assertions', which led to the meaning of 'argument' as a dispute.

- Some commands can appear anywhere, generally within a sentence, and are followed by the argument text in braces, such as `@code{a+1}` (which marks text as being code, `a+1` being the argument in this case).

- Some commands are written at the start of a line, with general text on following lines, terminated by a matching `@end` command on a line of its own. For example, `@example`, then the lines of a coding example, then `@end example`.

As a general rule, a command requires braces if it mingles among other text; but it does not need braces if it is on a line of its own. The non-alphabetic commands, such as `@:`, are exceptions to the rule; they do not need braces.

As you gain experience with Texinfo, you will rapidly learn how to write the different commands: the different ways to write commands actually make it easier to write and read Texinfo files than if all commands followed exactly the same syntax. See Section A.1 [@-Command Syntax], page 256, for all the details.

1.9 General Syntactic Conventions

This section describes the general conventions used in all Texinfo documents.

- All printable ASCII characters except '`@`', '`{`' and '`}`' can appear in a Texinfo file and stand for themselves. '`@`' is the escape character which introduces commands, while '`{`' and '`}`' are used to surround arguments to certain commands. To put one of these special characters into the document, put an '`@`' character in front of it, like this: '`@@`', '`@{`', and '`@}`'.

- Texinfo supports the usual quotation marks used in English and in other languages; see Section 14.5 [Inserting Quotation Marks], page 125.

- Use three hyphens in a row, '`---`', to produce a long dash—like this (called an *em dash*), used for punctuation in sentences. Use two hyphens, '`--`', to produce a medium dash (called an *en dash*), used primarily for numeric ranges, as in "June 25–26". Use a single hyphen, '`-`', to produce a standard hyphen used in compound words. For display on the screen, Info reduces three hyphens to two and two hyphens to one (not transitively!). Of course, any number of hyphens in the source remain as they are in literal contexts, such as `@code` and `@example`.

- Form feed (*CTRL-l*) characters in the input are handled as follows:

  PDF/DVI   In normal text, treated as ending any open paragraph; essentially ignored between paragraphs.

  Info   Output as-is between paragraphs (their most common use); in other contexts, they may be treated as regular spaces (and thus consolidated with surrounding whitespace).

  HTML   Written as a numeric entity except contexts where spaces are ignored; for example, in '`@footnote{ ^L foo}`', the form feed is ignored.

  XML   Keep them everywhere; in attributes, escaped as '`\f`'; also, '`\`' is escaped as '`\\`' and newline as '`\n`'.

  Docbook   Completely removed, as they are not allowed.

As you can see, because of these differing requirements of the output formats, it's not possible to use form feeds completely portably.

- **Caution:** Last, do not use tab characters in a Texinfo file! (Except perhaps in verbatim modes.) TEX uses variable-width fonts, which means that it is impractical at best to define a tab to work in all circumstances. Consequently, TEX treats tabs like single spaces, and that is not what they look like in the source. Furthermore, `makeinfo` does nothing special with tabs, and thus a tab character in your input file will usually have a different appearance in the output.

  To avoid this problem, Texinfo mode in GNU Emacs inserts multiple spaces when you press the `TAB` key. Also, you can run `untabify` in Emacs to convert tabs in a region to multiple spaces, or use the `unexpand` command from the shell.

1.10 Comments

You can write comments in a Texinfo file by using the `@comment` command, which may be abbreviated to `@c`. Such comments are for a person looking at the Texinfo source file. All the text on a line that follows either `@comment` or `@c` is a comment; the rest of the line does not appear in the visible output. (To be precise, the character after the `@c` or `@comment` must be something other than a dash or alphanumeric, or it will be taken as part of the command.)

Often, you can write the `@comment` or `@c` in the middle of a line, and only the text that follows after the `@comment` or `@c` command does not appear; but some commands, such as `@settitle` and `@setfilename`, work on a whole line. You cannot use `@comment` or `@c` within a line beginning with such a command.

In cases of nested command invocations, complicated macro definitions, etc., `@c` and `@comment` may provoke an error when processing with TEX. Therefore, you can also use the *DEL* character (ASCII 127 decimal, 0x7f hex, 0177 octal) as a true TEX comment character (catcode 14, in TEX internals). Everything on the line after the *DEL* will be ignored.

You can also have long stretches of text ignored by the Texinfo processors with the `@ignore` and `@end ignore` commands. Write each of these commands on a line of its own, starting each command at the beginning of the line. Text between these two commands does not appear in the processed output. You can use `@ignore` and `@end ignore` for writing comments. (For some caveats regarding nesting of such commands, see Section 18.7 [Conditional Nesting], page 164.)

1.11 What a Texinfo File Must Have

By convention, the name of a Texinfo file ends with (in order of preference) one of the extensions `.texinfo`, `.texi`, `.txi`, or `.tex`. The longer extensions are preferred since they describe more clearly to a human reader the nature of the file. The shorter extensions are for operating systems that cannot handle long file names.

In order to be made into a good printed manual and other output formats, a Texinfo file *must* begin with lines like this:

```
\input texinfo
@setfilename info-file-name
@settitle name-of-manual
```

The contents of the file follow this beginning, and then you *must* end the Texinfo source with a line like this:

```
@bye
```

Here's an explanation:

- The '\input texinfo' line tells TEX to use the `texinfo.tex` file, which tells TEX how to translate the Texinfo @-commands into TEX typesetting commands. (Note the use of the backslash, '\'; this is correct for TEX.)

- The `@setfilename` line provides a name for the Info file and tells TEX to open auxiliary files. **All text before `@setfilename` is ignored!**

- The `@settitle` line specifies a title for the page headers (or footers) of the printed manual, and the default title and document description for the '`<head>`' in HTML. Strictly speaking, `@settitle` is optional—if you don't mind your document being titled 'Untitled'.

- The `@bye` line at the end of the file on a line of its own tells the formatters that the file is ended and to stop formatting.

If you use Emacs, it is also useful to include mode setting and start-of-header and end-of-header lines at the beginning of a Texinfo file, like this:

```
\input texinfo    @c -*-texinfo-*-
@c %**start of header
@setfilename info-file-name
@settitle name-of-manual
@c %**end of header
```

In the first line, '-*-texinfo-*-' causes Emacs to switch into Texinfo mode when you edit the file.

The `@c ...header` lines above which surround the `@setfilename` and `@settitle` lines allow you to process, within Emacs, just part of the Texinfo source. (See Section 3.2.2 [Start of Header], page 31.)

Furthermore, you will usually provide a Texinfo file with a title page, indices, and the like, all of which are explained in this manual. But the minimum, which can be useful for short documents, is just the three lines at the beginning and the one line at the end.

1.12 Six Parts of a Texinfo File

Generally, a Texinfo file contains more than the minimal beginning and end described in the previous section—it usually contains the six parts listed below. These are described fully in the following sections.

1. Header   The *Header* names the file, tells TEX which definitions file to use, and other such housekeeping tasks.

2. Summary and Copyright

    The *Summary and Copyright* segment describes the document and contains the copyright notice and copying permissions. This is done with the `@copying` command.

3. Title and Copyright

The *Title and Copyright* segment contains the title and copyright pages for the printed manual. The segment must be enclosed between `@titlepage` and `@end titlepage` commands. The title and copyright page appear only in the printed manual.

4. 'Top' Node and Master Menu

The 'Top' node starts off the online output; it does not appear in the printed manual. We recommend including the copying permissions here as well as the segments above. And it contains at least a top-level menu listing the chapters, and possibly a *Master Menu* listing all the nodes in the entire document.

5. Body   The *Body* of the document is typically structured like a traditional book or encyclopedia, but it may be free form.

6. End   The *End* segment may contain commands for printing indices, and closes with the `@bye` command on a line of its own.

1.13 A Short Sample Texinfo File

Here is a very short but complete Texinfo file, in the six conventional parts enumerated in the previous section, so you can see how Texinfo source appears in practice. The first three parts of the file, from '\input texinfo' through to '@end titlepage', look more intimidating than they are: most of the material is standard boilerplate; when writing a manual, you simply change the names as appropriate.

See Chapter 3 [Beginning a File], page 29, for full documentation on the commands listed here. See Section C.2 [GNU Sample Texts], page 264, for the full texts to be used in GNU manuals.

In the following, the sample text is *indented*; comments on it are not. The complete file, without interspersed comments, is shown in Section C.1 [Short Sample Texinfo File], page 263.

Part 1: Header

The header does not appear in either the Info file or the printed output. It sets various parameters, including the name of the Info file and the title used in the header.

```
\input texinfo   @c -*-texinfo-*-
@c %**start of header
@setfilename sample.info
@settitle Sample Manual 1.0
@c %**end of header
```

Part 2: Summary Description and Copyright

A real manual includes more text here, according to the license under which it is distributed. See Section C.2 [GNU Sample Texts], page 264.

```
@copying
This is a short example of a complete Texinfo file, version 1.0.

Copyright @copyright{} 2015 Free Software Foundation, Inc.
@end copying
```

Part 3: Titlepage, Contents, Copyright

The titlepage segment does not appear in the online output, only in the printed manual. We use the `@insertcopying` command to include the permission text from the previous section, instead of writing it out again; it is output on the back of the title page. The `@contents` command generates a table of contents.

```
@titlepage
@title Sample Title

@c The following two commands start the copyright page.
@page
@vskip 0pt plus 1filll
@insertcopying
@end titlepage

@c Output the table of contents at the beginning.
@contents
```

Part 4: 'Top' Node and Master Menu

The 'Top' node contains the master menu for the Info file. Since the printed manual uses a table of contents rather than a menu, it excludes the 'Top' node. We repeat the short description from the beginning of the '`@copying`' text, but there's no need to repeat the copyright information, so we don't use '`@insertcopying`' here. The '`@top`' command itself helps `makeinfo` determine the relationships between nodes.

```
@ifnottex
@node Top
@top Short Sample

This is a short sample Texinfo file.
@end ifnottex

@menu
* First Chapter::    The first chapter is the
                       only chapter in this sample.
* Index::            Complete index.
@end menu
```

Part 5: The Body of the Document

The body segment contains all the text of the document, but not the indices or table of contents. This example illustrates a node and a chapter containing an enumerated list.

```
@node First Chapter
@chapter First Chapter

@cindex chapter, first

This is the first chapter.
@cindex index entry, another
```

```
Here is a numbered list.

@enumerate
@item
This is the first item.

@item
This is the second item.
@end enumerate
```

Part 6: The End of the Document

The end segment contains commands for generating an index in a node and unnumbered chapter of its own, and the @bye command that marks the end of the document.

```
@node Index
@unnumbered Index

@printindex cp

@bye
```

Some Results

Here is what the contents of the first chapter of the sample look like:

This is the first chapter.

Here is a numbered list.

1. This is the first item.

2. This is the second item.

1.14 History

Richard M. Stallman invented the Texinfo format, wrote the initial processors, and created Edition 1.0 of this manual. Robert J. Chassell greatly revised and extended the manual, starting with Edition 1.1. Brian Fox was responsible for the standalone Texinfo distribution until version 3.8, and originally wrote the standalone `makeinfo` and `info` programs. Karl Berry has continued maintenance since Texinfo 3.8 (manual edition 2.22).

Our thanks go out to all who helped improve this work, particularly the indefatigable Eli Zaretskii and Andreas Schwab, who have provided patches beyond counting. François Pinard and David D. Zuhn, tirelessly recorded and reported mistakes and obscurities. Zack Weinberg did the impossible by implementing the macro syntax in `texinfo.tex`. Thanks to Melissa Weisshaus for her frequent reviews of nearly similar editions. Dozens of others have contributed patches and suggestions, they are gratefully acknowledged in the `ChangeLog` file. Our mistakes are our own.

Beginnings

In the 1970's at CMU, Brian Reid developed a program and format named Scribe to mark up documents for printing. It used the @ character to introduce commands, as Texinfo does. Much more consequentially, it strove to describe document contents rather than formatting, an idea wholeheartedly adopted by Texinfo.

Meanwhile, people at MIT developed another, not too dissimilar format called Bolio. This then was converted to using TeX as its typesetting language: BoTeX. The earliest BoTeX version seems to have been 0.02 on October 31, 1984.

BoTeX could only be used as a markup language for documents to be printed, not for online documents. Richard Stallman (RMS) worked on both Bolio and BoTeX. He also developed a nifty on-line help format called Info, and then combined BoTeX and Info to create Texinfo, a mark up language for text that is intended to be read both online and as printed hard copy.

Moving forward, the original translator to create Info was written (primarily by RMS and Bob Chassell) in Emacs Lisp, namely the `texinfo-format-buffer` and other functions. In the early 1990s, Brian Fox reimplemented the conversion program in C, now called `makeinfo`.

Reimplementing in Perl

In 2012, the C `makeinfo` was itself replaced by a Perl implementation generically called `texi2any`. This version supports the same level of output customization as `texi2html`, an independent program originally written by Lionel Cons, later with substantial work by many others. The many additional features needed to make `texi2html` a replacement for `makeinfo` were implemented by Patrice Dumas. The first never-released version of `texi2any` was based on the `texi2html` code. That implementation, however, was abandoned in favor of the current program, which parses the Texinfo input into a tree for processing. It still supports nearly all the features of `texi2html`.

The new Perl program is much slower than the old C program. We hope the speed gap will close in the future, but it may not ever be entirely comparable. So why did we switch? In short, we intend and hope that the present program will be much easier than the previous C implementation of `makeinfo` to extend to different output styles, back-end output formats, and all other customizations. In more detail:

- HTML customization. Many GNU and other free software packages had been happily using the HTML customization features in `texi2html` for years. Thus, in effect two independent implementations of the Texinfo language had developed, and keeping them in sync was not simple. Adding the HTML customization possible in `texi2html` to a C program would have been an enormous effort.

- Unicode, and multilingual support generally, especially of east Asian languages. Although of course it's perfectly plausible to write such support in C, in the particular case of `makeinfo`, it would have been tantamount to rewriting the entire program. In Perl, much of that comes essentially for free.

- Additional back-ends. The `makeinfo` code had become convoluted to the point where adding a new back-end was quite complex, requiring complex interactions with existing back-ends. In contrast, our Perl implementation provides a clean tree-based representation for all back-ends to work from. People have requested numerous different back-ends (LATEX, the latest (X)HTML, . . .), and they will now be much more feasible to implement. Which leads to the last item:

- Making contributions easier. In general, due to the cleaner structure, the Perl program should be considerably easier than the C for anyone to read and contribute to, with the resulting obvious benefits.

See Section 22.1 [Reference Implementation], page 189, for more on the rationale for and role of `texi2any`.

2 Using Texinfo Mode

You may edit a Texinfo file with any text editor you choose. A Texinfo file is no different from any other ASCII file. However, GNU Emacs comes with a special mode, called Texinfo mode, that provides Emacs commands and tools to help ease your work.

This chapter describes features of GNU Emacs' Texinfo mode but not any features of the Texinfo formatting language. So if you are reading this manual straight through from the beginning, you may want to skim through this chapter briefly and come back to it after reading succeeding chapters which describe the Texinfo formatting language in detail.

2.1 Texinfo Mode Overview

Texinfo mode provides special features for working with Texinfo files. You can:

- Insert frequently used @-commands.
- Automatically create `@node` lines.
- Show the structure of a Texinfo source file.
- Automatically create or update the 'Next', 'Previous', and 'Up' pointers of a node.
- Automatically create or update menus.
- Automatically create a master menu.
- Format a part or all of a file for Info.
- Typeset and print part or all of a file.

Perhaps the two most helpful features are those for inserting frequently used @-commands and for creating node pointers and menus.

2.2 The Usual GNU Emacs Editing Commands

In most cases, the usual Text mode commands work the same in Texinfo mode as they do in Text mode. Texinfo mode adds new editing commands and tools to GNU Emacs' general purpose editing features. The major difference concerns filling. In Texinfo mode, the paragraph separation variable and syntax table are redefined so that Texinfo commands that should be on lines of their own are not inadvertently included in paragraphs. Thus, the `M-q` (`fill-paragraph`) command will refill a paragraph but not mix an indexing command on a line adjacent to it into the paragraph.

In addition, Texinfo mode sets the `page-delimiter` variable to the value of `texinfo-chapter-level-regexp`; by default, this is a regular expression matching the commands for chapters and their equivalents, such as appendices. With this value for the page delimiter, you can jump from chapter title to chapter title with the `C-x ]` (`forward-page`) and `C-x [` (`backward-page`) commands and narrow to a chapter with the `C-x n p` (`narrow-to-page`) command. (See Section "Pages" in *The GNU Emacs Manual*, for details about the page commands.)

You may name a Texinfo file however you wish, but the convention is to end a Texinfo file name with one of the extensions `.texinfo`, `.texi`, `.txi`, or `.tex`. A longer extension is preferred, since it is explicit, but a shorter extension may be necessary for operating systems that limit the length of file names. GNU Emacs automatically enters Texinfo mode when you visit a file with a `.texinfo`, `.texi` or `.txi` extension. Also, Emacs switches to

Texinfo mode when you visit a file that has '-*-texinfo-*-' in its first line. If ever you are in another mode and wish to switch to Texinfo mode, type M-x texinfo-mode.

Like all other Emacs features, you can customize or enhance Texinfo mode as you wish. In particular, the keybindings are very easy to change. The keybindings described here are the default or standard ones.

2.3 Inserting Frequently Used Commands

Texinfo mode provides commands to insert various frequently used @-commands into the buffer. You can use these commands to save keystrokes.

The insert commands are invoked by typing *C-c* twice and then the first letter of the @-command:

C-c C-c c
M-x texinfo-insert-@code
>   Insert @code{} and put the cursor between the braces.

C-c C-c d
M-x texinfo-insert-@dfn
>   Insert @dfn{} and put the cursor between the braces.

C-c C-c e
M-x texinfo-insert-@end
>   Insert @end and attempt to insert the correct following word, such as 'example' or 'table'. (This command does not handle nested lists correctly, but inserts the word appropriate to the immediately preceding list.)

C-c C-c i
M-x texinfo-insert-@item
>   Insert @item and put the cursor at the beginning of the next line.

C-c C-c k
M-x texinfo-insert-@kbd
>   Insert @kbd{} and put the cursor between the braces.

C-c C-c n
M-x texinfo-insert-@node
>   Insert @node and a comment line listing the sequence for the 'Next', 'Previous', and 'Up' nodes. Leave point after the @node.

C-c C-c o
M-x texinfo-insert-@noindent
>   Insert @noindent and put the cursor at the beginning of the next line.

C-c C-c s
M-x texinfo-insert-@samp
>   Insert @samp{} and put the cursor between the braces.

C-c C-c t
M-x texinfo-insert-@table
>   Insert @table followed by a SPC and leave the cursor after the SPC.

`C-c C-c v`
`M-x texinfo-insert-@var`

> Insert @var{} and put the cursor between the braces.

`C-c C-c x`
`M-x texinfo-insert-@example`

> Insert @example and put the cursor at the beginning of the next line.

`C-c C-c {`
`M-x texinfo-insert-braces`

> Insert {} and put the cursor between the braces.

`C-c }`
`C-c ]`
`M-x up-list`

> Move from between a pair of braces forward past the closing brace. Typing `C-c ]` is easier than typing `C-c }`, which is, however, more mnemonic; hence the two keybindings. (Also, you can move out from between braces by typing `C-f`.)

To put a command such as @code{...} around an *existing* word, position the cursor in front of the word and type `C-u 1 C-c C-c c`. This makes it easy to edit existing plain text. The value of the prefix argument tells Emacs how many words following point to include between braces—'1' for one word, '2' for two words, and so on. Use a negative argument to enclose the previous word or words. If you do not specify a prefix argument, Emacs inserts the @-command string and positions the cursor between the braces. This feature works only for those @-commands that operate on a word or words within one line, such as @kbd and @var.

This set of insert commands was created after analyzing the frequency with which different @-commands are used in the *GNU Emacs Manual* and the *GDB Manual*. If you wish to add your own insert commands, you can bind a keyboard macro to a key, use abbreviations, or extend the code in `texinfo.el`.

`C-c C-c C-d` (texinfo-start-menu-description) is an insert command that works differently from the other insert commands. It inserts a node's section or chapter title in the space for the description in a menu entry line. (A menu entry has three parts, the entry name, the node name, and the description. Only the node name is required, but a description helps explain what the node is about. See Section 7.3 [The Parts of a Menu], page 63.)

To use `texinfo-start-menu-description`, position point in a menu entry line and type `C-c C-c C-d`. The command looks for and copies the title that goes with the node name, and inserts the title as a description; it positions point at beginning of the inserted text so you can edit it. The function does not insert the title if the menu entry line already contains a description.

This command is only an aid to writing descriptions; it does not do the whole job. You must edit the inserted text since a title tends to use the same words as a node name but a useful description uses different words.

2.4 Showing the Sectioning Structure of a File

You can show the sectioning structure of a Texinfo file by using the `C-c C-s` command (`texinfo-show-structure`). This command lists the lines that begin with the @-commands for @chapter, @section, and the like. It constructs what amounts to a table of contents. These lines are displayed in another buffer called the '*Occur*' buffer. In that buffer, you can position the cursor over one of the lines and use the `C-c C-c` command (occur-mode-goto-occurrence), to jump to the corresponding spot in the Texinfo file.

`C-c C-s`
`M-x texinfo-show-structure`
> Show the @chapter, @section, and such lines of a Texinfo file.

`C-c C-c`
`M-x occur-mode-goto-occurrence`
> Go to the line in the Texinfo file corresponding to the line under the cursor in the *Occur* buffer.

If you call `texinfo-show-structure` with a prefix argument by typing `C-u C-c C-s`, it will list not only those lines with the @-commands for @chapter, @section, and the like, but also the @node lines. You can use `texinfo-show-structure` with a prefix argument to check whether the 'Next', 'Previous', and 'Up' pointers of an @node line are correct.

Often, when you are working on a manual, you will be interested only in the structure of the current chapter. In this case, you can mark off the region of the buffer that you are interested in by using the `C-x n n` (narrow-to-region) command and `texinfo-show-structure` will work on only that region. To see the whole buffer again, use `C-x n w` (widen). (See Section "Narrowing" in *The GNU Emacs Manual*, for more information about the narrowing commands.)

In addition to providing the `texinfo-show-structure` command, Texinfo mode sets the value of the page delimiter variable to match the chapter-level @-commands. This enables you to use the `C-x ]` (forward-page) and `C-x [` (backward-page) commands to move forward and backward by chapter, and to use the `C-x n p` (narrow-to-page) command to narrow to a chapter. See Section "Pages" in *The GNU Emacs Manual*, for more information about the page commands.

2.5 Updating Nodes and Menus

Texinfo mode provides commands for automatically creating or updating menus and node pointers. The commands are called "update" commands because their most frequent use is for updating a Texinfo file after you have worked on it; but you can use them to insert the 'Next', 'Previous', and 'Up' pointers into an @node line that has none and to create menus in a file that has none.

If you do not use any updating commands, you need to write menus and node pointers by hand, which is a tedious task.

2.5.1 The Updating Commands

You can use the updating commands to:

- insert or update the 'Next', 'Previous', and 'Up' pointers of a node,

- insert or update the menu for a section, and

- create a master menu for a Texinfo source file.

You can also use the commands to update all the nodes and menus in a region or in a whole Texinfo file.

The updating commands work only with conventional Texinfo files, which are structured hierarchically like books. In such files, a structuring command line must follow closely after each @node line, except for the 'Top' @node line. (A *structuring command line* is a line beginning with @chapter, @section, or other similar command.)

You can write the structuring command line on the line that follows immediately after an @node line or else on the line that follows after a single @comment line or a single @ifinfo line. You cannot interpose more than one line between the @node line and the structuring command line; and you may interpose only an @comment line or an @ifinfo line.

Commands which work on a whole buffer require that the 'Top' node be followed by a node with an @chapter or equivalent-level command. The menu updating commands will not create a main or master menu for a Texinfo file that has only @chapter-level nodes! The menu updating commands only create menus *within* nodes for lower level nodes. To create a menu of chapters, you must provide a 'Top' node.

The menu updating commands remove menu entries that refer to other Info files since they do not refer to nodes within the current buffer. This is a deficiency. Rather than use menu entries, you can use cross references to refer to other Info files. None of the updating commands affect cross references.

Texinfo mode has five updating commands that are used most often: two are for updating the node pointers or menu of a single node (or a region); two are for updating every node pointer and menu in a file; and one, the texinfo-master-menu command, is for creating a master menu for a complete file, and optionally, for updating every node and menu in the whole Texinfo file.

The texinfo-master-menu command is the primary command:

C-c C-u m
M-x texinfo-master-menu
> Create or update a master menu that includes all the other menus (incorporating the descriptions from pre-existing menus, if any).
>
> With an argument (prefix argument, *C-u,* if interactive), first create or update all the nodes and all the regular menus in the buffer before constructing the master menu. (See Section 3.6 [The Top Node and Master Menu], page 39, for more about a master menu.)
>
> For texinfo-master-menu to work, the Texinfo file must have a 'Top' node and at least one subsequent node.
>
> After extensively editing a Texinfo file, you can type the following:
>
> ```
>     C-u M-x texinfo-master-menu
> ```
> or
> ```
>     C-u C-c C-u m
> ```
> This updates all the nodes and menus completely and all at once.

The other major updating commands do smaller jobs and are designed for the person who updates nodes and menus as he or she writes a Texinfo file.

The commands are:

C-c C-u C-n
M-x texinfo-update-node

>Insert the 'Next', 'Previous', and 'Up' pointers for the node that point is within (i.e., for the @node line preceding point). If the @node line has pre-existing 'Next', 'Previous', or 'Up' pointers in it, the old pointers are removed and new ones inserted. With an argument (prefix argument, *C-u*, if interactive), this command updates all @node lines in the region (which is the text between point and mark).

C-c C-u C-m
M-x texinfo-make-menu

>Create or update the menu in the node that point is within. With an argument (*C-u* as prefix argument, if interactive), the command makes or updates menus for the nodes which are either within or a part of the region.

>Whenever texinfo-make-menu updates an existing menu, the descriptions from that menu are incorporated into the new menu. This is done by copying descriptions from the existing menu to the entries in the new menu that have the same node names. If the node names are different, the descriptions are not copied to the new menu.

C-c C-u C-e
M-x texinfo-every-node-update

>Insert or update the 'Next', 'Previous', and 'Up' pointers for every node in the buffer.

C-c C-u C-a
M-x texinfo-all-menus-update

>Create or update all the menus in the buffer. With an argument (*C-u* as prefix argument, if interactive), first insert or update all the node pointers before working on the menus.

>If a master menu exists, the texinfo-all-menus-update command updates it; but the command does not create a new master menu if none already exists. (Use the texinfo-master-menu command for that.)

>When working on a document that does not merit a master menu, you can type the following:

>>C-u C-c C-u C-a

>or

>>C-u M-x texinfo-all-menus-update

>This updates all the nodes and menus.

The texinfo-column-for-description variable specifies the column to which menu descriptions are indented. By default, the value is 32 although it can be useful to reduce it to as low as 24. You can set the variable via customization (see Section "Customization" in *The GNU Emacs Manual*) or with the *M-x set-variable* command (see Section "Examining and Setting Variables" in *The GNU Emacs Manual*).

Also, the `texinfo-indent-menu-description` command may be used to indent existing menu descriptions to a specified column. Finally, if you wish, you can use the `texinfo-insert-node-lines` command to insert missing `@node` lines into a file. (See Section 2.5.3 [Other Updating Commands], page 23, for more information.)

2.5.2 Updating Requirements

To use the updating commands, you must organize the Texinfo file hierarchically with chapters, sections, subsections, and the like. When you construct the hierarchy of the manual, do not 'jump down' more than one level at a time: you can follow the 'Top' node with a chapter, but not with a section; you can follow a chapter with a section, but not with a subsection. However, you may 'jump up' any number of levels at one time—for example, from a subsection to a chapter.

Each `@node` line, with the exception of the line for the 'Top' node, must be followed by a line with a structuring command such as `@chapter`, `@section`, or `@unnumberedsubsec`.

Each `@node` line/structuring-command line combination must look either like this:

```
@node      Comments,  Minimum, Conventions, Overview
@comment   node-name, next,     previous,    up
@section Comments
```

or like this (without the `@comment` line):

```
@node Comments, Minimum, Conventions, Overview
@section Comments
```

or like this (without the explicit node pointers):

```
@node Comments
@section Comments
```

In this example, 'Comments' is the name of both the node and the section. The next node is called 'Minimum' and the previous node is called 'Conventions'. The 'Comments' section is within the 'Overview' node, which is specified by the 'Up' pointer. (Instead of an `@comment` line, you may also write an `@ifinfo` line.)

If a file has a 'Top' node, it must be called 'top' or 'Top' and be the first node in the file.

The menu updating commands create a menu of sections within a chapter, a menu of subsections within a section, and so on. This means that you must have a 'Top' node if you want a menu of chapters.

Incidentally, the `makeinfo` command will create an Info file for a hierarchically organized Texinfo file that lacks 'Next', 'Previous' and 'Up' pointers. Thus, if you can be sure that your Texinfo file will be formatted with `makeinfo`, you have no need for the update node commands. (See Section 23.1 [Creating an Info File], page 213, for more information about `makeinfo`.) However, both `makeinfo` and the `texinfo-format-...` commands require that you insert menus in the file.

2.5.3 Other Updating Commands

In addition to the five major updating commands, Texinfo mode possesses several less frequently used updating commands:

M-x texinfo-insert-node-lines

Insert @node lines before the @chapter, @section, and other sectioning commands wherever they are missing throughout a region in a Texinfo file.

With an argument (*C-u* as prefix argument, if interactive), the command texinfo-insert-node-lines not only inserts @node lines but also inserts the chapter or section titles as the names of the corresponding nodes. In addition, it inserts the titles as node names in pre-existing @node lines that lack names. Since node names should be more concise than section or chapter titles, you must manually edit node names so inserted.

For example, the following marks a whole buffer as a region and inserts @node lines and titles throughout:

```
C-x h C-u M-x texinfo-insert-node-lines
```

This command inserts titles as node names in @node lines; the texinfo-start-menu-description command (see Section 2.3 [Inserting], page 18) inserts titles as descriptions in menu entries, a different action. However, in both cases, you need to edit the inserted text.

M-x texinfo-multiple-files-update

Update nodes and menus in a document built from several separate files. With *C-u* as a prefix argument, create and insert a master menu in the outer file. With a numeric prefix argument, such as *C-u 2*, first update all the menus and all the 'Next', 'Previous', and 'Up' pointers of all the included files before creating and inserting a master menu in the outer file. The texinfo-multiple-files-update command is described in the appendix on @include files. See Section 20.2 [texinfo-multiple-files-update], page 174.

M-x texinfo-indent-menu-description

Indent every description in the menu following point to the specified column. You can use this command to give yourself more space for descriptions. With an argument (*C-u* as prefix argument, if interactive), the texinfo-indent-menu-description command indents every description in every menu in the region. However, this command does not indent the second and subsequent lines of a multi-line description.

M-x texinfo-sequential-node-update

Insert the names of the nodes immediately following and preceding the current node as the 'Next' or 'Previous' pointers regardless of those nodes' hierarchical level. This means that the 'Next' node of a subsection may well be the next chapter. Sequentially ordered nodes are useful for novels and other documents that you read through sequentially. (However, in Info, the *g* * command lets you look through the file sequentially, so sequentially ordered nodes are not strictly necessary.) With an argument (prefix argument, if interactive), the texinfo-sequential-node-update command sequentially updates all the nodes in the region.

2.6 Formatting for Info

Texinfo mode provides several commands for formatting part or all of a Texinfo file for Info. Often, when you are writing a document, you want to format only part of a file—that is, a region.

You can use either the `texinfo-format-region` or the `makeinfo-region` command to format a region:

```
C-c C-e C-r
M-x texinfo-format-region
C-c C-m C-r
M-x makeinfo-region
```
> Format the current region for Info.

You can use either the `texinfo-format-buffer` or the `makeinfo-buffer` command to format a whole buffer:

```
C-c C-e C-b
M-x texinfo-format-buffer
C-c C-m C-b
M-x makeinfo-buffer
```
> Format the current buffer for Info.

For example, after writing a Texinfo file, you can type the following:

```
C-u C-c C-u m
```
or

```
C-u M-x texinfo-master-menu
```

This updates all the nodes and menus. Then type the following to create an Info file:

```
C-c C-m C-b
```
or

```
M-x makeinfo-buffer
```

For TeX or the Info formatting commands to work, the file *must* include a line that has `@setfilename` in its header.

See Section 23.1 [Creating an Info File], page 213, for details about Info formatting.

2.7 Printing

Typesetting and printing a Texinfo file is a multi-step process in which you first create a file for printing (called a DVI file), and then print the file. Optionally, you may also create indices. To do this, you must run the `texindex` command after first running the `tex` typesetting command; and then you must run the `tex` command again. Or else run the `texi2dvi` command which automatically creates indices as needed (see Section 21.2 [Format with `texi2dvi`], page 177).

Often, when you are writing a document, you want to typeset and print only part of a file to see what it will look like. You can use the `texinfo-tex-region` and related commands for this purpose. Use the `texinfo-tex-buffer` command to format all of a buffer.

C-c C-t C-b
M-x texinfo-tex-buffer

> Run `texi2dvi` on the buffer. In addition to running TEX on the buffer, this command automatically creates or updates indices as needed.

C-c C-t C-r
M-x texinfo-tex-region

> Run TEX on the region.

C-c C-t C-i
M-x texinfo-texindex

> Run `texindex` to sort the indices of a Texinfo file formatted with `texinfo-tex-region`. The `texinfo-tex-region` command does not run `texindex` automatically; it only runs the `tex` typesetting command. You must run the `texinfo-tex-region` command a second time after sorting the raw index files with the `texindex` command. (Usually, you do not format an index when you format a region, only when you format a buffer. Now that the `texi2dvi` command exists, there is little or no need for this command.)

C-c C-t C-p
M-x texinfo-tex-print

> Print the file (or the part of the file) previously formatted with `texinfo-tex-buffer` or `texinfo-tex-region`.

For `texinfo-tex-region` or `texinfo-tex-buffer` to work, the file *must* start with a '\input texinfo' line and must include an `@settitle` line. The file must end with `@bye` on a line by itself. (When you use `texinfo-tex-region`, you must surround the `@settitle` line with start-of-header and end-of-header lines.)

See Chapter 21 [Hardcopy], page 177, for a description of the other TEX related commands, such as `tex-show-print-queue`.

2.8 Texinfo Mode Summary

In Texinfo mode, each set of commands has default keybindings that begin with the same keys. All the commands that are custom-created for Texinfo mode begin with *C-c*. The keys are somewhat mnemonic.

Insert Commands

The insert commands are invoked by typing *C-c* twice and then the first letter of the @-command to be inserted. (It might make more sense mnemonically to use *C-c C-i*, for 'custom insert', but *C-c C-c* is quick to type.)

C-c C-c c	Insert '@code'.
C-c C-c d	Insert '@dfn'.
C-c C-c e	Insert '@end'.
C-c C-c i	Insert '@item'.
C-c C-c n	Insert '@node'.
C-c C-c s	Insert '@samp'.
C-c C-c v	Insert '@var'.
C-c {	Insert braces.

```
C-c ]
C-c }          Move out of enclosing braces.

C-c C-c C-d    Insert a node's section title
               in the space for the description
               in a menu entry line.
```

Show Structure

The `texinfo-show-structure` command is often used within a narrowed region.

```
C-c C-s        List all the headings.
```

The Master Update Command

The `texinfo-master-menu` command creates a master menu; and can be used to update every node and menu in a file as well.

```
C-c C-u m
M-x texinfo-master-menu
               Create or update a master menu.

C-u C-c C-u m  With C-u as a prefix argument, first
               create or update all nodes and regular
               menus, and then create a master menu.
```

Update Pointers

The update pointer commands are invoked by typing *C-c C-u* and then either *C-n* for `texinfo-update-node` or *C-e* for `texinfo-every-node-update`.

```
C-c C-u C-n    Update a node.
C-c C-u C-e    Update every node in the buffer.
```

Update Menus

Invoke the update menu commands by typing *C-c C-u* and then either *C-m* for `texinfo-make-menu` or *C-a* for `texinfo-all-menus-update`. To update both nodes and menus at the same time, precede *C-c C-u C-a* with *C-u*.

```
C-c C-u C-m    Make or update a menu.

C-c C-u C-a    Make or update all
               menus in a buffer.

C-u C-c C-u C-a With C-u as a prefix argument,
               first create or update all nodes and
               then create or update all menus.
```

Format for Info

The Info formatting commands that are written in Emacs Lisp are invoked by typing *C-c C-e* and then either *C-r* for a region or *C-b* for the whole buffer.

The Info formatting commands that are written in C and based on the `makeinfo` program are invoked by typing *C-c C-m* and then either *C-r* for a region or *C-b* for the whole buffer.

Use the `texinfo-format...` commands:

C-c C-e C-r	Format the region.
C-c C-e C-b	Format the buffer.

Use `makeinfo`:

C-c C-m C-r	Format the region.
C-c C-m C-b	Format the buffer.
C-c C-m C-l	Recenter the `makeinfo` output buffer.
C-c C-m C-k	Kill the `makeinfo` formatting job.

Typeset and Print

The TEX typesetting and printing commands are invoked by typing *C-c C-t* and then another control command: *C-r* for `texinfo-tex-region`, *C-b* for `texinfo-tex-buffer`, and so on.

C-c C-t C-r	Run TEX on the region.
C-c C-t C-b	Run `texi2dvi` on the buffer.
C-c C-t C-i	Run `texindex`.
C-c C-t C-p	Print the DVI file.
C-c C-t C-q	Show the print queue.
C-c C-t C-d	Delete a job from the print queue.
C-c C-t C-k	Kill the current TEX formatting job.
C-c C-t C-x	Quit a currently stopped TEX formatting job.
C-c C-t C-l	Recenter the output buffer.

Other Updating Commands

The remaining updating commands do not have standard keybindings because they are rarely used.

M-x texinfo-insert-node-lines
> Insert missing @node lines in region.
> With *C-u* as a prefix argument,
> use section titles as node names.

M-x texinfo-multiple-files-update
> Update a multi-file document.
> With *C-u 2* as a prefix argument,
> create or update all nodes and menus
> in all included files first.

M-x texinfo-indent-menu-description
> Indent descriptions.

M-x texinfo-sequential-node-update
> Insert node pointers in strict sequence.

3 Beginning a Texinfo File

Certain pieces of information must be provided at the beginning of a Texinfo file, such as the name for the output file(s), the title of the document, and the Top node. A table of contents is also generally produced here.

This chapter expands on the minimal complete Texinfo source file previously given (see Section 1.12 [Six Parts], page 11). It describes the numerous commands for handling the traditional frontmatter items in Texinfo.

Straight text outside of any command before the Top node should be avoided. Such text is treated differently in the different output formats: at the time of writing, it is visible in TeX and HTML, by default not shown in Info readers, and so on.

3.1 Sample Texinfo File Beginning

The following sample shows what is needed. The elements given here are explained in more detail in the following sections. Other commands are often included at the beginning of Texinfo files, but the ones here are the most critical.

See Section C.2 [GNU Sample Texts], page 264, for the full texts to be used in GNU manuals.

```
\input texinfo   @c -*-texinfo-*-
@c %**start of header
@setfilename infoname.info
@settitle name-of-manual version
@c %**end of header

@copying
This manual is for program, version version.

Copyright @copyright{} years copyright-owner.

@quotation
Permission is granted to ...
@end quotation
@end copying

@titlepage
@title name-of-manual-when-printed
@subtitle subtitle-if-any
@subtitle second-subtitle
@author author

@c  The following two commands
@c  start the copyright page.
@page
@vskip 0pt plus 1filll
@insertcopying
```

```
Published by ...
@end titlepage

@c So the toc is printed at the start.
@contents

@ifnottex
@node Top
@top title

This manual is for program, version version.
@end ifnottex

@menu
* First Chapter::     Getting started ...
* Second Chapter::          ...
  ...
* Copying::          Your rights and freedoms.
@end menu

@node First Chapter
@chapter First Chapter

@cindex first chapter
@cindex chapter, first
...
```

3.2 Texinfo File Header

Texinfo files start with at least three lines that provide Texinfo translators with necessary information. These are the \input texinfo line, the @settitle line, and the @setfilename line.

Also, if you want to format just part of the Texinfo file in Emacs, you must write the @settitle and @setfilename lines between start-of-header and end-of-header lines. These start- and end-of-header lines are optional, but they do no harm, so you might as well always include them.

Any command that affects document formatting as a whole makes sense to include in the header. @synindex (see Section 13.4.2 [@synindex], page 117), for instance, is another command often included in the header.

Thus, the beginning of a Texinfo file generally looks approximately like this:

```
\input texinfo   @c -*-texinfo-*-
@c %**start of header
@setfilename sample.info
@settitle Sample Manual 1.0
@c %**end of header
```

(See Section C.2 [GNU Sample Texts], page 264, for complete sample texts.)

3.2.1 The First Line of a Texinfo File

Every Texinfo file that is to be the top-level input to TeX must begin with a line that looks like this:

```
\input texinfo    @c -*-texinfo-*-
```

This line serves two functions:

1. When the file is processed by TeX, the '\input texinfo' command tells TeX to load the macros needed for processing a Texinfo file. These are in a file called `texinfo.tex`, which should have been installed on your system along with either the TeX or Texinfo software. TeX uses the backslash, '\', to mark the beginning of a command, exactly as Texinfo uses '@'. The `texinfo.tex` file causes the switch from '\' to '@'; before the switch occurs, TeX requires '\', which is why it appears at the beginning of the file.

2. When the file is edited in GNU Emacs, the '-*-texinfo-*-' mode specification tells Emacs to use Texinfo mode.

3.2.2 Start of Header

A start-of-header line is a Texinfo comment that looks like this:

```
@c %**start of header
```

Write the start-of-header line on the second line of a Texinfo file. Follow the start-of-header line with `@setfilename` and `@settitle` lines and, optionally, with other commands that globally affect the document formatting, such as `@synindex` or `@footnotestyle`; and then by an end-of-header line (see Section 3.2.5 [End of Header], page 33).

The start- and end-of-header lines allow you to format only part of a Texinfo file for Info or printing. See Section 23.1.3 [`texinfo-format` commands], page 214.

The odd string of characters, '%**', is to ensure that no other comment is accidentally taken for a start-of-header line. You can change it if you wish by setting the `tex-start-of-header` and/or `tex-end-of-header` Emacs variables. See Section 21.6 [Texinfo Mode Printing], page 181.

3.2.3 @setfilename: Set the Output File Name

The first Texinfo command (that is, after the `\input texinfo`) in a document is generally `@setfilename`:

```
@setfilename info-file-name
```

This command is required for TeX, and very strongly recommended for `makeinfo`.

Write the `@setfilename` command at the beginning of a line and follow it on the same line by the Info file name. Do not write anything else on the line.

When an `@setfilename` line is present, the Texinfo processors ignore everything written before the `@setfilename` line. This is why the very first line of the file (the `\input` line) does not show up in the output.

The `@setfilename` line specifies the name of the output file to be generated. This name must be different from the name of the Texinfo file. There are two conventions for choosing the name: you can either remove the extension (such as '.texi') entirely from the input file name, or (recommended) replace it with the '.info' extension.

Although an explicit '.info' extension is preferable, some operating systems cannot handle long file names. You can run into a problem even when the file name you specify is itself short enough. This occurs because the Info formatters split a long Info file into short indirect subfiles, and name them by appending '-1', '-2', ..., '-10', '-11', and so on, to the original file name. (See Section 23.1.5 [Tag and Split Files], page 215.) The subfile name `texinfo.info-10`, for example, is too long for old systems with a 14-character limit on filenames; so the Info file name for this document is `texinfo` rather than `texinfo.info`. When `makeinfo` is running on operating systems such as MS-DOS which impose severe limits on file names, it may remove some characters from the original file name to leave enough space for the subfile suffix, thus producing files named `texin-10`, `gcc.i12`, etc.

When producing another output format, `makeinfo` will replace any final extension with the output format-specific extension ('html' when generating HTML, for example), or add a dot followed by the extension ('.html' for HTML) if the given name has no extension.

The `@setfilename` line produces no output when you typeset a manual with TeX, but it is nevertheless essential: it opens the index and other auxiliary files used by Texinfo, and also reads `texinfo.cnf` if that file is present on your system (see Section 21.9 [Preparing for TeX], page 184).

If there is no `@setfilename` line, `makeinfo` uses the input file name to determine the output name: first, any of the extensions .texi, .tex, .txi or .texinfo is removed from the input file name; then, the output format specific extension is added—.html when generating HTML, .info when generating Info, etc. The \input line is still ignored in this processing, as well as leading blank lines.

See also the `--output` option in Section 22.2 [Invoking `texi2any`], page 190.

3.2.4 `@settitle`: Set the Document Title

A Texinfo file should contain a line that looks like this:

    @settitle *title*

Write the `@settitle` command at the beginning of a line and follow it on the same line by the title. Do not write anything else on the line. The `@settitle` command should precede everything that generates actual output. The best place for it is right after the `@setfilename` command (described in the previous section).

This command tells TeX the title to use in a header or footer for double-sided output, in case such headings are output. For more on headings for TeX, see Section 3.4.5 [Heading Generation], page 38.

In the HTML file produced by `makeinfo`, *title* serves as the document '<title>'. It also becomes the default document description in the '<head>' part (see Section 3.7.1 [@documentdescription], page 41).

When the title page is used in the output, the title in the `@settitle` command does not affect the title as it appears on the title page. Thus, the two do not need not to match exactly. A practice we recommend is to include the version or edition number of the manual in the `@settitle` title; on the title page, the version number generally appears as an `@subtitle` so it would be omitted from the `@title`. See Section 3.4.1 [@titlepage], page 34.

3.2.5 End of Header

Follow the header lines with an end-of-header line, which is a Texinfo comment that looks like this:

```
@c %**end of header
```

See Section 3.2.2 [Start of Header], page 31.

3.3 Document Permissions

The copyright notice and copying permissions for a document need to appear in several places in the various Texinfo output formats. Therefore, Texinfo provides a command (`@copying`) to declare this text once, and another command (`@insertcopying`) to insert the text at appropriate points.

This section is about the license of the Texinfo document. If the document is a software manual, the software is typically under a different license—for GNU and many other free software packages, software is usually released under the GNU GPL, and manuals are released under the GNU FDL. It is helpful to state the license of the software of the manual, but giving the complete text of the software license is not necessarily required.

3.3.1 @copying: Declare Copying Permissions

The `@copying` command should be given very early in the document; the recommended location is right after the header material (see Section 3.2 [Texinfo File Header], page 30). It conventionally consists of a sentence or two about what the program is, identification of the documentation itself, the legal copyright line, and the copying permissions. Here is a skeletal example:

```
@copying
This manual is for program (version version, updated
date), which ...

Copyright @copyright{} years copyright-owner.

@quotation
Permission is granted to ...
@end quotation
@end copying
```

The `@quotation` has no legal significance; it's there to improve readability in some contexts.

The text of `@copying` is output as a comment at the beginning of Info, HTML, XML, and Docbook output files. It is *not* output implicitly in plain text or TeX; it's up to you to use `@insertcopying` to emit the copying information. See the next section for details.

The `@copyright{}` command generates a 'c' inside a circle when the output format supports this glyph (print and HTML always do, for instance). When the glyph is not supported in the output, it generates the three-character sequence '(C)'.

The copyright notice itself has the following legally-prescribed form:

```
Copyright © years copyright-owner.
```

The word 'Copyright' must always be written in English, even if the document is otherwise written in another language. This is due to international law.

The list of years should include all years in which a version was completed (even if it was released in a subsequent year). It is simplest for each year to be written out individually and in full, separated by commas.

The copyright owner (or owners) is whoever holds legal copyright on the work. In the case of works assigned to the FSF, the owner is 'Free Software Foundation, Inc.'.

The copyright 'line' may actually be split across multiple lines, both in the source document and in the output. This often happens for documents with a long history, having many different years of publication. If you do use several lines, do not indent any of them (or anything else in the `@copying` block) in the source file.

See Section "Copyright Notices" in *GNU Maintainer Information*, for additional information. See Section C.2 [GNU Sample Texts], page 264, for the full text to be used in GNU manuals. See Appendix G [GNU Free Documentation License], page 287, for the license itself under which GNU and other free manuals are distributed.

3.3.2 `@insertcopying`: Include Permissions Text

The `@insertcopying` command is simply written on a line by itself, like this:

```
@insertcopying
```

This inserts the text previously defined by `@copying`. To meet legal requirements, it must be used on the copyright page in the printed manual (see Section 3.4.4 [Copyright], page 37).

The `@copying` command itself causes the permissions text to appear in an Info file *before* the first node. The text is also copied into the beginning of each split Info output file, as is legally necessary. This location implies a human reading the manual using Info does *not* see this text (except when using the advanced Info command **g ***), but this does not matter for legal purposes, because the text is present.

Similarly, the `@copying` text is automatically included at the beginning of each HTML output file, as an HTML comment. Again, this text is not visible (unless the reader views the HTML source).

The permissions text defined by `@copying` also appears automatically at the beginning of the XML and Docbook output files.

3.4 Title and Copyright Pages

In hard copy output, the manual's name and author are usually printed on a title page. Copyright information is usually printed on the back of the title page.

The title and copyright pages appear in printed manuals, but not in most other output formats. Because of this, it is possible to use several slightly obscure typesetting commands that are not to be used in the main text. In addition, this part of the beginning of a Texinfo file contains the text of the copying permissions that appears in the printed manual.

3.4.1 `@titlepage`

Start the material for the title page and following copyright page with `@titlepage` on a line by itself and end it with `@end titlepage` on a line by itself.

The `@end titlepage` command starts a new page and turns on page numbering (see Section 3.4.5 [Heading Generation], page 38). All the material that you want to appear on unnumbered pages should be put between the `@titlepage` and `@end titlepage` commands. You can force the table of contents to appear there with the `@setcontentsaftertitlepage` command (see Section 3.5 [Contents], page 38).

By using the `@page` command you can force a page break within the region delineated by the `@titlepage` and `@end titlepage` commands and thereby create more than one unnumbered page. This is how the copyright page is produced. (The `@titlepage` command might perhaps have been better named the `@titleandadditionalpages` command, but that would have been rather long!)

When you write a manual about a computer program, you should write the version of the program to which the manual applies on the title page. If the manual changes more frequently than the program or is independent of it, you should also include an edition number[1] for the manual. This helps readers keep track of which manual is for which version of the program. (The 'Top' node should also contain this information; see Section 3.6 [The Top Node], page 39.)

Texinfo provides two main methods for creating a title page. One method uses the `@titlefont`, `@sp`, and `@center` commands to generate a title page in which the words on the page are centered.

The second method uses the `@title`, `@subtitle`, and `@author` commands to create a title page with black rules under the title and author lines and the subtitle text set flush to the right hand side of the page. With this method, you do not specify any of the actual formatting of the title page. You specify the text you want, and Texinfo does the formatting.

You may use either method, or you may combine them; see the examples in the sections below.

For sufficiently simple documents, and for the bastard title page in traditional book frontmatter, Texinfo also provides a command `@shorttitlepage` which takes the rest of the line as the title. The argument is typeset on a page by itself and followed by a blank page.

3.4.2 `@titlefont`, `@center`, and `@sp`

You can use the `@titlefont`, `@sp`, and `@center` commands to create a title page for a printed document. (This is the first of the two methods for creating a title page in Texinfo.)

Use the `@titlefont` command to select a large font suitable for the title itself. You can use `@titlefont` more than once if you have an especially long title.

For HTML output, each `@titlefont` command produces an `<h1>` heading, but the HTML document `<title>` is not affected. For that, you must put an `@settitle` command before the `@titlefont` command (see Section 3.2.4 [`@settitle`], page 32).

For example:

```
@titlefont{Texinfo}
```

Use the `@center` command at the beginning of a line to center the remaining text on that line. Thus,

---

[1] We have found that it is helpful to refer to versions of independent manuals as 'editions' and versions of programs as 'versions'; otherwise, we find we are liable to confuse each other in conversation by referring to both the documentation and the software with the same words.

```
@center @titlefont{Texinfo}
```
centers the title, which in this example is "Texinfo" printed in the title font.

Use the `@sp` command to insert vertical space. For example:

```
@sp 2
```
This inserts two blank lines on the printed page. (See Section 15.7 [`@sp`], page 137, for more information about the `@sp` command.)

A template for this method looks like this:

```
@titlepage
@sp 10
@center @titlefont{name-of-manual-when-printed}
@sp 2
@center subtitle-if-any
@sp 2
@center author
...
@end titlepage
```
The spacing of the example fits an 8.5 by 11 inch manual.

You can in fact use these commands anywhere, not just on a title page, but since they are not logical markup commands, we don't recommend them.

3.4.3 `@title`, `@subtitle`, and `@author`

You can use the `@title`, `@subtitle`, and `@author` commands to create a title page in which the vertical and horizontal spacing is done for you automatically. This contrasts with the method described in the previous section, in which the `@sp` command is needed to adjust vertical spacing.

Write the `@title`, `@subtitle`, or `@author` commands at the beginning of a line followed by the title, subtitle, or author. The `@author` command may be used for a quotation in an `@quotation` block (see Section 10.2 [`@quotation`], page 90); except for that, it is an error to use any of these commands outside of `@titlepage`.

The `@title` command produces a line in which the title is set flush to the left-hand side of the page in a larger than normal font. The title is underlined with a black rule. The title must be given on a single line in the source file; it will be broken into multiple lines of output is needed.

For long titles, the `@*` command may be used to specify the line breaks in long titles if the automatic breaks do not suit. Such explicit line breaks are generally reflected in all output formats; if you only want to specify them for the printed output, use a conditional (see Chapter 18 [Conditionals], page 155). For example:

```
@title This Long Title@inlinefmt{tex,@*} Is Broken in @TeX{}
```

The `@subtitle` command sets subtitles in a normal-sized font flush to the right-hand side of the page.

The `@author` command sets the names of the author or authors in a middle-sized font flush to the left-hand side of the page on a line near the bottom of the title page. The names are followed by a black rule that is thinner than the rule that underlines the title.

There are two ways to use the `@author` command: you can write the name or names on the remaining part of the line that starts with an `@author` command:

```
@author by Jane Smith and John Doe
```

or you can write the names one above each other by using multiple `@author` commands:

```
@author Jane Smith
@author John Doe
```

A template for this method looks like this:

```
@titlepage
@title name-of-manual-when-printed
@subtitle subtitle-if-any
@subtitle second-subtitle
@author author
@page
...
@end titlepage
```

3.4.4 Copyright Page

By international treaty, the copyright notice for a book must be either on the title page or on the back of the title page. When the copyright notice is on the back of the title page, that page is customarily not numbered. Therefore, in Texinfo, the information on the copyright page should be within `@titlepage` and `@end titlepage` commands.

Use the `@page` command to cause a page break. To push the copyright notice and the other text on the copyright page towards the bottom of the page, use the following incantation after `@page`:

```
@vskip 0pt plus 1filll
```

The `@vskip` command inserts whitespace in the TeX output; it is ignored in all other output formats. The `0pt plus 1filll` means to put in zero points of mandatory whitespace, and as much optional whitespace as needed to push the following text to the bottom of the page. Note the use of three 'l's in the word 'filll'; this is correct.

To insert the copyright text itself, write `@insertcopying` next (see Section 3.3 [Document Permissions], page 33):

```
@insertcopying
```

Follow the copying text by the publisher, ISBN numbers, cover art credits, and other such information.

Here is an example putting all this together:

```
@titlepage
...
@page
@vskip 0pt plus 1filll
@insertcopying

Published by ...

Cover art by ...
```

```
@end titlepage
```

We have one more special case to consider: for plain text output, you must insert the copyright information explicitly if you want it to appear. For instance, you could have the following after the copyright page:

```
@ifplaintext
@insertcopying
@end ifplaintext
```

You could include other title-like information for the plain text output in the same place.

3.4.5 Heading Generation

Like all `@end` commands (see Chapter 10 [Quotations and Examples], page 89), the `@end titlepage` command must be written at the beginning of a line by itself, with only one space between the `@end` and the `titlepage`. It not only marks the end of the title and copyright pages, but also causes TEX to start generating page headings and page numbers.

Texinfo has two standard page heading formats, one for documents printed on one side of each sheet of paper (single-sided printing), and the other for documents printed on both sides of each sheet (double-sided printing).

In full generality, you can control the headings in different ways:

- The conventional way is to write an `@setchapternewpage` command before the title page commands, if required, and then have the `@end titlepage` command start generating page headings in the manner desired.

  Most documents are formatted with the standard single-sided or double-sided headings, (sometimes) using `@setchapternewpage odd` for double-sided printing and (almost always) no `@setchapternewpage` command for single-sided printing (see Section 3.7.2 [@setchapternewpage], page 41).

- Alternatively, you can use the `@headings` command to prevent page headings from being generated or to start them for either single or double-sided printing. Write an `@headings` command immediately after the `@end titlepage` command. To turn off headings, write `@headings off`. See Section 3.7.3 [@headings], page 42.

- Or, you may specify your own page heading and footing format. See Appendix D [Headings], page 269.

3.5 Generating a Table of Contents

The `@chapter`, `@section`, and other structuring commands (see Chapter 5 [Chapter Structuring], page 47) supply the information to make up a table of contents, but they do not cause an actual table to appear in the manual. To do this, you must use the `@contents` and/or `@summarycontents` command(s).

`@contents`

Generates a table of contents in a printed manual, including all chapters, sections, subsections, etc., as well as appendices and unnumbered chapters. Headings generated by `@majorheading`, `@chapheading`, and the other `@...heading` commands do not appear in the table of contents (see Section 5.2 [Structuring Command Types], page 47).

`@shortcontents`
`@summarycontents`

>   (`@summarycontents` is a synonym for `@shortcontents`.)
>
>   Generates a short or summary table of contents that lists only the chapters, appendices, and unnumbered chapters. Sections, subsections and subsubsections are omitted. Only a long manual needs a short table of contents in addition to the full table of contents.

Both contents commands should be written on a line by themselves, and placed near the beginning of the file, after the `@end titlepage` (see Section 3.4.1 [`@titlepage`], page 34), before any sectioning command. The contents commands automatically generate a chapter-like heading at the top of the first table of contents page, so don't include any sectioning command such as `@unnumbered` before them.

Since an Info file uses menus instead of tables of contents, the Info formatting commands ignore the contents commands. But the contents are included in plain text output (generated by `makeinfo --plaintext`) and in other output formats, such as HTML.

When `makeinfo` writes a short table of contents while producing HTML output, the links in the short table of contents point to corresponding entries in the full table of contents rather than the text of the document. The links in the full table of contents point to the main text of the document.

In the past, the contents commands were sometimes placed at the end of the file, after any indices and just before the `@bye`, but we no longer recommend this.

However, since many existing Texinfo documents still do have the `@contents` at the end of the manual, if you are a user printing a manual, you may wish to force the contents to be printed after the title page. You can do this by specifying `@setcontentsaftertitlepage` and/or `@setshortcontentsaftertitlepage`. The first prints only the main contents after the `@end titlepage`; the second prints both the short contents and the main contents. In either case, any subsequent `@contents` or `@shortcontents` is ignored.

You need to include the `@set...contentsaftertitlepage` commands early in the document (just after `@setfilename`, for example). We recommend using `texi2dvi` (see Section 21.2 [Format with `texi2dvi`], page 177) to specify this without altering the source file at all. For example:

```
texi2dvi --texinfo=@setcontentsaftertitlepage foo.texi
```

An alternative invocation, using `texi2any`:

```
texi2any --dvi --Xopt --texinfo=@setcontentsaftertitlepage foo.texi
```

3.6 The 'Top' Node and Master Menu

The 'Top' node is the node in which a reader enters an Info manual. As such, it should begin with a brief description of the manual (including the version number), and end with a master menu for the whole manual. Of course you should include any other general information you feel a reader would find helpful.

It is conventional and desirable to write an `@top` sectioning command line containing the title of the document immediately after the `@node Top` line (see Section 6.1.5 [`@top` Command], page 58).

The contents of the 'Top' node should appear only in the online output; none of it should appear in printed output, so enclose it between `@ifnottex` and `@end ifnottex` commands. (TEX does not print either an `@node` line or a menu; they appear only in Info; strictly speaking, you are not required to enclose these parts between `@ifnottex` and `@end ifnottex`, but it is simplest to do so. See Chapter 18 [Conditionally Visible Text], page 155.)

3.6.1 Top Node Example

Here is an example of a Top node.

```
@ifnottex
@node Top
@top Sample Title

This is the text of the top node.
@end ifnottex

Additional general information.

@menu
* First Chapter::
* Second Chapter::

...

* Index::
@end menu
```

3.6.2 Parts of a Master Menu

A *master menu* is the main menu. It is customary to include a detailed menu listing all the nodes in the document in this menu.

Like any other menu, a master menu is enclosed in `@menu` and `@end menu` and does not appear in the printed output.

Generally, a master menu is divided into parts.

- The first part contains the major nodes in the Texinfo file: the nodes for the chapters, chapter-like sections, and the appendices.
- The second part contains nodes for the indices.
- The third and subsequent parts contain a listing of the other, lower-level nodes, often ordered by chapter. This way, rather than go through an intermediary menu, an inquirer can go directly to a particular node when searching for specific information. These menu items are not required; add them if you think they are a convenience. If you do use them, put `@detailmenu` before the first one, and `@end detailmenu` after the last; otherwise, `makeinfo` will get confused.

Each section in the menu can be introduced by a descriptive line. So long as the line does not begin with an asterisk, it will not be treated as a menu entry. (See Section 7.2 [Writing a Menu], page 62, for more information.)

For example, the master menu for this manual looks like the following (but has many more entries):

```
@menu
* Copying Conditions::   Your rights.
* Overview::             Texinfo in brief.
...
* Command and Variable Index::
* General Index::

@detailmenu
--- The Detailed Node Listing ---

Overview of Texinfo

* Reporting Bugs:: ...
...

Beginning a Texinfo File

* Sample Beginning:: ...
...
@end detailmenu
@end menu
```

3.7 Global Document Commands

Besides the basic commands mentioned in the previous sections, here are additional commands which affect the document as a whole. They are generally all given before the Top node, if they are given at all.

3.7.1 @documentdescription: Summary Text

When producing HTML output for a document, `makeinfo` writes a '`<meta>`' element in the '`<head>`' to give some idea of the content of the document. By default, this *description* is the title of the document, taken from the `@settitle` command (see Section 3.2.4 [`@settitle`], page 32). To change this, use the `@documentdescription` environment, as in:

```
@documentdescription
descriptive text.
@end documentdescription
```

This will produce the following output in the '`<head>`' of the HTML:

```
<meta name=description content="descriptive text.">
```

`@documentdescription` must be specified before the first node of the document.

3.7.2 @setchapternewpage: Blank Pages Before Chapters

In an officially bound book, text is usually printed on both sides of the paper, chapters start on right-hand pages, and right-hand pages have odd numbers. But in short reports, text often is printed only on one side of the paper. Also in short reports, chapters sometimes do not start on new pages, but are printed on the same page as the end of the preceding chapter, after a small amount of vertical whitespace.

You can use the `@setchapternewpage` command with various arguments to specify how TEX should start chapters and whether it should format headers for printing on one or both sides of the paper (single-sided or double-sided printing).

Write the `@setchapternewpage` command at the beginning of a line followed by its argument.

For example, you would write the following to cause each chapter to start on a fresh odd-numbered page:

```
@setchapternewpage odd
```

You can specify one of three alternatives with the `@setchapternewpage` command:

`@setchapternewpage off`

> Cause TEX to typeset a new chapter on the same page as the last chapter, after skipping some vertical whitespace. Also, cause TEX to format page headers for single-sided printing.

`@setchapternewpage on`

> Cause TEX to start new chapters on new pages and to format page headers for single-sided printing. This is the form most often used for short reports or personal printing. This is the default.

`@setchapternewpage odd`

> Cause TEX to start new chapters on new, odd-numbered pages (right-handed pages) and to typeset for double-sided printing. This is the form most often used for books and manuals.

Texinfo does not have an `@setchapternewpage even` command, because there is no printing tradition of starting chapters or books on an even-numbered page.

If you don't like the default headers that `@setchapternewpage` sets, you can explicit control them with the `@headings` command. See Section 3.7.3 [@headings], page 42.

At the beginning of a manual or book, pages are not numbered—for example, the title and copyright pages of a book are not numbered. By convention, table of contents and frontmatter pages are numbered with roman numerals and not in sequence with the rest of the document.

The `@setchapternewpage` has no effect in output formats that do not have pages, such as Info and HTML.

We recommend not including any `@setchapternewpage` command in your document source at all, since such desired pagination is not intrinsic to the document. For a particular hard copy run, if you don't want the default output (no blank pages, same headers on all pages) use the `--texinfo` option to `texi2dvi` to specify the output you want.

3.7.3 The `@headings` Command

The `@headings` command is rarely used. It specifies what kind of page headings and footings to print on each page. Usually, this is controlled by the `@setchapternewpage` command. You need the `@headings` command only if the `@setchapternewpage` command does not do what you want, or if you want to turn off predefined page headings prior to defining your own. Write an `@headings` command immediately after the `@end titlepage` command.

You can use `@headings` as follows:

`@headings off`
> Turn off printing of page headings.

`@headings single`
> Turn on page headings appropriate for single-sided printing.

`@headings double`
> Turn on page headings appropriate for double-sided printing.

`@headings singleafter`
`@headings doubleafter`
> Turn on `single` or `double` headings, respectively, after the current page is output.

`@headings on`
> Turn on page headings: `single` if '`@setchapternewpage on`', `double` otherwise.

For example, suppose you write `@setchapternewpage off` before the `@titlepage` command to tell TEX to start a new chapter on the same page as the end of the last chapter. This command also causes TEX to typeset page headers for single-sided printing. To cause TEX to typeset for double sided printing, write `@headings double` after the `@end titlepage` command.

You can stop TEX from generating any page headings at all by writing `@headings off` on a line of its own immediately after the line containing the `@end titlepage` command, like this:

```
@end titlepage
@headings off
```

The `@headings off` command overrides the `@end titlepage` command, which would otherwise cause TEX to print page headings.

You can also specify your own style of page heading and footing. See Appendix D [Page Headings], page 269, for more information.

3.7.4 `@paragraphindent`: Controlling Paragraph Indentation

The Texinfo processors may insert whitespace at the beginning of the first line of each paragraph, thereby indenting that paragraph. You can use the `@paragraphindent` command to specify this indentation. Write an `@paragraphindent` command at the beginning of a line followed by either 'asis' or a number:

```
@paragraphindent indent
```

The indentation is according to the value of *indent*:

`asis`   Do not change the existing indentation (not implemented in TEX).

`none`
`0`   Omit all indentation.

n   Indent by *n* space characters in Info output, by *n* ems in TEX.

The default value of *indent* is 3. `@paragraphindent` is ignored for HTML output.

It is best to write the `@paragraphindent` command before the end-of-header line at the beginning of a Texinfo file, so the region formatting commands indent paragraphs as specified. See Section 3.2.2 [Start of Header], page 31.

A peculiarity of the `texinfo-format-buffer` and `texinfo-format-region` commands is that they do not indent (nor fill) paragraphs that contain `@w` or `@*` commands.

3.7.5 `@firstparagraphindent`: **Indenting After Headings**

As you can see in the present manual, the first paragraph in any section is not indented by default. Typographically, indentation is a paragraph separator, which means that it is unnecessary when a new section begins. This indentation is controlled with the `@firstparagraphindent` command:

> `@firstparagraphindent` *word*

The first paragraph after a heading is indented according to the value of *word*:

none   Prevents the first paragraph from being indented (default). This option is ignored by `makeinfo` if `@paragraphindent asis` is in effect.

insert   Include normal paragraph indentation. This respects the paragraph indentation set by an `@paragraphindent` command (see Section 3.7.4 [`@paragraphindent`], page 43).

`@firstparagraphindent` is ignored for HTML and Docbook output.

It is best to write the `@firstparagraphindent` command before the end-of-header line at the beginning of a Texinfo file, so the region formatting commands indent paragraphs as specified. See Section 3.2.2 [Start of Header], page 31.

3.7.6 `@exampleindent`: **Environment Indenting**

The Texinfo processors indent each line of `@example` and similar environments. You can use the `@exampleindent` command to specify this indentation. Write an `@exampleindent` command at the beginning of a line followed by either 'asis' or a number:

> `@exampleindent` *indent*

The indentation is according to the value of *indent*:

asis   Do not change the existing indentation (not implemented in TeX).

0   Omit all indentation.

n Indent environments by n space characters in Info output, by n ems in TeX.

The default value of *indent* is 5 spaces in Info, and 0.4 in in TeX, which is somewhat less. (The reduction is to help TeX fit more characters onto physical lines.)

It is best to write the `@exampleindent` command before the end-of-header line at the beginning of a Texinfo file, so the region formatting commands indent paragraphs as specified. See Section 3.2.2 [Start of Header], page 31.

4 Ending a Texinfo File

The end of a Texinfo file should include commands to create indices, and the `@bye` command to mark the last line to be processed. For example:

```
@node Index
@unnumbered Index

@printindex cp

@bye
```

4.1 Printing Indices and Menus

To print an index means to include it as part of a manual or Info file. This does not happen automatically just because you use `@cindex` or other index-entry generating commands in the Texinfo file; those just cause the raw data for the index to be accumulated. To generate an index, you must include the `@printindex` command at the place in the document where you want the index to appear. Also, as part of the process of creating a printed manual, you must run a program called **texindex** (see Chapter 21 [Hardcopy], page 177) to sort the raw data to produce a sorted index file. The sorted index file is what is actually used to print the index.

Texinfo offers six separate types of predefined index, which suffice in most cases. See Chapter 13 [Indices], page 114, for information on this, as well defining your own new indices, combining indices, and, most importantly advice on writing the actual index entries. This section focuses on printing indices, which is done with the `@printindex` command.

`@printindex` takes one argument, a two-letter index abbreviation. It reads the corresponding sorted index file (for printed output), and formats it appropriately into an index.

The `@printindex` command does not generate a chapter heading for the index, since different manuals have different needs. Consequently, you should precede the `@printindex` command with a suitable section or chapter command (usually `@appendix` or `@unnumbered`) to supply the chapter heading and put the index into the table of contents. Precede the chapter heading with an `@node` line as usual.

For example:

```
@node Variable Index
@unnumbered Variable Index

@printindex vr

@node Concept Index
@unnumbered Concept Index

@printindex cp
```

If you have more than one index, we recommend placing the concept index last.

- In printed output, `@printindex` produces a traditional two-column index, with dot leaders between the index terms and page numbers.

- In Info output, `@printindex` produces a special menu containing the line number of the entry, relative to the start of the node. Info readers can use this to go to the exact line of an entry, not just the containing node. (Older Info readers will just go to the node.) Here's an example:

```
* First index entry:   Top.   (line  7)
```

The actual number of spaces is variable, to right-justify the line number; it's been reduced here to make the line fit in the printed manual.

- In plain text output, `@printindex` produces the same menu, but the line numbers are relative to the start of the file, since that's more convenient for that format.

- In HTML output, `@printindex` produces links to the index entries.

- In XML and Docbook output, it simply records the index to be printed.

4.2 @bye File Ending

An `@bye` command terminates Texinfo processing. None of the formatters process anything following `@bye`; any such text is completely ignored. The `@bye` command should be on a line by itself.

Thus, if you wish, you may follow the `@bye` line with arbitrary notes. Also, you may follow the `@bye` line with a local variables list for Emacs, most typically a `compile-command` (see Section 21.7 [Using the Local Variables List], page 183).

5 Chapter Structuring

Texinfo's *chapter structuring* commands (could more generally be called *sectioning structuring*, but that is awkward) divide a document into a hierarchy of chapters, sections, subsections, and subsubsections. These commands generate large headings in the text, like the one above. They also provide information for generating the table of contents (see Section 3.5 [Generating a Table of Contents], page 38), and for implicitly determining node pointers, as is recommended (see Section 6.2 [makeinfo Pointer Creation], page 58).

The chapter structuring commands do not create a node structure, so normally you put an @node command immediately before each chapter structuring command (see Chapter 6 [Nodes], page 54). The only time you are likely to use the chapter structuring commands without also using nodes is if you are writing a document that contains no cross references and will only be printed, not transformed into Info, HTML, or other formats.

5.1 Tree Structure of Sections

A Texinfo file is usually structured like a book with chapters, sections, subsections, and the like. This structure can be visualized as a tree (or rather as an upside-down tree) with the root at the top and the levels corresponding to chapters, sections, subsection, and subsubsections.

Here is a diagram that shows a Texinfo file with three chapters, each with two sections.

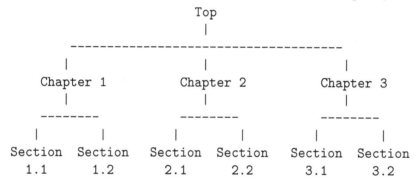

```
                            Top
                             |
       ---------------------------------------------
       |                     |                     |
    Chapter 1            Chapter 2             Chapter 3
       |                     |                     |
    --------              --------              --------
    |      |              |      |              |      |
 Section Section       Section Section       Section Section
   1.1    1.2            2.1    2.2            3.1    3.2
```

In a Texinfo file that has this structure, the beginning of Chapter 2 would normally (with implicitly-determined node pointers) be written like this:

```
@node     Chapter 2
@chapter Chapter 2
```

But for purposes of example, here is how it would be written with explicit node pointers:

```
@node     Chapter 2,  Chapter 3, Chapter 1, Top
@chapter Chapter 2
```

The chapter structuring commands are described in the sections that follow; the @node command is described in the following chapter (see Chapter 6 [Nodes], page 54).

5.2 Structuring Command Types

The chapter structuring commands fall into four groups or series, each of which contains structuring commands corresponding to the hierarchical levels of chapters, sections, subsections, and subsubsections.

The four groups of commands are the `@chapter` series, the `@unnumbered` series, the `@appendix` series, and the `@heading` series. Each command produces a title with a different appearance in the body of the document. Some of the commands list their titles in the tables of contents, while others do not. Here are the details:

- The `@chapter` and `@appendix` series of commands produce numbered or lettered entries both in the body of a document and in its table of contents.

- The `@unnumbered` series of commands produce unnumbered entries both in the body of a document and in its table of contents. The `@top` command, which has a special use, is a member of this series (see Section 6.1.5 [`@top` Command], page 58). An `@unnumbered` section is a normal part of the document structure.

- The `@heading` series of commands produce simple unnumbered headings that do not appear in a table of contents, are not associated with nodes, and cannot be cross-referenced. These heading commands never start a new page.

When an `@setchapternewpage` command says to do so, the `@chapter`, `@unnumbered`, and `@appendix` commands start new pages in the printed manual; the `@heading` commands do not. See Section 3.7.2 [`@setchapternewpage`], page 41.

Here is a summary:

Numbered	Unnumbered	Lettered/numbered	No new page Unnumbered
In contents	In contents	In contents	Not in contents
	@top		@majorheading
@chapter	@unnumbered	@appendix	@chapheading
@section	@unnumberedsec	@appendixsec	@heading
@subsection	@unnumberedsubsec	@appendixsubsec	@subheading
@subsubsection	@unnumberedsubsubsec	@appendixsubsubsec	@subsubheading

5.3 `@chapter`: Chapter Structuring

`@chapter` identifies a chapter in the document–the highest level of the normal document structuring hierarchy. Write the command at the beginning of a line and follow it on the same line by the title of the chapter. The chapter is numbered automatically, starting from 1.

For example, the present chapter in this manual is entitled "`@chapter`: Chapter Structuring"; the `@chapter` line looks like this:

```
@chapter @code{@@chapter}: Chapter Structuring
```

In TeX, the `@chapter` command produces a chapter heading in the document.

In Info and plain text output, the `@chapter` command causes the title to appear on a line by itself, with a line of asterisks inserted underneath. So, the above example produces the following output:

```
5 Chapter Structuring
*********************
```

In HTML, the `@chapter` command produces an `<h2>`-level header by default (controlled by the `CHAPTER_HEADER_LEVEL` customization variable, see Section 22.5.4 [Other Customization Variables], page 204).

In the XML and Docbook output, a `<chapter>` element is produced that includes all the following sections, up to the next chapter.

5.4 @unnumbered, @appendix: Chapters with Other Labeling

Use the @unnumbered command to start a chapter-level element that appears without chapter numbers of any kind. Use the @appendix command to start an appendix that is labeled by letter ('A', 'B', ...) instead of by number; appendices are also at the chapter level of structuring.

Write an @appendix or @unnumbered command at the beginning of a line and follow it on the same line by the title, just as with @chapter.

Texinfo also provides a command @centerchap, which is analogous to @unnumbered, but centers its argument in the printed and HTML outputs. This kind of stylistic choice is not usually offered by Texinfo. It may be suitable for short documents.

With @unnumbered, if the name of the associated node is one of these English words (case-insensitive):

```
Acknowledgements  Colophon  Dedication  Preface
```

then the Docbook output uses corresponding special tags (<preface>, etc.) instead of the default <chapter>. The argument to @unnumbered itself can be anything, and is output as the following <title> text as usual.

5.5 @majorheading, @chapheading: Chapter-level Headings

The @majorheading and @chapheading commands produce chapter-like headings in the body of a document.

However, neither command produces an entry in the table of contents, and neither command causes TEX to start a new page in a printed manual.

In TEX, an @majorheading command generates a larger vertical whitespace before the heading than an @chapheading command but is otherwise the same.

In Info and plain text, the @majorheading and @chapheading commands produce the same output as @chapter: the title is printed on a line by itself with a line of asterisks underneath. Similarly for HTML. The only difference is the lack of numbering and the lack of any association with nodes. See Section 5.3 [@chapter], page 48.

5.6 @section: Sections Below Chapters

An @section command identifies a section within a chapter unit, whether created with @chapter, @unnumbered, or @appendix, following the numbering scheme of the chapter-level command. Thus, within an @chapter chapter numbered '1', the sections are numbered '1.1', '1.2', etc.; within an @appendix "chapter" labeled 'A', the sections are numbered 'A.1', 'A.2', etc.; within an @unnumbered chapter, the section gets no number. The output is underlined with '=' in Info and plain text.

To make a section, write the @section command at the beginning of a line and follow it on the same line by the section title. For example,

```
@section This is a section
```

might produce the following in Info:

```
5.7 This is a section
=====================
```

Section titles are listed in the table of contents.

The TeX, HTML, Docbook, and XML output is all analogous to the chapter-level output, just "one level down"; see Section 5.3 [@chapter], page 48.

5.7 @unnumberedsec, @appendixsec, @heading

The @unnumberedsec, @appendixsec, and @heading commands are, respectively, the unnumbered, appendix-like, and heading-like equivalents of the @section command (see the previous section).

@unnumberedsec and @appendixsec do not need to be used in ordinary circumstances, because @section may also be used within @unnumbered and @appendix chapters; again, see the previous section.

@unnumberedsec

> The @unnumberedsec command may be used within an unnumbered chapter or within a regular chapter or appendix to produce an unnumbered section.

@appendixsec
@appendixsection

> @appendixsection is a longer spelling of the @appendixsec command; the two are synonymous.
>
> Conventionally, the @appendixsec or @appendixsection command is used only within appendices.

@heading   You may use the @heading command (almost) anywhere for a section-style heading that will not appear in the table of contents. The @heading-series commands can appear inside most environments, for example, though pathological and useless locations such as inside @titlepage, as an argument to another command, etc., are not allowed.

5.8 @subsection: Subsections Below Sections

Subsections are to sections as sections are to chapters; see Section 5.6 [@section], page 49. In Info and plain text, subsection titles are underlined with '-'. For example,

```
@subsection This is a subsection
```

might produce

```
1.2.3 This is a subsection
-------------------------
```

Subsection titles are listed in the table of contents.

The TeX, HTML, Docbook, and XML output is all analogous to the chapter-level output, just "two levels down"; see Section 5.3 [@chapter], page 48.

5.9 The @subsection-like Commands

The @unnumberedsubsec, @appendixsubsec, and @subheading commands are, respectively, the unnumbered, appendix-like, and heading-like equivalents of the @subsection command. (See Section 5.8 [@subsection], page 50.)

@unnumberedsubsec and @appendixsubsec do not need to be used in ordinary circumstances, because @subsection may also be used within sections of @unnumbered and @appendix chapters (see Section 5.6 [@section], page 49).

An @subheading command produces a heading like that of a subsection except that it is not numbered and does not appear in the table of contents. Similarly, an @unnumberedsubsec command produces an unnumbered heading like that of a subsection and an @appendixsubsec command produces a subsection-like heading labeled with a letter and numbers; both of these commands produce headings that appear in the table of contents. In Info and plain text, the @subsection-like commands generate a title underlined with hyphens.

5.10 @subsection and Other Subsub Commands

The fourth and lowest level sectioning commands in Texinfo are the 'subsub' commands. They are:

@subsubsection

> Subsubsections are to subsections as subsections are to sections. (See Section 5.8 [@subsection], page 50.) Subsubsection titles appear in the table of contents.

@unnumberedsubsubsec

> Unnumbered subsubsection titles appear in the table of contents, but lack numbers. Otherwise, unnumbered subsubsections are the same as subsubsections.

@appendixsubsubsec

> Conventionally, appendix commands are used only for appendices and are lettered and numbered appropriately. They also appear in the table of contents.

@subsubheading

> The @subsubheading command may be used anywhere that you want a small heading that will not appear in the table of contents.

As with subsections, @unnumberedsubsubsec and @appendixsubsubsec do not need to be used in ordinary circumstances, because @subsubsection may also be used within subsections of @unnumbered and @appendix chapters (see Section 5.6 [@section], page 49).

In Info, 'subsub' titles are underlined with periods. For example,

    @subsubsection This is a subsubsection

might produce

    1.2.3.4 This is a subsubsection
    ....

The TeX, HTML, Docbook, and XML output is all analogous to the chapter-level output, just "three levels down"; see Section 5.3 [@chapter], page 48.

5.11 @part: Groups of Chapters

The final sectioning command is @part, to mark a *part* of a manual, that is, a group of chapters or (rarely) appendices. This behaves quite differently from the other sectioning commands, to fit with the way such "parts" are conventionally used in books.

No `@node` command is associated with `@part`. Just write the command on a line by itself, including the part title, at the place in the document you want to mark off as starting that part. For example:

```
@part Part I:@* The beginning
```

As can be inferred from this example, no automatic numbering or labeling of the `@part` text is done. The text is taken as-is.

Because parts are not associated with nodes, no general text can follow the `@part` line. To produce the intended output, it must be followed by a chapter-level command (including its node). Thus, to continue the example:

```
@part Part I:@* The beginning


@node Introduction
@chapter Introduction
...
```

In the TeX output, the `@part` text is included in both the normal and short tables of contents (see Section 3.5 [Contents], page 38), without a page number (since that is the normal convention). In addition, a "part page" is output in the body of the document, with just the `@part` text. In the example above, the `@*` causes a line break on the part page (but is replaced with a space in the tables of contents). This part page is always forced to be on an odd (right-hand) page, regardless of the chapter pagination (see Section 3.7.2 [`@setchapternewpage`], page 41).

In the HTML output, the `@part` text is similarly included in the tables of contents, and a heading is included in the main document text, as part of the following chapter or appendix node.

In the XML and Docbook output, the `<part>` element includes all the following chapters, up to the next `<part>`. A `<part>` containing chapters is also closed at an appendix.

In the Info and plain text output, `@part` has no effect.

`@part` is ignored when raising or lowering sections (see next section). That is, it is never lowered and nothing can be raised to it.

5.12 Raise/lower Sections: `@raisesections` and `@lowersections`

The `@raisesections` and `@lowersections` commands implicitly raise and lower the hierarchical level of following chapters, sections and the other sectioning commands (excluding parts).

That is, the `@raisesections` command changes sections to chapters, subsections to sections, and so on. Conversely, the `@lowersections` command changes chapters to sections, sections to subsections, and so on. Thus, an `@lowersections` command cancels an `@raisesections` command, and vice versa.

You can use `@lowersections` to include text written as an outer or standalone Texinfo file in another Texinfo file as an inner, included file (see Chapter 20 [Include Files], page 174). Typical usage looks like this:

```
@lowersections
```

```
@include somefile.texi
@raisesections
```

(Without the `@raisesections`, all the subsequent sections in the main file would also be lowered.)

If the included file being lowered has an `@top` node, you'll need to conditionalize its inclusion with a flag (see Section 18.5.1 [`@set @value`], page 159).

Another difficulty can arise with documents that use the (recommended) feature of `makeinfo` for implicitly determining node pointers. Since `makeinfo` must assume a hierarchically organized document to determine the pointers, you cannot just arbitrarily sprinkle `@raisesections` and `@lowersections` commands throughout the document. The final result has to have menus that take the raising and lowering into account. So, as a practical matter, you generally only want to raise or lower large chunks, usually in external files as shown above.

Repeated use of the commands continues to raise or lower the hierarchical level a step at a time. An attempt to raise above 'chapter' reproduces chapter commands; an attempt to lower below 'subsubsection' reproduces subsubsection commands. Also, lowered subsubsections and raised chapters will not work with `makeinfo`'s feature of implicitly determining node pointers, since the menu structure cannot be represented correctly.

Write each `@raisesections` and `@lowersections` command on a line of its own.

6 Nodes

Nodes are the primary segments of a Texinfo file. They do not in and of themselves impose a hierarchical or any other kind of structure on a file. Nodes contain *node pointers* that name other nodes, and can contain *menus* which are lists of nodes. In Info, the movement commands can carry you to a pointed-to node or to a node listed in a menu.

Node pointers and menus provide structure for Info files just as chapters, sections, subsections, and the like provide structure for printed books. The two structures are theoretically distinct. In practice, however, the tree structure of printed books is essentially always used for the node and menu structure also, as this leads to a document which is easiest to follow. See Section 1.5 [Texinfo Document Structure], page 6.

Because node names are used in cross references, it is not desirable to casually change them once published. Such name changes invalidate references from other manuals, from mail archives, and so on. See Section 24.4.7 [HTML Xref Link Preservation], page 232.

6.1 The @node Command

A *node* is a stretch of text that begins at an @node command and continues until the next @node command. The definition of node is different from that for chapter or section. A chapter may contain sections and a section may contain subsections, but a node cannot contain subnodes: the text of a node continues only until the next @node command in the file. A node usually contains only one chapter structuring command, immediately following the @node line.

To specify a node, write an @node command at the beginning of a line, and follow it with up to four arguments, separated by commas, on the rest of the same line. The first argument is required; it is the name of this node (for details of node names, see Section 6.1.3 [Node Line Requirements], page 56). The subsequent arguments are optional—they are the names of the 'Next', 'Previous', and 'Up' pointers, in that order. We strongly recommend omitting them if your Texinfo document is hierarchically organized, as virtually all are (see Section 6.2 [makeinfo Pointer Creation], page 58). You may insert spaces before or after each name on the @node line if you wish; such spaces are ignored.

Whether the node pointers are specified implicitly or explicitly, the Info and HTML output from makeinfo for each node includes links to the 'Next', 'Previous', and 'Up' nodes. The HTML also uses the accesskey attribute with the values 'n', 'p', and 'u' respectively. This allows people using web browsers to follow the navigation using (typically) *M-letter*, e.g., *M-n* for the 'Next' node, from anywhere within the node.

Usually, you write one of the chapter-structuring command lines immediately after an @node line—for example, an @section or @subsection line. See Section 5.2 [Structuring Command Types], page 47.

TEX uses both @node names and chapter-structuring names in the output for cross references. For this reason, you must write @node lines in a Texinfo file that you intend to format for printing, even if you do not intend to format it for Info; and you must include a chapter-structuring command after a node for it to be a valid cross reference target (to TEX). You can use @anchor (see Section 6.3 [@anchor], page 59) to make cross references to an arbitrary position in a document.

Cross references, such as the one at the end of this sentence, are made with `@xref` and related commands; see Chapter 8 [Cross References], page 66.

6.1.1 Choosing Node and Pointer Names

The name of a node identifies the node. For all the details of node names, see Section 6.1.3 [Node Line Requirements], page 56).

Here are some suggestions for node names:

- Try to pick node names that are informative but short.

  In the Info file, the file name, node name, and pointer names are all inserted on one line, which may run into the right edge of the window. (This does not cause a problem with Info, but is ugly.)

- Try to pick node names that differ from each other near the beginnings of their names. This way, it is easy to use automatic name completion in Info.

- Conventionally, node names are capitalized in the same way as section and chapter titles. In this manual, initial and significant words are capitalized; others are not. In other manuals, just initial words and proper nouns are capitalized. Either way is fine; we recommend just being consistent.

The pointers from a given node enable you to reach other nodes and consist simply of the names of those nodes. The pointers are usually not specified explicitly, as `makeinfo` can determine them (see Section 6.2 [`makeinfo` Pointer Creation], page 58).

Normally, a node's 'Up' pointer contains the name of the node whose menu mentions that node. The node's 'Next' pointer contains the name of the node that follows the present node in that menu and its 'Previous' pointer contains the name of the node that precedes it in that menu. When a node's 'Previous' node is the same as its 'Up' node, both pointers name the same node.

Usually, the first node of a Texinfo file is the 'Top' node, and its 'Up' pointer points to the `dir` file, which contains the main menu for all of Info.

6.1.2 Writing an `@node` Line

The easiest and preferred way to write an `@node` line is to write `@node` at the beginning of a line and then the name of the node, like this:

```
@node node-name
```

If you are using GNU Emacs, you can use the update node commands provided by Texinfo mode to insert the names of the pointers; or (recommended), you can leave the pointers out of the Texinfo file and let `makeinfo` insert node pointers into the Info file it creates. (See Chapter 2 [Texinfo Mode], page 17, and Section 6.2 [`makeinfo` Pointer Creation], page 58.)

Alternatively, you can insert the 'Next', 'Previous', and 'Up' pointers yourself. If you do this, you may find it helpful to use the Texinfo mode keyboard command `C-c C-c n`. This command inserts '`@node`' and a comment line listing the names of the pointers in their proper order. The comment line helps you keep track of which arguments are for which pointers. This comment line is especially useful if you are not familiar with Texinfo.

The template for a fully-written-out node line with 'Next', 'Previous', and 'Up' pointers looks like this:

```
@node node-name, next, previous, up
```

The *node-name* argument must be present, but the others are optional. If you wish to specify some but not others, just insert commas as needed, as in: '@node mynode,,,uppernode'. However, we recommend leaving off all the pointers and letting makeinfo determine them, as described above.

If you wish, you can ignore @node lines altogether in your first draft and then use the texinfo-insert-node-lines command to create @node lines for you. However, we do not recommend this practice. It is better to name the node itself at the same time that you write a segment so you can easily make cross references. Useful cross references are an especially important feature of a good Texinfo manual.

After you have inserted an @node line, you should immediately write an @-command for the chapter or section and insert its name. Next (and this is important!), put in several index entries. Usually, you will find at least two and often as many as four or five ways of referring to the node in the index. Use them all. This will make it much easier for people to find the node.

Even when you explicitly specify all pointers, you cannot write the nodes in the Texinfo source file in an arbitrary order! Because formatters must process the file sequentially, irrespective of node pointers, you must write the nodes in the order you wish them to appear in the output. For Info format one can imagine that the order may not matter, but it matters for the other formats.

6.1.3 @node Line Requirements

Names used with @node have several requirements:

- All the node names in a single Texinfo file must be unique.

  This means, for example, that if you end every chapter with a summary, you must name each summary node differently. You cannot just call them all "Summary". You may, however, duplicate the titles of chapters, sections, and the like. Thus you can end each chapter with a section called "Summary", so long as the node names for those sections are all different.

- The next/previous/up pointers on @node lines must be the names of nodes. (It's recommended to leave out these explicit node pointer names, which automatically avoids any problem here; see Section 6.2 [makeinfo Pointer Creation], page 58.)

- Node names can contain @-commands. The output is generally the natural result of the command; for example, using @TeX{} in a node name results in the TeX logo being output, as it would be in normal text. Cross references should use @TeX{} just as the node name does.

  For Info and HTML output, especially, it is necessary to expand commands to some sequence of plain characters; for instance, @TeX{} expands to the three letters 'TeX' in the Info node name. However, cross references to the node should not take the "shortcut" of using 'TeX'; stick to the actual node name, commands and all.

  Some commands do not make sense in node names; for instance, environments (e.g., @quotation), commands that read a whole line as their argument (e.g., @sp), and plenty of others.

  For the complete list of commands that are allowed, and their expansion for HTML identifiers and file names, see Section 24.4.3 [HTML Xref Command Expansion], page 228. The expansions for Info are generally given with main the description of the command.

Prior to the Texinfo 5 release in 2013, this feature was supported in an ad hoc way (the `--commands-in-node-names` option to `makeinfo`). Now it is part of the language.

- Unfortunately, you cannot reliably use periods, commas, or colons within a node name; these can confuse the Info reader. Also, a node name may not start with a left parenthesis preceding a right parenthesis, as in `(not)allowed`, since this syntax is used to specify an external manual. (Perhaps these limitations will be removed some day.)

  `makeinfo` warns about such problematic usage in node names, menu items, and cross references. If you don't want to see the warnings, you can set the customization variable `INFO_SPECIAL_CHARS_WARNING` to '0' (see Section 22.5.4 [Other Customization Variables], page 204).

  Also, if you insist on using these characters in node names (accepting the resulting substandard Info output), in order not to confuse the Texinfo processors you must still escape those characters, by using either special insertions (see Section 14.1.3 [Inserting a Comma], page 120) or `@asis` (see [@asis], page 103). For example:

      @node foo@asis{::}bar

  As an example of avoiding the special characters, the following is a section title in this manual:

      @section @code{@@unnumbered}, @code{@@appendix}: ...

  But the corresponding node name lacks the commas and the subtitle:

      @node @unnumbered @appendix

- Case is significant in node names.
- Spaces before and after names on the '`@node`' line are ignored. Multiple whitespace characters "inside" a name are collapsed to a single space. For example:

      @node foo bar
      @node foo bar,
      @node foo bar ,
      @node foo bar,
      @node foo bar ,

  all define the same node, namely '`foo bar`'. In menu entries, this is the name that should be used: no leading or trailing spaces, and a single internal space. (For cross-references, the node name used in the Texinfo sources is automatically normalized in this way.)

6.1.4 The First Node

The first node of a Texinfo file is the *Top* node, except in an included file (see Chapter 20 [Include Files], page 174). The Top node should contain a short summary, copying permissions, and a master menu. See Section 3.6 [The Top Node], page 39, for more information on the Top node contents and examples.

Here is a description of the node pointers to be used in the Top node:

- The Top node (which must be named '`top`' or '`Top`') should have as its '`Up`' node the name of a node in another file, where there is a menu that leads to this file. Specify the file name in parentheses.

Usually, all Info files are available through a single virtual Info tree, constructed from multiple directories. In this case, use '(dir)' as the parent of the Top node; this specifies the top-level node in the dir file, which contains the main menu for the Info system as a whole. (Each directory with Info files is intended to contain a file named dir.)

That's fine for Info, but for HTML output, one might well want the Up link from the Top node to go somewhere other than 'dir.html'. For example, for GNU the natural place would be http://www.gnu.org/manual/ (a web page collecting links to most GNU manuals), better specified as just /manual/ if the manual will be installed on www.gnu.org. This can be specified with the TOP_NODE_UP_URL customization variable (see Section 22.5.3 [HTML Customization Variables], page 199), as in

```
$ makeinfo --html -c TOP_NODE_UP_URL=/manual/ ...
```

All links to (dir) will be replaced by the given url.

- The 'Prev' node of the Top node is usually either omitted or also set to (dir). Either is fine.

- The 'Next' node of the Top node should be the first chapter in your document.

See Section 23.2 [Installing an Info File], page 216, for more information about installing an Info file in the info directory.

It is usually best to leave the pointers off entirely and let the tools implicitly define them, with this simple result:

```
@node Top
```

6.1.5 The @top Sectioning Command

The @top command is a special sectioning command that you should only use after an '@node Top' line at the beginning of a Texinfo file. The @top command tells the makeinfo formatter which node is to be used as the root of the node tree (needed if your manual uses implicit node pointers).

It produces the same sort of output as @unnumbered (see Section 5.4 [@unnumbered @appendix], page 49).

The @top node is conventionally wrapped in an @ifnottex conditional so that it will not appear in TeX output (see Chapter 18 [Conditionals], page 155). Thus, in practice, a Top node usually looks like this:

```
@ifnottex
@node Top
@top your-manual-title

very-high-level-summary
@end ifnottex
```

@top is ignored when raising or lowering sections. That is, it is never lowered and nothing can be raised to it (see Section 5.12 [Raise/lower sections], page 52).

6.2 makeinfo Pointer Creation

The makeinfo program can automatically determine node pointers for a hierarchically organized document. This implicit node pointer creation feature in makeinfo relieves you from the need to update menus and pointers manually or with Texinfo mode commands. (See Section 2.5 [Updating Nodes and Menus], page 20.) We highly recommend taking advantage of this.

To do so, write your `@node` lines with just the name of the node:

```
@node My Node
```

You do not need to write out the 'Next', 'Previous', and 'Up' pointers.

Then, you must write a sectioning command, such as `@chapter` or `@section`, on the line immediately following each truncated `@node` line (except that comment lines may intervene). This is where it normally goes.

Also, you must write the name of each node (except for the 'Top' node) in a menu that is one or more hierarchical levels above the node's level.

Finally, you must follow the 'Top' `@node` line with a line beginning with `@top` to mark the top-level node in the file. See Section 6.1.5 [`@top` Command], page 58.

If you use a detailed menu in your master menu (see Section 3.6.2 [Master Menu Parts], page 40), mark it with the `@detailmenu ... @end detailmenu` environment, or `makeinfo` will get confused, typically about the last and/or first node in the document.

In most cases, you will want to take advantage of this feature and not redundantly specify node pointers that the programs can determine. However, Texinfo documents are not required to be organized hierarchically or in fact to contain sectioning commands at all (for example, if you never intend the document to be printed), so node pointers may still be specified explicitly, in full generality.

6.3 `@anchor`: Defining Arbitrary Cross Reference Targets

An *anchor* is a position in your document, labeled so that cross references can refer to it, just as they can to nodes. You create an anchor with the `@anchor` command, and give the label as a normal brace-delimited argument. For example:

```
This marks the @anchor{x-spot}spot.
...
@xref{x-spot,,the spot}.
```

produces:

```
This marks the spot.
...
See [the spot], page 1.
```

As you can see, the `@anchor` command itself produces no output. This example defines an anchor 'x-spot' just before the word 'spot'. You can refer to it later with an `@xref` or other cross reference command, as shown (see Chapter 8 [Cross References], page 66).

It is best to put `@anchor` commands just before the position you wish to refer to; that way, the reader's eye is led on to the correct text when they jump to the anchor. You can put the `@anchor` command on a line by itself if that helps readability of the source. Whitespace (including newlines) is ignored after `@anchor`.

Anchor names and node names may not conflict. Anchors and nodes are given similar treatment in some ways; for example, the `goto-node` command takes either an anchor name or a node name as an argument. (See Section "Go to node" in *Info*.)

Also like node names, anchor names cannot include some characters (see Section 6.1.3 [Node Line Requirements], page 56).

Because of this duality, when you delete or rename a node, it is usually a good idea to define an @anchor with the old name. That way, any links to the old node, whether from other Texinfo manuals or general web pages, keep working. You can also do this with the RENAMED_NODES_FILE feature of makeinfo (see Section 24.4.7 [HTML Xref Link Preservation], page 232). Both methods keep links on the web working; the only substantive difference is that defining anchors also makes the old node names available when reading the document in Info.

6.4 Node and Menu Illustration

Here is a copy of the diagram shown earlier that illustrates a Texinfo file with three chapters, each of which contains two sections.

The "root" is at the top of the diagram and the "leaves" are at the bottom. This is how such a diagram is drawn conventionally; it illustrates an upside-down tree. For this reason, the root node is called the 'Top' node, and 'Up' node pointers carry you closer to the root.

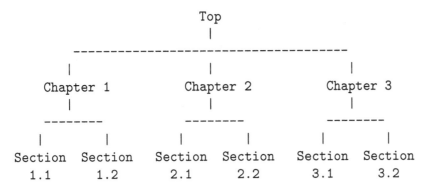

```
                              Top
                               |
         ------------------------------------------
         |                     |                    |
         |                     |                    |
     Chapter 1             Chapter 2            Chapter 3
         |                     |                    |
     ---------             ---------            ---------
     |       |             |       |            |       |
     |       |             |       |            |       |
  Section  Section     Section  Section     Section  Section
   1.1      1.2         2.1      2.2          3.1      3.2
```

Using explicit pointers (not recommended, but for shown for purposes of the example), the fully-written command to start Chapter 2 would be this:

```
@node      Chapter 2,  Chapter 3, Chapter 1, Top
@comment   node-name,  next,      previous,  up
```

This @node line says that the name of this node is "Chapter 2", the name of the 'Next' node is "Chapter 3", the name of the 'Previous' node is "Chapter 1", and the name of the 'Up' node is "Top". You can (and should) omit writing out these node names if your document is hierarchically organized (see Section 6.2 [makeinfo Pointer Creation], page 58), but the pointer relationships still obtain.

Note: 'Next' and 'Previous' refer to nodes at the *same hierarchical level* in the manual, not necessarily to the next node within the Texinfo file. In the Texinfo file, the subsequent node may be at a lower level—a section-level node most often follows a chapter-level node, for example. (The 'Top' node contains the exception to this rule. Since the 'Top' node is the only node at that level, 'Next' refers to the first following node, which is almost always a chapter or chapter-level node.)

To go to Sections 2.1 and 2.2 using Info, you need a menu inside Chapter 2. (See Chapter 7 [Menus], page 62.) You would write the menu just before the beginning of Section 2.1, like this:

```
@menu
* Sect. 2.1::   Description of this section.
* Sect. 2.2::   Description.
@end menu
```

Using explicit pointers, the node for Sect. 2.1 is written like this:

```
@node      Sect. 2.1, Sect. 2.2, Chapter 2, Chapter 2
@comment  node-name, next,      previous, up
```

In Info format, the 'Next' and 'Previous' pointers of a node usually lead to other nodes at the same level—from chapter to chapter or from section to section (sometimes, as shown, the 'Previous' pointer points up); an 'Up' pointer usually leads to a node at the level above (closer to the 'Top' node); and a 'Menu' leads to nodes at a level below (closer to 'leaves'). (A cross reference can point to a node at any level; see Chapter 8 [Cross References], page 66.)

Usually, an @node command and a chapter structuring command are conventionally used together, in that order, often followed by indexing commands. (As shown in the example above, you may follow the @node line with a comment line, e.g., to show which pointer is which if explicit pointers are used.) The Texinfo processors use this construct to determine the relationships between nodes and sectioning commands.

Here is the beginning of the chapter in this manual called "Ending a Texinfo File". This shows an @node line followed by an @chapter line, and then by indexing lines. The manual uses implictly determined node pointers; therefore, nothing else is needed on the @node line.

```
@node Ending a File
@chapter Ending a Texinfo File
@cindex Ending a Texinfo file
@cindex Texinfo file ending
@cindex File ending
```

An earlier version of the manual used explicit node pointers. Here is the beginning of the same chapter for that case. This shows an @node line followed by a comment line, an @chapter line, and then by indexing lines.

```
@node      Ending a File, Structuring, Beginning a File, Top
@comment node-name,      next,        previous,          up
@chapter Ending a Texinfo File
@cindex Ending a Texinfo file

...
```

7 Menus

Menus contain pointers to subordinate nodes. In online output, you use menus to go to such nodes. Menus have no effect in printed manuals and do not appear in them.

It's usually best if a node with a menu does not contain much text. If you find yourself with a lot of text before a menu, we generally recommend moving all but a couple of paragraphs into a new subnode. Otherwise, it is easy for readers to miss the menu.

7.1 Menu Location

There may be at most one menu in a node. A menu is conventionally located at the end of a node, without any regular text or additional commands between the `@end menu` and the beginning of the next node.

This convention is useful, since a reader who uses the menu could easily miss any such text. Also, any such post-menu text will be considered part of the menu in Info output (which has no marker for the end of a menu). Thus, a line beginning with '* ' will likely be incorrectly handled.

Technically, menus can carry you to any node, regardless of the structure of the document; even to nodes in a different Info file. However, we do not recommend making use of this, because it is hard for readers to follow. Also, the `makeinfo` implicit pointer creation feature (see Section 6.2 [`makeinfo` Pointer Creation], page 58) and GNU Emacs Texinfo mode updating commands work only to create menus of subordinate nodes in a hierarchically structured document. It is much better to use cross references to refer to arbitrary nodes.

Years ago, we recommended using an '`@heading`' command within an `@ifinfo` conditional instead of the normal sectioning commands after a very short node with a menu. This had the advantage of making the printed output look better, because there was no very short text between two headings on the page. But it does not work with `makeinfo`'s implicit pointer creation, and it also makes the XML output incorrect, since it does not reflect the true document structure. So, we no longer recommend this.

7.2 Writing a Menu

A menu consists of an `@menu` command on a line by itself followed by menu entry lines or menu comment lines and then by an `@end menu` command on a line by itself.

A menu looks like this:

```
@menu
Larger Units of Text

* Files::                      All about handling files.
* Multiples: Buffers.          Multiple buffers; editing
                               several files at once.

@end menu
```

In a menu, every line that begins with an '* ' is a *menu entry*. (Note the space after the asterisk.) A line that does not start with an '* ' may also appear in a menu. Such a line is not a menu entry but rather a *menu comment* line that appears in the Info file. In the example above, the line 'Larger Units of Text' is such a menu comment line; the two lines starting with '* ' are menu entries. Space characters in a menu are preserved as-is in the Info output; this allows you to format the menu as you wish. Unfortunately you must type node names without any extra spaces or some versions of some Info readers will not find the node (see Section 6.1.3 [Node Line Requirements], page 56).

In the HTML output from `makeinfo`, the `accesskey` attribute is used with the values '1'...'9' for the first nine entries. This allows people using web browsers to follow the first menu entries using (typically) *M-digit*, e.g., *M-1* for the first entry.

7.3 The Parts of a Menu

A menu entry has three parts, only the second of which is required:

1. The menu entry name (optional).

2. The name of the node (required).

3. A description of the item (optional).

The template for a generic menu entry looks like this (but see the next section for one more possibility):

```
* menu-entry-name: node-name.   description
```

Follow the menu entry name with a single colon and follow the node name with tab, comma, newline, or the two characters period and space ('. ').

`makeinfo` warns when the text of a menu item (and node names and cross references) contains a problematic construct that will interfere with its parsing in Info. If you don't want to see the warnings, you can set the customization variable `INFO_SPECIAL_CHARS_WARNING` to '0' (see Section 22.5.4 [Other Customization Variables], page 204).

In Info, a user selects a node with the `m` (`Info-menu`) command. The menu entry name is what the user types after the `m` command.

The third part of a menu entry is a descriptive phrase or sentence. Menu entry names and node names are often short; the description explains to the reader what the node is about. A useful description complements the node name rather than repeats it. The description, which is optional, can spread over multiple lines; if it does, some authors prefer to indent the second line while others prefer to align it with the first (and all others). It's up to you. An empty line, or the next menu entry, ends a description.

7.4 Less Cluttered Menu Entry

When the menu entry name and node name are the same, you can write the name immediately after the asterisk and space at the beginning of the line and follow the name with two colons.

For example, write

```
* Name::                        description
```

instead of

```
* Name: Name.                   description
```

We recommend using the node name for the menu entry name whenever possible, since it reduces visual clutter in the menu.

7.5 A Menu Example

A menu looks like this in Texinfo:

```
@menu
* menu entry name: Node name.    A short description.
* Node name::                    This form is preferred.
@end menu
```

This produces:

```
* menu:

* menu entry name: Node name.    A short description.
* Node name::                    This form is preferred.
```

Here is an example as you might see it in a Texinfo file:

```
@menu
Larger Units of Text

* Files::                        All about handling files.
* Multiples: Buffers.            Multiple buffers; editing
                                 several files at once.

@end menu
```

This produces:

```
* menu:
Larger Units of Text

* Files::                        All about handling files.
* Multiples: Buffers.            Multiple buffers; editing
                                 several files at once.
```

In this example, the menu has two entries. 'Files' is both a menu entry name and the name of the node referred to by that name. 'Multiples' is the menu entry name; it refers to the node named 'Buffers'. The line 'Larger Units of Text' is a comment; it appears in the menu, but is not an entry.

Since no file name is specified with either 'Files' or 'Buffers', they must be the names of nodes in the same Info file (see Section 7.6 [Referring to Other Info Files], page 64).

7.6 Referring to Other Info Files

You can create a menu entry that enables a reader in Info to go to a node in another Info file by writing the file name in parentheses just before the node name. Some examples:

```
@menu
* first-entry-name:(filename)nodename.    description
* (filename)second-node::                 description
@end menu
```

For example, to refer directly to the 'Outlining' and 'Rebinding' nodes in the *Emacs Manual*, you could write a menu like this:

```
@menu
* Outlining: (emacs)Outline Mode.  The major mode for
                                   editing outlines.
* (emacs)Rebinding::               How to redefine the
                                   meaning of a key.
@end menu
```

If you do not list the node name, but only name the file, then Info presumes that you are referring to the 'Top' node. Examples:

```
* Info: (info).          Documentation browsing system.
* (emacs)::              The extensible, self-documenting
                         text editor.
```

The GNU Emacs Texinfo mode menu updating commands only work with nodes within the current buffer, so you cannot use them to create menus that refer to other files. You must write such menus by hand.

8 Cross References

Cross references are used to refer the reader to other parts of the same or different Texinfo files. In Texinfo, nodes and anchors are the places to which cross references can refer.

8.1 What References Are For

Often, but not always, a printed document should be designed so that it can be read sequentially. People tire of flipping back and forth to find information that should be presented to them as they need it.

However, in any document, some information will be too detailed for the current context, or incidental to it; use cross references to provide access to such information. Also, an online help system or a reference manual is not like a novel; few read such documents in sequence from beginning to end. Instead, people look up what they need. For this reason, such creations should contain many cross references to help readers find other information that they may not have read.

In a printed manual, a cross reference results in a page reference, unless it is to another manual altogether, in which case the cross reference names that manual.

In Info, a cross reference results in an entry that you can follow using the Info 'f' command. (See Section "Following cross-references" in *Info*.)

In HTML, a cross reference results in an hyperlink.

The various cross reference commands use nodes (or anchors, see Section 6.3 [@anchor], page 59) to define cross reference locations. This is evident in Info and HTML, in which a cross reference takes you to the specified location.

TeX also needs nodes to define cross reference locations, but the action is less obvious. When TeX generates a DVI file, it records each node's page number and uses the page numbers in making references. Thus, even if you are writing a manual that will only be printed, and not used online, you must nonetheless write @node lines in order to name the places to which you make cross references.

8.2 Different Cross Reference Commands

There are four different cross reference commands:

@xref   Used to start a sentence in the printed manual and in HTML with 'See ...' or an Info cross reference saying '*Note *name*: *node*.'.

@ref   Used within or, more often, at the end of a sentence; produces just the reference in the printed manual and in HTML without the preceding 'See' (same as @xref for Info).

@pxref   Used within parentheses, at the end of a sentence, or otherwise before punctuation, to make a reference. Its output starts with a lowercase 'see' in the printed manual and in HTML, and a lowercase '*note' in Info. ('p' is for 'parenthesis'.)

@inforef   Used to make a reference to an Info file for which there is no printed manual.

The @cite command is used to make references to books and manuals for which there is no corresponding Info file and, therefore, no node to which to point. See Section 8.10 [@cite], page 77.

8.3 Parts of a Cross Reference

A cross reference command to a node requires only one argument, which is the name of the node to which it refers. But a cross reference command may contain up to four additional arguments. By using these arguments, you can provide a cross reference name, a topic description or section title for the printed output, the name of a different manual file, and the name of a different printed manual. To refer to another manual as a whole, the manual file and/or the name of the printed manual are the only required arguments (see Section 8.5 [Top Node Naming], page 72).

Here is a simple cross reference example:

```
@xref{Node name}.
```

which produces

```
*Note Node name::.
```

in Info and

See Section *nnn* [Node name], page *ppp*.

in a printed manual.

Here is an example of a full five-part cross reference:

```
@xref{Node name, Cross Reference Name, Particular Topic,
info-file-name, A Printed Manual}, for details.
```

which produces

```
*Note Cross Reference Name: (info-file-name)Node name,
for details.
```

in Info and

See section "Particular Topic" in *A Printed Manual*, for details.

in a printed book.

The five possible arguments for a cross reference are:

1. The node or anchor name (required, except for reference to whole manuals). This is the location to which the cross reference takes you. In a printed document, the location of the node provides the page reference only for references within the same document.

2. The cross reference name. If you include this argument, it becomes the first part of the cross reference. It is usually omitted; then the topic description (third argument) is used if it was specified; if that was omitted as well, the node name is used.

3. A topic description or section name. Often, this is the title of the section. This is used as the name of the reference in the printed manual. If omitted, the node name is used.

4. The name of the manual file in which the reference is located, if it is different from the current file. This name is used both for Info and HTML.

5. The name of a printed manual from a different Texinfo file.

The template for a full five argument cross reference looks like this:

```
@xref{node-name, cross-reference-name, title-or-topic,
info-file-name, printed-manual-title}.
```

Cross references with one, two, three, four, and five arguments are described separately following the description of @xref.

Write a node name in a cross reference in exactly the same way as in the `@node` line, including the same capitalization; otherwise, the formatters may not find the reference.

`makeinfo` warns when the text of a cross reference (and node names and menu items) contains a problematic construct that will interfere with its parsing in Info. If you don't want to see the warnings, you can set the customization variable `INFO_SPECIAL_CHARS_WARNING` to '0' (see Section 22.5.4 [Other Customization Variables], page 204).

8.4 `@xref`

The `@xref` command generates a cross reference for the beginning of a sentence. The Info formatting commands convert it into an Info cross reference, which the Info 'f' command can use to bring you directly to another node. The TeX typesetting commands convert it into a page reference, or a reference to another book or manual. In the HTML output format the cross reference is output as a hyperlink.

8.4.1 What a Reference Looks Like and Requires

Most often, an Info cross reference looks like this:

    *Note node-name::.

or like this

    *Note cross-reference-name: node-name.

In TeX, a cross reference looks like this:

    See Section section-number [node-name], page page.

or like this

    See Section section-number [title-or-topic], page page.

The `@xref` command does not generate a period or comma to end the cross reference automatically. You must write that period or comma yourself; otherwise, Info will not recognize the end of the reference. (The `@pxref` command works differently; see Section 8.7 [@pxref], page 73.)

> **Caution:** A period or comma *must* follow the closing brace of an `@xref`. It is required to terminate the cross reference. This period or comma will appear in the output.

`@xref` must refer to a node by name. Use `@node` to define the node (see Section 6.1.2 [Writing a Node], page 55), or `@anchor` (see Section 6.3 [@anchor], page 59).

`@xref` is followed by several arguments inside braces, separated by commas. Whitespace before and after these commas is ignored.

A cross reference to a node within the current file requires only the name of a node; but it may contain up to four additional arguments. Each of these variations produces a cross reference that looks somewhat different. A cross reference to another manual as a whole only requires the fourth or fifth argument.

> **Note:** Commas separate arguments in a cross reference, so you must not include a comma in the title or any other part lest the formatters mistake them for separators. `@comma{}` may be used to protect such commas (see Section 14.1.3 [Inserting a Comma], page 120).

8.4.2 @xref with One Argument

The simplest form of @xref takes one argument, the name of another node in the same Texinfo file. The Info formatters produce output that the Info readers can use to jump to the reference; TEX produces output that specifies the page and section number for you; the HTML output is a normal hyperlink.

For example,

    @xref{Tropical Storms}.

produces

    *Note Tropical Storms::.

in Info and

    See Section 3.1 [Tropical Storms], page 24.

in a printed manual. (Note that in the preceding example the closing brace to @xref's argument is followed by a period.)

You can write a clause after the cross reference, like this:

    @xref{Tropical Storms}, for more info.

which produces

    *Note Tropical Storms::, for more info.

in Info and

    See Section 3.1 [Tropical Storms], page 24, for more info.

in a printed manual. Note that in the preceding example the closing brace to @xref is followed by a comma, then the additional text. It's a common mistake to follow an @xref command with a space, but this is never correct.

8.4.3 @xref with Two Arguments

With two arguments, the second is used as the name of the cross reference, while the first is still the name of the node to which the cross reference points.

The template is like this:

    @xref{node-name, cross-reference-name}.

For example,

    @xref{Electrical Effects, Lightning}.

produces:

    *Note Lightning: Electrical Effects.

in Info and

    See Section 5.2 [Electrical Effects], page 57.

in a printed manual. (Note that in the preceding example the closing brace is followed by a period; and that the node name is printed, not the cross reference name.)

You can write a clause after the cross reference, like this:

    @xref{Electrical Effects, Lightning}, for more info.

which produces

```
*Note Lightning: Electrical Effects, for more info.
```
in Info and

See Section 5.2 [Electrical Effects], page 57, for more info.

in a printed manual. (Note that in the preceding example the closing brace is followed by a comma, and then by the clause, which is followed by a period.)

The second argument to cross references must observe some of the restrictions for node names (see Section 6.1.3 [Node Line Requirements], page 56). The most common issue is that colons cannot be used, since that interferes with the parsing of the Info file.

8.4.4 `@xref` with Three Arguments

A third argument replaces the node name in the TeX output. The third argument should be the name of the section in the printed output, or else state the topic discussed by that section. Often, you will want to use initial uppercase letters so it will be easier to read when the reference is printed. Use a third argument when the node name is unsuitable because of syntax or meaning.

Remember to write a comma or period after the closing brace of an `@xref` to terminate the cross reference. In the following examples, a clause follows a terminating comma.

The template is like this:

```
@xref{node-name, cross-reference-name, title-or-topic}.
```
For example,

```
@xref{Electrical Effects, Lightning, Thunder and Lightning},
for details.
```
produces

```
*Note Lightning: Electrical Effects, for details.
```
in Info and

See Section 5.2 [Thunder and Lightning], page 57, for details.

in a printed manual.

If a third argument is given and the second one is empty, then the third argument serves for both. (Note how two commas, side by side, mark the empty second argument.)

```
@xref{Electrical Effects, , Thunder and Lightning},
for details.
```
produces

```
*Note Thunder and Lightning: Electrical Effects, for details.
```
in Info and

See Section 5.2 [Thunder and Lightning], page 57, for details.

in a printed manual.

The third argument to cross references must observe some of the restrictions for node names (see Section 6.1.3 [Node Line Requirements], page 56). The most common issue is that colons cannot be used, since that interferes with the parsing of the Info file.

As a practical matter, it is often best to write cross references with just the first argument if the node name and the section title are the same (or nearly so), and with the first and third arguments only if the node name and title are different.

Texinfo offers a setting to use the section title instead of node names by default in cross references (an explicitly specified third argument still takes precedence):

```
@xrefautomaticsectiontitle on
```

Typically this line would be given near the beginning of the document and used for the whole manual. But you can turn it off if you want (`@xrefautomaticsectiontitle off`), for example, if you're including some other sub-document that doesn't have suitable section names.

8.4.5 @xref with Four and Five Arguments

In a cross reference, a fourth argument specifies the name of another Info file, different from the file in which the reference appears, and a fifth argument specifies its title as a printed manual.

Remember that a comma or period must follow the closing brace of an `@xref` command to terminate the cross reference.

The full template is:

```
@xref{node-name, cross-reference-name, title-or-topic,
info-file-name, printed-manual-title}.
```

For example,

```
@xref{Electrical Effects, Lightning, Thunder and Lightning,
weather, An Introduction to Meteorology}.
```

produces this output in Info:

```
*Note Lightning: (weather)Electrical Effects.
```

As you can see, the name of the Info file is enclosed in parentheses and precedes the name of the node.

In a printed manual, the reference looks like this:

See section "Thunder and Lightning" in *An Introduction to Meteorology*.

The title of the printed manual is typeset like `@cite`; and the reference lacks a page number since TEX cannot know to which page a reference refers when that reference is to another manual.

Next case: often, you will leave out the second argument when you use the long version of `@xref`. In this case, the third argument, the topic description, will be used as the cross reference name in Info. For example,

```
@xref{Electrical Effects, , Thunder and Lightning,
weather, An Introduction to Meteorology}.
```

produces

```
*Note Thunder and Lightning: (weather)Electrical Effects.
```

in Info and

See section "Thunder and Lightning" in *An Introduction to Meteorology*.

in a printed manual.

Next case: If the node name and the section title are the same in the other manual, you may also leave out the section title. In this case, the node name is used in both instances. For example,

```
@xref{Electrical Effects,,,
weather, An Introduction to Meteorology}.
```
produces
```
*Note (weather)Electrical Effects::.
```
in Info and

See section "Electrical Effects" in *An Introduction to Meteorology.*

in a printed manual.

A very unusual case: you may want to refer to another manual file that is within a single printed manual—when multiple Texinfo files are incorporated into the same TeX run but can create separate Info or HTML output files. In this case, you need to specify only the fourth argument, and not the fifth.

Finally, it's also allowed to leave out all the arguments *except* the fourth and fifth, to refer to another manual as a whole. See the next section.

8.5 Naming a 'Top' Node

Ordinarily, you must always name a node in a cross reference. However, it's not unusual to want to refer to another manual as a whole, rather than a particular section within it. In this case, giving any section name is an unnecessary distraction.

So, with cross references to other manuals (see Section 8.4.5 [Four and Five Arguments], page 71), if the first argument is either 'Top' (capitalized just that way) or omitted entirely, and the third argument is omitted, the printed output includes no node or section name. (The Info output includes 'Top' if it was given.) For example,
```
@xref{Top,,, make, The GNU Make Manual}.
```
produces
```
*Note (make)Top::.
```
and

See *The GNU Make Manual.*

Info readers will go to the Top node of the manual whether or not the 'Top' node is explicitly specified.

It's also possible (and is historical practice) to refer to a whole manual by specifying the 'Top' node and an appropriate entry for the third argument to the @xref command. Using this idiom, to make a cross reference to *The GNU Make Manual,* you would write:
```
@xref{Top,, Overview, make, The GNU Make Manual}.
```
which produces
```
*Note Overview: (make)Top.
```
in Info and

See section "Overview" in *The GNU Make Manual.*

in a printed manual.

In this example, 'Top' is the name of the first node, and 'Overview' is the name of the first section of the manual. There is no widely-used convention for naming the first section in a printed manual, this is just what the Make manual happens to use. This arbitrariness of the first name is a principal reason why omitting the third argument in whole-manual cross references is preferable.

8.6 @ref

`@ref` is nearly the same as `@xref` except that it does not generate a 'See' in the printed output, just the reference itself. This makes it useful as the last part of a sentence.

For example,

```
For more information, @pxref{This}, and @ref{That}.
```

produces in Info:

```
For more information, *note This::, and *note That::.
```

and in printed output:

> For more information, see Section 1.1 [This], page 1, and Section 1.2 [That], page 2.

The `@ref` command can tempt writers to express themselves in a manner that is suitable for a printed manual but looks awkward in the Info format. Bear in mind that your audience could be using both the printed and the Info format. For example:

```
Sea surges are described in @ref{Hurricanes}.
```

looks ok in the printed output:

> Sea surges are described in Section 6.7 [Hurricanes], page 72.

but is awkward to read in Info, "note" being a verb:

```
Sea surges are described in *note Hurricanes::.
```

You should write a period or comma immediately after an `@ref` command with two or more arguments. If there is no such following punctuation, `makeinfo` will generate a (grammatically incorrect) period in the Info output; otherwise, the cross reference would fail completely, due to the current syntax of Info format.

In general, it is best to use `@ref` only when you need some word other than "see" to precede the reference. When "see" (or "See") is ok, `@xref` and `@pxref` are preferable.

8.7 @pxref

The parenthetical reference command, `@pxref`, is nearly the same as `@xref`, but it is best used at the end of a sentence or before a closing parenthesis. The command differs from `@xref` in two ways:

1. TEX typesets the reference for the printed manual with a lowercase 'see' rather than an uppercase 'See'.

2. The Info formatting commands automatically end the reference with a closing colon or period, if necessary.

`@pxref` is designed so that the output looks right and works right at the end of a sentence or parenthetical phrase, both in printed output and in an Info file. In a printed manual, a closing comma or period should not follow a cross reference within parentheses; such punctuation is wrong. But in an Info file, suitable closing punctuation must follow the cross reference so Info can recognize its end. `@pxref` spares you the need to use complicated methods to put a terminator into one form of the output and not the other.

With one argument, a parenthetical cross reference looks like this:

```
      ... storms cause flooding (@pxref{Hurricanes}) ...
```
which produces
```
      ... storms cause flooding (*note Hurricanes::) ...
```
in Info and

     ... storms cause flooding (see Section 6.7 [Hurricanes], page 72) ...

in a printed manual.

     With two arguments, a parenthetical cross reference has this template:
```
      ... (@pxref{node-name, cross-reference-name}) ...
```
which produces
```
      ... (*note cross-reference-name: node-name.) ...
```
in Info and

     ... (see Section *nnn* [*node-name*], page *ppp*) ...

in a printed manual.

     `@pxref` can be used with up to five arguments, just like `@xref` (see Section 8.4 [`@xref`], page 68).

     In past versions of Texinfo, it was not allowed to write punctuation after an `@pxref`, so it could be used *only* before a right parenthesis. This is no longer the case, so now it can be used (for example) at the end of a sentence, where a lowercase "see" works best. For instance:
```
      ... For more information, @pxref{More}.
```
which outputs (in Info):
```
      ... For more information, *note More::.
```
In general, `@pxref` should only be followed by a comma, period, or right parenthesis; in other cases, `makeinfo` has to insert a period to make the cross reference work correctly in Info, and that period looks wrong.

     As a matter of style, `@pxref` is best used at the ends of sentences. Although it technically works in the middle of a sentence, that location breaks up the flow of reading.

8.8 `@inforef`: Cross References to Info-only Material

`@inforef` is used for making cross references to Info documents—even from a printed manual. This might be because you want to refer to conditional `@ifinfo` text (see Chapter 18 [Conditionals], page 155), or because printed output is not available (perhaps because there is no Texinfo source), among other possibilities.

     The command takes either two or three arguments, in the following order:

1. The node name.
2. The cross reference name (optional).
3. The Info file name.

Separate the arguments with commas, as with `@xref`. Also, you must terminate the reference with a comma or period after the '`}`', as you do with `@xref`.

The template is:

```
@inforef{node-name, cross-reference-name, info-file-name},
```
For example,
```
@inforef{Advanced, Advanced Info commands, info},
for more information.
```
produces (in Info):
```
*Note Advanced Info commands: (info)Advanced,
for more information.
```
and (in the printed output):

See Info file `info`, node 'Advanced', for more information.

(This particular example is not realistic, since the Info manual is written in Texinfo, so all formats are available. In fact, we don't know of any extant Info-only manuals.)

The converse of `@inforef` is `@cite`, which is used to refer to printed works for which no Info form exists. See Section 8.10 [`@cite`], page 77.

8.9 @url, @uref{url[, text] [, replacement]}

`@uref` produces a reference to a uniform resource locator (url). It takes one mandatory argument, the url, and two optional arguments which control the text that is displayed. In HTML and PDF output, `@uref` produces a link you can follow. (To merely indicate a url without creating a link people can follow, use `@indicateurl`, see Section 9.1.15 [`@indicateurl`], page 86.)

`@url` is a synonym for `@uref`. (Originally, `@url` had the meaning of `@indicateurl`, but in practice it was almost always misused. So we've changed the meaning.)

The second argument, if specified, is the text to display (the default is the url itself); in Info, DVI, and PDF output, but not in HTML output, the url is output in addition to this text.

The third argument, if specified, is the text to display, but in this case the url is not output in any format. This is useful when the text is already sufficiently referential, as in a man page. Also, if the third argument is given, the second argument is ignored.

8.9.1 @url Examples

First, here is an example of the simplest form of `@url`, with just one argument. The given url is both the target and the visible text of the link:
```
The official GNU ftp site is @uref{http://ftp.gnu.org/gnu}.
```
produces:

The official GNU ftp site is `http://ftp.gnu.org/gnu`.

Two-argument form of @url

Here is an example of the two-argument form:
```
The official @uref{http://ftp.gnu.org/gnu, GNU ftp site}
holds programs and texts.
```
which produces:

> The official GNU ftp site (`http://ftp.gnu.org/gnu`)
> holds programs and texts.

that is, the Info (and TEX, etc.) output is this:

```
The official GNU ftp site (http://ftp.gnu.org/gnu)
holds programs and texts.
```

while the HTML output is this:

```
The official <a href="http://ftp.gnu.org/gnu">GNU ftp site</a>
holds programs and texts.
```

Three-argument form of `@url`

Finally, an example of the three-argument form:

```
The @uref{/man.cgi/1/ls,,ls} program ...
```

which, except for HTML, produces:

> The ls program ...

but with HTML:

```
The <a href="/man.cgi/1/ls">ls</a> program ...
```

By the way, some people prefer to display urls in the unambiguous format:

> <URL:http://*host*/*path*>

You can use this form in the input file if you wish. We feel it's not necessary to include the '`<URL:`' and '`>`' in the output, since to be useful any software that tries to detect urls in text already has to detect them without the '`<URL:`'.

8.9.2 URL Line Breaking

TEX allows line breaking within urls at only a few characters (which are special in urls): '`&`', '`.`', '`#`', '`?`', and '`/`' (but not between two '`/`' characters). A tiny amount of stretchable space is also inserted around these characters to help with line breaking.

For HTML output, modern browsers will also do line breaking within displayed urls. If you need to allow breaks at other characters you can insert `@/` as needed (see Section 15.2 [Line Breaks], page 135).

By default, in TEX any such breaks at special characters will occur after the character. Some people prefer such breaks to happen after the special character. This can be controlled with the `@urefbreakstyle` command (this command has effect only in TEX):

```
@urefbreakstyle how
```

where the argument *how* is one of these words:

'`after`'   (the default) Potentially break after the special characters.

'`before`'   Potentially break before the special characters.

'`none`'   Do not consider breaking at the special characters at all; any potential breaks must be manually inserted.

8.9.3 @url PDF Output Format

If the ultimate purpose of a PDF is only to be viewed online, perhaps similar to HTML in some inchoate way, you may not want the urls to be included in the visible text (just as urls are not visible to readers of web pages). Texinfo provides a PDF-specific option for this, which must be used inside @tex:

```
@tex
\global\urefurlonlylinktrue
@end tex
```

The result is that @url{http://www.gnu.org, GNU} has the visible output of just 'GNU', with a link target of http://www.gnu.org. Ordinarily, the visible output would include both the label and the url: 'GNU (http://www.gnu.org)'.

This option only has effect when the PDF output is produced with the pdfTEX program, not with other ways of getting from Texinfo to PDF (e.g., TEX to DVI to PDF). Consequently, it is ok to specify this option unconditionally within @tex, as shown above. It is ignored when DVI is being produced.

8.9.4 PDF Colors

By default, urls and cross-reference links are printed in black in PDF output. Very occasionally, however, you may want to highlight such "live" links with a different color, as is commonly done on web pages. Texinfo provides a PDF-specific option for specifying these colors, which must be used inside @tex:

```
@tex
\global\def\linkcolor{1 0 0}  % red
\global\def\urlcolor{0 1 0}   % green
@end tex
```

\urlcolor changes the color of @url output (both the actual url and any textual label), while \linkcolor changes the color for cross-references to nodes, etc. They are independent.

The three given values must be numbers between 0 and 1, specifying the amount of red, green, and blue respectively.

These definitions only have an effect when the PDF output is produced with the pdfTEX program, not with other ways of getting from Texinfo to PDF (e.g., TEX to DVI to PDF). Consequently, it is ok to specify this option unconditionally within @tex, as shown above. It is ignored when DVI is being produced.

We do not recommend colorizing just for fun; unless you have a specific reason to use colors, best to skip it.

8.10 @cite{reference}

Use the @cite command for the name of a book that lacks a companion Info file. The command produces italics in the printed manual, and quotation marks in the Info file.

If a book is written in Texinfo, it is better to use a cross reference command since a reader can easily follow such a reference in Info. See Section 8.4 [@xref], page 68.

9 Marking Text, Words and Phrases

In Texinfo, you can mark words and phrases in a variety of ways. The Texinfo formatters use this information to determine how to highlight the text. You can specify, for example, whether a word or phrase is a defining occurrence, a metasyntactic variable, or a symbol used in a program. Also, you can emphasize text, in several different ways.

9.1 Indicating Definitions, Commands, etc.

Texinfo has commands for indicating just what kind of object a piece of text refers to. For example, email addresses are marked by `@email`; that way, the result can be a live link to send email when the output format supports it. If the email address was simply marked as "print in a typewriter font", that would not be possible.

9.1.1 Highlighting Commands are Useful

The commands serve a variety of purposes:

`@code{sample-code}`
> Indicate text that is a literal example of a piece of a program. See Section 9.1.2 [@code], page 79.

`@kbd{keyboard-characters}`
> Indicate keyboard input. See Section 9.1.3 [@kbd], page 80.

`@key{key-name}`
> Indicate the conventional name for a key on a keyboard. See Section 9.1.4 [@key], page 81.

`@samp{text}`
> Indicate text that is a literal example of a sequence of characters. See Section 9.1.5 [@samp], page 82.

`@verb{text}`
> Write a verbatim sequence of characters. See Section 9.1.6 [@verb], page 82.

`@var{metasyntactic-variable}`
> Indicate a metasyntactic variable. See Section 9.1.7 [@var], page 83.

`@env{environment-variable}`
> Indicate an environment variable. See Section 9.1.8 [@env], page 83.

`@file{file-name}`
> Indicate the name of a file. See Section 9.1.9 [@file], page 84.

`@command{command-name}`
> Indicate the name of a command. See Section 9.1.10 [@command], page 84.

`@option{option}`
> Indicate a command-line option. See Section 9.1.11 [@option], page 84.

`@dfn{term}`
> Indicate the introductory or defining use of a term. See Section 9.1.12 [@dfn], page 84.

`@cite{`*reference*`}`
> Indicate the name of a book. See Section 8.10 [`@cite`], page 77.

`@abbr{`*abbreviation*`}`
> Indicate an abbreviation, such as 'Comput.'.

`@acronym{`*acronym*`}`
> Indicate an acronym. See Section 9.1.14 [`@acronym`], page 85.

`@indicateurl{`*uniform-resource-locator*`}`
> Indicate an example (that is, nonfunctional) uniform resource locator. See Section 9.1.15 [`@indicateurl`], page 86. (Use `@url` (see Section 8.9 [`@url`], page 75) for live urls.)

`@email{`*email-address*`[, `*displayed-text*`]}`
> Indicate an electronic mail address. See Section 9.1.16 [`@email`], page 86.

9.1.2 `@code{`*sample-code*`}`

Use the `@code` command to indicate text that is a piece of a program and which consists of entire syntactic tokens. Enclose the text in braces.

Thus, you should use `@code` for an expression in a program, for the name of a variable or function used in a program, or for a keyword in a programming language.

Use `@code` for command names in languages that resemble programming languages, such as Texinfo. For example, `@code` and `@samp` are produced by writing '`@code{@@code}`' and '`@code{@@samp}`' in the Texinfo source, respectively.

It is incorrect to alter the case of a word inside an `@code` command when it appears at the beginning of a sentence. Most computer languages are case sensitive. In C, for example, `Printf` is different from the identifier `printf`, and most likely is a misspelling of it. Even in languages which are not case sensitive, it is confusing to a human reader to see identifiers spelled in different ways. Pick one spelling and always use that. If you do not want to start a sentence with a command name written all in lowercase, you should rearrange the sentence.

In the Info output, `@code` results in single quotation marks around the text. In other formats, `@code` argument is typeset in a typewriter (monospace) font. For example,

        The function returns @code{nil}.

produces this:

        The function returns `nil`.

Here are some cases for which it is preferable *not* to use `@code`:

- For shell command names such as `ls` (use `@command`).
- For environment variable such as `TEXINPUTS` (use `@env`).
- For shell options such as '`-c`' when such options stand alone (use `@option`).
- An entire shell command often looks better if written using `@samp` rather than `@code`. In this case, the rule is to choose the more pleasing format.
- For a string of characters shorter than a syntactic token. For example, if you are writing about '`goto-ch`', which is just a part of the name for the `goto-char` Emacs Lisp function, you should use `@samp`.

- In general, when writing about the characters used in a token; for example, do not use @code when you are explaining what letters or printable symbols can be used in the names of functions. (Use @samp.) Also, you should not use @code to mark text that is considered input to programs unless the input is written in a language that is like a programming language. For example, you should not use @code for the keystroke commands of GNU Emacs (use @kbd instead) although you may use @code for the names of the Emacs Lisp functions that the keystroke commands invoke.

By default, TEX will consider breaking lines at '-' and '_' characters within @code and related commands. This can be controlled with @allowcodebreaks (see Section 15.4 [@allowcodebreaks], page 136). The HTML output attempts to respect this for '-', but ultimately it is up to the browser's behavior. For Info, it seems better never to make such breaks.

For Info, the quotes are omitted in the output of the @code command and related commands (e.g., @kbd, @command), in typewriter-like contexts such as the @example environment (see Section 10.4 [@example], page 91) and @code itself, etc.

To control which quoting characters are implicitly inserted by Texinfo processors in the output of '@code', etc., see the OPEN_QUOTE_SYMBOL and CLOSE_QUOTE_SYMBOL customization variables (see Section 22.5.4 [Other Customization Variables], page 204). This is separate from how actual quotation characters in the input document are handled (see Section 14.2 [Inserting Quote Characters], page 121).

9.1.3 @kbd{*keyboard-characters*}

Use the @kbd command for characters of input to be typed by users. For example, to refer to the characters *M-a*, write:

    @kbd{M-a}

and to refer to the characters *M-x shell*, write:

    @kbd{M-x shell}

By default, the @kbd command produces a different font (slanted typewriter instead of normal typewriter), so users can distinguish the characters that they are supposed to type from those that the computer outputs.

Since the usage of @kbd varies from manual to manual, you can control the font switching with the @kbdinputstyle command. This command has no effect on Info output. Write this command at the beginning of a line with a single word as an argument, one of the following:

'code'   Always use the same font for @kbd as @code.

'example'   Use the distinguishing font for @kbd only in @example and similar environments.

'distinct'
            (the default) Always use the distinguishing font for @kbd.

You can embed another @-command inside the braces of an @kbd command. Here, for example, is the way to describe a command that would be described more verbosely as "press the 'r' key and then press the RETURN key":

    @kbd{r @key{RET}}

This produces: *r RET*. (The present manual uses the default for @kbdinputstyle.)

You also use the `@kbd` command if you are spelling out the letters you type; for example:

```
To give the @code{logout} command,
type the characters @kbd{l o g o u t @key{RET}}.
```

This produces:

To give the `logout` command, type the characters *l o g o u t RET*.

(Also, this example shows that you can add spaces for clarity. If you explicitly want to mention a space character as one of the characters of input, write *@key{SPC}* for it.)

9.1.4 @key{*key-name*}

Use the `@key` command for the conventional name for a key on a keyboard, as in:

```
@key{RET}
```

You can use the `@key` command within the argument of an `@kbd` command when the sequence of characters to be typed includes one or more keys that are described by name.

For example, to produce *C-x ESC* and *M-TAB* you would type:

```
@kbd{C-x @key{ESC}}
@kbd{M-@key{TAB}}
```

Here is a list of the recommended names for keys:

SPC	Space
RET	Return
LFD	Linefeed (however, since most keyboards nowadays do not have a Linefeed key, it might be better to call this character *C-j*)
TAB	Tab
BS	Backspace
ESC	Escape
DELETE	Delete
SHIFT	Shift
CTRL	Control
META	Meta

There are subtleties to handling words like 'meta' or 'ctrl' that are names of modifier keys. When mentioning a character in which the modifier key is used, such as *Meta-a*, use the `@kbd` command alone; do not use the `@key` command; but when you are referring to the modifier key in isolation, use the `@key` command. For example, write '`@kbd{Meta-a}`' to produce *Meta-a* and '`@key{META}`' to produce META.

As a convention in GNU manuals, `@key` should not be used in index entries.

9.1.5 @samp{*text*}

Use the `@samp` command to indicate text that is a literal example or 'sample' of a sequence of characters in a file, string, pattern, etc. Enclose the text in braces. The argument appears within single quotation marks in both the Info file and the printed manual; in addition, it is printed in a fixed-width font.

```
To match @samp{foo} at the end of the line,
use the regexp @samp{foo$}.
```

produces

> To match 'foo' at the end of the line, use the regexp 'foo$'.

Any time you are referring to single characters, you should use `@samp` unless `@kbd` or `@key` is more appropriate. Also, you may use `@samp` for entire statements in C and for entire shell commands—in this case, `@samp` often looks better than `@code`. Basically, `@samp` is a catchall for whatever is not covered by `@code`, `@kbd`, `@key`, `@command`, etc.

Only include punctuation marks within braces if they are part of the string you are specifying. Write punctuation marks outside the braces if those punctuation marks are part of the English text that surrounds the string. In the following sentence, for example, the commas and period are outside of the braces:

```
In English, the vowels are @samp{a}, @samp{e},
@samp{i}, @samp{o}, @samp{u}, and sometimes
@samp{y}.
```

This produces:

> In English, the vowels are 'a', 'e', 'i', 'o', 'u', and sometimes 'y'.

9.1.6 @verb{*chartextchar*}

Use the `@verb` command to print a verbatim sequence of characters.

Like LaTeX's `\verb` command, the verbatim text can be quoted using any unique delimiter character. Enclose the verbatim text, including the delimiters, in braces. Text is printed in a fixed-width font:

```
How many @verb{|@|}-escapes does one need to print this
@verb{.@a @b.@c.} string or @verb{+@'e?'{}!'\+} this?
```

produces

```
How many @-escapes does one need to print this
@a @b.@c string or @'e?'{}!'\ this?
```

This is in contrast to `@samp` (see the previous section), `@code`, and similar commands; in those cases, the argument is normal Texinfo text, where the three characters `@{}` are special, as usual. With `@verb`, nothing is special except the delimiter character you choose.

The delimiter character itself may appear inside the verbatim text, as shown above. As another example, '`@verb{...}`' prints a single (fixed-width) period.

It is not reliable to use `@verb` inside other Texinfo constructs. In particular, it does not work to use `@verb` in anything related to cross referencing, such as section titles or figure captions.

9.1.7 @var{*metasyntactic-variable*}

Use the @var command to indicate metasyntactic variables. A *metasyntactic variable* is something that stands for another piece of text. For example, you should use a metasyntactic variable in the documentation of a function to describe the arguments that are passed to that function.

Do not use @var for the names of normal variables in computer programs. These are specific names, so @code is correct for them (@code). For example, the Emacs Lisp variable `texinfo-tex-command` is not a metasyntactic variable; it is properly formatted using @code.

Do not use @var for environment variables either; @env is correct for them (see the next section).

The effect of @var in the Info file is to change the case of the argument to all uppercase. In the printed manual and HTML output, the argument is output in slanted type.

For example,

```
To delete file @var{filename},
type @samp{rm @var{filename}}.
```

produces

> To delete file *filename*, type '`rm `*`filename`*'.

(Note that @var may appear inside @code, @samp, @file, etc.)

Write a metasyntactic variable all in lowercase without spaces, and use hyphens to make it more readable. Thus, the Texinfo source for the illustration of how to begin a Texinfo manual looks like this:

```
\input texinfo
@@setfilename @var{info-file-name}
@@settitle @var{name-of-manual}
```

This produces:

```
\input texinfo
@setfilename info-file-name
@settitle name-of-manual
```

In some documentation styles, metasyntactic variables are shown with angle brackets, for example:

```
..., type rm <filename>
```

However, that is not the style that Texinfo uses.

9.1.8 @env{*environment-variable*}

Use the @env command to indicate environment variables, as used by many operating systems, including GNU. Do not use it for *meta*syntactic variables; use @var for those (see the previous section).

@env is equivalent to @code in its effects. For example:

```
The @env{PATH} environment variable ...
```

produces

> The `PATH` environment variable ...

9.1.9 @file{*file-name*}

Use the @file command to indicate text that is the name of a file, buffer, or directory, or is the name of a node in Info. You can also use the command for file name suffixes. Do not use @file for symbols in a programming language; use @code.

@file is equivalent to code in its effects. For example,

```
The @file{.el} files are in
the @file{/usr/local/emacs/lisp} directory.
```

produces

> The .el files are in the /usr/local/emacs/lisp directory.

9.1.10 @command{*command-name*}

Use the @command command to indicate command names, such as ls or cc.

@command is equivalent to @code in its effects. For example:

```
The command @command{ls} lists directory contents.
```

produces

> The command ls lists directory contents.

You should write the name of a program in the ordinary text font, rather than using @command, if you regard it as a new English word, such as 'Emacs' or 'Bison'.

When writing an entire shell command invocation, as in 'ls -l', you should use either @samp or @code at your discretion.

9.1.11 @option{*option-name*}

Use the @option command to indicate a command-line option; for example, -l or --version or --output=*filename*.

@option is equivalent to @code in its effects. For example:

```
The option @option{-l} produces a long listing.
```

produces

> The option -l produces a long listing.

9.1.12 @dfn{*term*}

Use the @dfn command to identify the introductory or defining use of a technical term. Use the command only in passages whose purpose is to introduce a term which will be used again or which the reader ought to know. Mere passing mention of a term for the first time does not deserve @dfn. The command generates italics in the printed manual, and double quotation marks in the Info file. For example:

```
Getting rid of a file is called @dfn{deleting} it.
```

produces

> Getting rid of a file is called *deleting* it.

As a general rule, a sentence containing the defining occurrence of a term should be a definition of the term. The sentence does not need to say explicitly that it is a definition, but it should contain the information of a definition—it should make the meaning clear.

9.1.13 @abbr{*abbreviation*[, *meaning*]}

You can use the **@abbr** command for general abbreviations. The abbreviation is given as the single argument in braces, as in '**@abbr{Comput.}**'. As a matter of style, or for particular abbreviations, you may prefer to omit periods, as in '**@abbr{Mr} Stallman**'.

@abbr accepts an optional second argument, intended to be used for the meaning of the abbreviation.

If the abbreviation ends with a lowercase letter and a period, and is not at the end of a sentence, and has no second argument, remember to use the **@.** command (see Section 14.3.3 [Ending a Sentence], page 123) to get the correct spacing. However, you do not have to use **@.** within the abbreviation itself; Texinfo automatically assumes periods within the abbreviation do not end a sentence.

In TEX and in the Info output, the first argument is printed as-is; if the second argument is present, it is printed in parentheses after the abbreviation. In HTML the **<abbr>** tag is used; in Docbook, the **<abbrev>** tag is used. For instance:

```
@abbr{Comput. J., Computer Journal}
```

produces:

Comput. J. (Computer Journal)

For abbreviations consisting of all capital letters, you may prefer to use the **@acronym** command instead. See the next section for more on the usage of these two commands.

9.1.14 @acronym{*acronym*[, *meaning*]}

You can use the **@acronym** command for abbreviations written in all capital letters, such as 'NASA'. The abbreviation is given as the single argument in braces, as in '**@acronym{NASA}**'. As a matter of style, or for particular acronyms, you may prefer to use periods, as in '**@acronym{N.A.S.A.}**'.

@acronym accepts an optional second argument, intended to be used for the meaning of the acronym.

If the acronym is at the end of a sentence, and if there is no second argument, remember to use the **@.** or similar command (see Section 14.3.3 [Ending a Sentence], page 123) to get the correct spacing.

In TEX, the acronym is printed in slightly smaller font. In the Info output, the argument is printed as-is. In either format, if the second argument is present, it is printed in parentheses after the acronym. In HTML and Docbook the **<acronym>** tag is used.

For instance (since GNU is a recursive acronym, we use **@acronym** recursively):

```
@acronym{GNU, @acronym{GNU}'s Not Unix}
```

produces:

GNU (GNU's Not Unix)

In some circumstances, it is conventional to print family names in all capitals. Don't use **@acronym** for this, since a name is not an acronym. Use **@sc** instead (see Section 9.2.2 [Smallcaps], page 87).

@abbr and **@acronym** are closely related commands: they both signal to the reader that a shortened form is being used, and possibly give a meaning. When choosing whether to use these two commands, please bear the following in mind.

- In common English usage, acronyms are a subset of abbreviations: they include pronounceable words like 'NATO', 'radar', and 'snafu'; some sources also include syllable acronyms like 'Usenet', hybrids like 'SIGGRAPH', and unpronounceable initialisms like 'FBI'.

- In Texinfo, an acronym (but not an abbreviation) should consist only of capital letters and periods, no lowercase.

- In TeX, an acronym (but not an abbreviation) is printed in a slightly smaller font.

- Some browsers place a dotted bottom border under abbreviations but not acronyms.

- It usually turns out to be quite difficult and/or time-consuming to consistently use @acronym for all sequences of uppercase letters. Furthermore, it looks strange for some acronyms to be in the normal font size and others to be smaller. Thus, a simpler approach you may wish to consider is to avoid @acronym and just typeset everything as normal text in all capitals: 'GNU', producing the output 'GNU'.

- In general, it's not essential to use either of these commands for all abbreviations; use your judgment. Text is perfectly readable without them.

9.1.15 @indicateurl{*uniform-resource-locator*}

Use the @indicateurl command to indicate a uniform resource locator on the World Wide Web. This is purely for markup purposes and does not produce a link you can follow (use the @url or @uref command for that, see Section 8.9 [@url], page 75). @indicateurl is useful for urls which do not actually exist. For example:

> For example, the url might be @indicateurl{http://example.org/path}.

which produces:

> For example, the url might be 'http://example.org/path'.

The output from @indicateurl is more or less like that of @samp (see Section 9.1.5 [@samp], page 82).

9.1.16 @email{*email-address*[, *displayed-text*]}

Use the @email command to indicate an electronic mail address. It takes one mandatory argument, the address, and one optional argument, the text to display (the default is the address itself).

In Info, the address is shown in angle brackets, preceded by the text to display if any. In TeX, the angle brackets are omitted. In HTML output, @email produces a 'mailto' link that usually brings up a mail composition window. For example:

> Send bug reports to @email{bug-texinfo@@gnu.org},
> suggestions to the @email{bug-texinfo@@gnu.org, same place}.

produces

> Send bug reports to bug-texinfo@gnu.org,
> suggestions to the same place.

9.2 Emphasizing Text

Usually, Texinfo changes the font to mark words in the text according to the category the words belong to; an example is the @code command. Most often, this is the best way to mark words. However, sometimes you will want to emphasize text without indicating a category. Texinfo has two commands to do this. Also, Texinfo has several commands that specify the font in which text will be output. These commands have no effect in Info and only one of them, the `@r` command, has any regular use.

9.2.1 `@emph{`*text*`}` and `@strong{`*text*`}`

The `@emph` and `@strong` commands are for emphasis; `@strong` is stronger. In printed output, `@emph` produces *italics* and `@strong` produces **bold**. In the Info output, `@emph` surrounds the text with underscores ('`_`'), and `@strong` puts asterisks around the text.

For example,

```
@strong{Caution:} @samp{rm *}
removes @emph{all} normal files.
```

produces the following:

Caution: '`rm * .[^.]*`' removes *all* normal files.

The `@strong` command is seldom used except to mark what is, in effect, a typographical element, such as the word 'Caution' in the preceding example.

Caution: Do not use `@strong` with the word '`Note`' followed by a space; Info will mistake the combination for a cross reference. Use a phrase such as **Please notice** or **Caution** instead, or the optional argument to `@quotation`—'Note' is allowable there.

9.2.2 `@sc{`*text*`}`: The Small Caps Font

Use the '`@sc`' command to set text in A SMALL CAPS FONT (where possible). Write the text you want to be in small caps between braces in lowercase, like this:

```
Richard @sc{Stallman} commencé GNU.
```

This produces:

Richard STALLMAN commencé GNU.

As shown here, we recommend reserving `@sc` for special cases where you want typographic small caps; family names are one such, especially in languages other than English, though there are no hard-and-fast rules about such things.

TeX typesets any uppercase letters between the braces of an `@sc` command in full-size capitals; only lowercase letters are printed in the small caps font. In the Info output, the argument to `@sc` is printed in all uppercase. In HTML, the argument is uppercased and the output marked with the `<small>` tag to reduce the font size, since HTML cannot easily represent true small caps.

Overall, we recommend using standard upper- and lowercase letters wherever possible.

9.2.3 Fonts for Printing

Texinfo provides one command to change the size of the main body font in the TeX output for a document: `@fonttextsize`. It has no effect in other output. It takes a single argument on the remainder of the line, which must be either '10' or '11'. For example:

```
@fonttextsize 10
```

The effect is to reduce the body font to a 10 pt size (the default is 11 pt). Fonts for other elements, such as sections and chapters, are reduced accordingly. This should only be used in conjunction with `@smallbook` (see Section 21.11 [`@smallbook`], page 186) or similar, since 10 pt fonts on standard paper (8.5x11 or A4) are too small. One reason to use this command is to save pages, and hence printing cost, for physical books.

Texinfo does not at present have commands to switch the font family to use, or more general size-changing commands.

Texinfo also provides a number of font commands that specify font changes in the printed manual and (where possible) in the HTML output. They have no effect in Info. All the commands apply to a following argument surrounded by braces.

`@b`   selects **bold** face;

`@i`   selects an *italic* font;

`@r`   selects a roman font, which is the usual font in which text is printed. It may or may not be seriffed.

`@sansserif`
                    selects a sans serif font;

`@slanted`   selects a *slanted* font;

`@t`   selects the `fixed-width`, typewriter-style font used by `@code`;

(The commands with longer names were invented much later than the others, at which time it did not seem desirable to use very short names for such infrequently needed features.)

The `@r` command can be useful in example-like environments, to write comments in the standard roman font instead of the fixed-width font. This looks better in printed output, and produces a `<lineannotation>` tag in Docbook output.

For example,

```
@lisp
(+ 2 2)      ; @r{Add two plus two.}
@end lisp
```

produces

```
(+ 2 2)      ; Add two plus two.
```

The `@t` command can occasionally be useful to produce output in a typewriter font where that is supported (e.g., HTML and PDF), but no distinction is needed in Info or plain text: `@t{foo}` produces `foo`, cf. `@code{foo}` producing `foo`.

For example, we use `@t` in the `@node` commands for this manual to specify the Texinfo command names, because the quotes which `@code` outputs look extraneous in that particular context.

In general, the other font commands are unlikely to be useful; they exist primarily to make it possible to document the functionality of specific font effects, such as in TeX and related packages.

10 Quotations and Examples

Quotations and examples are blocks of text consisting of one or more whole paragraphs that are set off from the bulk of the text and treated differently. They are usually indented in the output.

In Texinfo, you always begin a quotation or example by writing an @-command at the beginning of a line by itself, and end it by writing an `@end` command that is also at the beginning of a line by itself. For instance, you begin an example by writing `@example` by itself at the beginning of a line and end the example by writing `@end example` on a line by itself, at the beginning of that line, and with only one space between the `@end` and the `example`.

10.1 Block Enclosing Commands

Here is a summary of commands that enclose blocks of text, also known as *environments*. They're explained further in the following sections.

`@quotation`

Indicate text that is quoted. The text is filled, indented (from both margins), and printed in a roman font by default.

`@indentedblock`

Like `@quotation`, but the text is indented only on the left.

`@example`   Illustrate code, commands, and the like. The text is printed in a fixed-width font, and indented but not filled.

`@lisp`   Like `@example`, but specifically for illustrating Lisp code. The text is printed in a fixed-width font, and indented but not filled.

`@verbatim`

Mark a piece of text that is to be printed verbatim; no character substitutions are made and all commands are ignored, until the next `@end verbatim`. The text is printed in a fixed-width font, and not indented or filled. Extra spaces and blank lines are significant, and tabs are expanded.

`@display`   Display illustrative text. The text is indented but not filled, and no font is selected (so, by default, the font is roman).

`@format`   Like `@display` (the text is not filled and no font is selected), but the text is not indented.

`@smallquotation`
`@smallindentedblock`
`@smallexample`
`@smalllisp`
`@smalldisplay`
`@smallformat`

These `@small...` commands are just like their non-small counterparts, except that they output text in a smaller font size, where possible.

`@flushleft`
`@flushright`
> Text is not filled, but is set flush with the left or right margin, respectively.

`@raggedright`
> Text is filled, but only justified on the left, leaving the right margin ragged.

`@cartouche`
> Highlight text, often an example or quotation, by drawing a box with rounded corners around it.

The `@exdent` command is used within the above constructs to undo the indentation of a line.

The `@noindent` command may be used after one of the above constructs (or at the beginning of any paragraph) to prevent the following text from being indented as a new paragraph.

10.2 `@quotation`: Block Quotations

The text of a quotation is processed like normal text (regular font, text is filled) except that:

- both the left and right margins are closer to the center of the page, so the whole of the quotation is indented;
- the first lines of paragraphs are indented no more than other lines; and
- an `@author` command may be given to specify the author of the quotation.

> This is an example of text written between an `@quotation` command and an `@end quotation` command. An `@quotation` command is most often used to indicate text that is excerpted from another (real or hypothetical) printed work.

Write an `@quotation` command as text on a line by itself. This line will disappear from the output. Mark the end of the quotation with a line beginning with and containing only `@end quotation`. The `@end quotation` line will likewise disappear from the output.

`@quotation` takes one optional argument, given on the remainder of the line. This text, if present, is included at the beginning of the quotation in bold or otherwise emphasized, and followed with a ':'. For example:

```
@quotation Note
This is
a foo.
@end quotation
```

produces

> **Note:** This is a foo.

If the `@quotation` argument is one of these English words (case-insensitive):

```
Caution  Important  Note  Tip  Warning
```

then the Docbook output uses corresponding special tags (`<note>`, etc.) instead of the default `<blockquote>`. HTML output always uses `<blockquote>`.

If the author of the quotation is specified in the `@quotation` block with the `@author` command, a line with the author name is displayed after the quotation:

```
@quotation
People sometimes ask me if it is a sin in the Church of Emacs to use
vi.  Using a free version of vi is not a sin; it is a penance.  So happy
hacking.

@author Richard Stallman
@end quotation
```

produces

> People sometimes ask me if it is a sin in the Church of Emacs to use vi. Using a free version of vi is not a sin; it is a penance. So happy hacking.
>
> —*Richard Stallman*

Texinfo also provides a command `@smallquotation`, which is just like `@quotation` but uses a smaller font size where possible. See Section 10.8 [`@small`...], page 94.

10.3 `@indentedblock`: Indented text blocks

The `@indentedblock` environment is similar to `@quotation`, except that text is only indented on the left (and there is no optional argument for an author). Thus, the text font remains unchanged, and text is gathered and filled as usual, but the left margin is increased. For example:

> This is an example of text written between an `@indentedblock` command and an `@end indentedblock` command. The `@indentedblock` environment can contain any text or other commands desired.

This is written in the Texinfo source as:

```
@indentedblock
This is an example ...
@end indentedblock
```

Texinfo also provides a command `@smallindentedblock`, which is just like `@indentedblock` but uses a smaller font size where possible. See Section 10.8 [`@small`...], page 94.

10.4 `@example`: Example Text

The `@example` environment is used to indicate an example that is not part of the running text, such as computer input or output. Write an `@example` command at the beginning of a line by itself. Mark the end of the example with an `@end example` command, also written at the beginning of a line by itself.

An `@example` environment has the following characteristics:

- Each line in the input file is a line in the output; that is, the source text is not filled as it normally is.
- Extra spaces and blank lines are significant.
- The output is indented.
- The output uses a fixed-width font.
- Texinfo commands *are* expanded; if you want the output to be the input verbatim, use the `@verbatim` environment instead (see Section 10.5 [`@verbatim`], page 92).

For example,

```
@example
cp foo @var{dest1}; \
 cp foo @var{dest2}
@end example
```

produces

```
cp foo dest1; \
 cp foo dest2
```

The lines containing `@example` and `@end example` will disappear from the output. To make the output look good, you should put a blank line before the `@example` and another blank line after the `@end example`. Blank lines inside the beginning `@example` and the ending `@end example`, on the other hand, do appear in the output.

> **Caution:** Do not use tabs in the lines of an example! (Or anywhere else in Texinfo, except in verbatim environments.) TeX treats tabs as single spaces, and that is not what they look like. In Emacs, you can use *M-x untabify* to convert tabs in a region to multiple spaces.

Examples are often, logically speaking, "in the middle" of a paragraph, and the text that continues afterwards should not be indented, as in the example above. The `@noindent` command prevents a piece of text from being indented as if it were a new paragraph (see Section 10.14 [`@noindent`], page 97.

If you want to embed code fragments within sentences, instead of displaying them, use the `@code` command or its relatives (see Section 9.1.2 [`@code`], page 79).

If you wish to write a "comment" on a line of an example in the normal roman font, you can use the `@r` command (see Section 9.2.3 [Fonts], page 87).

10.5 `@verbatim`: Literal Text

Use the `@verbatim` environment for printing of text that may contain special characters or commands that should not be interpreted, such as computer input or output (`@example` interprets its text as regular Texinfo commands). This is especially useful for including automatically generated files in a Texinfo manual.

In general, the output will be just the same as the input. No character substitutions are made, e.g., all spaces and blank lines are significant, including tabs. In the printed manual, the text is typeset in a fixed-width font, and not indented or filled.

Write an `@verbatim` command at the beginning of a line by itself. This line will disappear from the output. Mark the end of the verbatim block with an `@end verbatim` command, also written at the beginning of a line by itself. The `@end verbatim` will also disappear from the output.

For example:

```
@verbatim
{
TAB@command with strange characters: @'e
expandTABme
}
```

```
@end verbatim
```

This produces:

```
{
        @command with strange characters: @'e
expand   me
}
```

Since the lines containing `@verbatim` and `@end verbatim` produce no output, typically you should put a blank line before the `@verbatim` and another blank line after the `@end verbatim`. Blank lines between the beginning `@verbatim` and the ending `@end verbatim` will appear in the output.

You can get a "small" verbatim by enclosing the `@verbatim` in an `@smallformat` environment, as shown here:

```
@smallformat
@verbatim
... still verbatim, but in a smaller font ...
@end verbatim
@end smallformat
```

Finally, a word of warning: it is not reliable to use `@verbatim` inside other Texinfo constructs.

10.6 `@verbatiminclude` *file*: Include a File Verbatim

You can include the exact contents of a file in the document with the `@verbatiminclude` command:

```
@verbatiminclude filename
```

The contents of *filename* is printed in a verbatim environment (see Section 10.5 [`@verbatim`], page 92). Generally, the file is printed exactly as it is, with all special characters and white space retained. No indentation is added; if you want indentation, enclose the `@verbatiminclude` within `@example` (see Section 10.4 [`@example`], page 91).

The name of the file is taken literally, with a single exception: `@value{var}` references are expanded. This makes it possible to include files in other directories within a distribution, for instance:

```
@verbatiminclude @value{top_srcdir}/NEWS
```

(You still have to get `top_srcdir` defined in the first place.)

For a method on printing the file contents in a smaller font size, see the end of the previous section on `@verbatim`.

10.7 `@lisp`: Marking a Lisp Example

The `@lisp` command is used for Lisp code. It is synonymous with the `@example` command.

```
This is an example of text written between an
@lisp command and an @end lisp command.
```

Use `@lisp` instead of `@example` to preserve information regarding the nature of the example. This is useful, for example, if you write a function that evaluates only and all the Lisp code in a Texinfo file. Then you can use the Texinfo file as a Lisp library.[1]

Mark the end of `@lisp` with `@end lisp` on a line by itself.

10.8 `@small...` Block Commands

In addition to the regular `@example` and similar commands, Texinfo has "small" example-style commands. These are `@smallquotation`, `@smallindentedblock`, `@smalldisplay`, `@smallexample`, `@smallformat`, and `@smalllisp`.

In Info output, the `@small...` commands are equivalent to their non-small companion commands.

In TeX, however, the `@small...` commands typeset text in a smaller font than the non-small example commands. Thus, for instance, code examples can contain longer lines and still fit on a page without needing to be rewritten.

A smaller font size is also requested in HTML output, and (as usual) retained in the Texinfo XML transliteration.

Mark the end of an `@small...` block with a corresponding `@end small...`. For example, pair `@smallexample` with `@end smallexample`.

Here is an example of the font used by the `@smallexample` command (in Info, the output will be the same as usual):

```
... to make sure that you have the freedom to
distribute copies of free software (and charge for
this service if you wish), that you receive source
code or can get it if you want it, that you can
change the software or use pieces of it in new free
programs; and that you know you can do these things.
```

The `@small...` commands use the same font style as their normal counterparts: `@smallexample` and `@smalllisp` use a fixed-width font, and everything else uses the regular font. They also have the same behavior in other respects—whether filling is done and whether margins are narrowed.

As a general rule, a printed document looks better if you use only one of (for instance) `@example` or `@smallexample` consistently within a chapter.

10.9 `@display`: Examples Using the Text Font

The `@display` command begins another kind of environment, where the font is left unchanged, not switched to typewriter as with `@example`. Each line of input still produces a line of output, and the output is still indented.

This is an example of text written between an `@display` command and an `@end display` command. The `@display` command indents the text, but does not fill it.

Texinfo also provides the environment `@smalldisplay`, which is like `@display` but uses a smaller font size. See Section 10.8 [`@small...`], page 94.

---

[1] It would be straightforward to extend Texinfo to work in a similar fashion for C, Fortran, or other languages.

The @table command (see Section 11.4.1 [@table], page 103) is not supported inside @display. Since @display is line-oriented, it doesn't make sense to use them together. If you want to indent a table, try @quotation (see Section 10.2 [@quotation], page 90) or @indentedblock (see Section 10.3 [@indentedblock], page 91).

10.10 @format: Examples Using the Full Line Width

The @format command is similar to @display, except it leaves the text unindented. Like @display, it does not select the fixed-width font.

This is an example of text written between an @format command
and an @end format command. As you can see
from this example,
the @format command does not fill the text.

Texinfo also provides the environment @smallformat, which is like @format but uses a smaller font size. See Section 10.8 [@small...], page 94.

10.11 @exdent: Undoing a Line's Indentation

The @exdent command removes any indentation a line might have. The command is written at the beginning of a line and applies only to the text that follows the command that is on the same line. Do not use braces around the text. In a printed manual, the text on an @exdent line is printed in the roman font.

@exdent is usually used within examples. Thus,

```
@example
This line follows an @@example command.
@exdent This line is exdented.
This line follows the exdented line.
The @@end example comes on the next line.
@end example
```

produces

```
This line follows an @example command.
```
This line is exdented.
```
This line follows the exdented line.
The @end example comes on the next line.
```

In practice, the @exdent command is rarely used. Usually, you un-indent text by ending the example and returning the page to its normal width.

@exdent has no effect in HTML output.

10.12 @flushleft and @flushright

The @flushleft and @flushright commands line up the ends of lines on the left and right margins of a page, but do not fill the text. The commands are written on lines of their own, without braces. The @flushleft and @flushright commands are ended by @end flushleft and @end flushright commands on lines of their own.

For example,

```
@flushleft
This text is
written flushleft.
@end flushleft
```

produces

This text is
written flushleft.

`@flushright` produces the type of indentation often used in the return address of letters. For example,

```
@flushright
Here is an example of text written
flushright.  The @code{@flushright} command
right justifies every line but leaves the
left end ragged.
@end flushright
```

produces

> Here is an example of text written
> flushright. The `@flushright` command
> right justifies every line but leaves the
> left end ragged.

10.13 `@raggedright`: Ragged Right Text

The `@raggedright` fills text as usual, but the text is only justified on the left; the right margin is ragged. The command is written on a line of its own, without braces. The `@raggedright` command is ended by `@end raggedright` on a line of its own. This command has no effect in Info and HTML output, where text is always set ragged right.

The `@raggedright` command can be useful with paragraphs containing lists of commands with long names, when it is known in advance that justifying the text on both margins will make the paragraph look bad.

An example (from elsewhere in this manual):

```
@raggedright
Commands for double and single angle quotation marks:
@code{@@guillemetleft@{@}}, @code{@@guillemetright@{@}},
@code{@@guillemotleft@{@}}, @code{@@guillemotright@{@}},
@code{@@guilsinglleft@{@}}, @code{@@guilsinglright@{@}}.
@end raggedright
```

produces

Commands for double and single angle quotation marks: `@guillemetleft{}`, `@guillemetright{}`, `@guillemotleft{}`, `@guillemotright{}`, `@guilsinglleft{}`, `@guilsinglright{}`.

10.14 @noindent: Omitting Indentation

An example or other inclusion can break a paragraph into segments. Ordinarily, the formatters indent text that follows an example as a new paragraph. You can prevent this on a case-by-case basis by writing @noindent at the beginning of a line, preceding the continuation text. You can also disable indentation for all paragraphs globally with @paragraphindent (see Section 3.7.4 [@paragraphindent], page 43).

Here is an example showing how to eliminate the normal indentation of the text after an @example, a common situation:

```
@example
This is an example
@end example

@noindent
This line is not indented.  As you can see, the
beginning of the line is fully flush left with the
line that follows after it.
```

produces:

```
    This is an example
```

This line is not indented. As you can see, the
beginning of the line is fully flush left with the
line that follows after it.

The standard usage of @indent is just as above: at the beginning of what would otherwise be a paragraph, to eliminate the indentation that normally happens there. It can either be followed by text or be on a line by itself. There is no reason to use it in other contexts, such as in the middle of a paragraph or inside an environment (see Chapter 10 [Quotations and Examples], page 89).

You can control the number of blank lines in the Info file output by adjusting the input as desired: a line containing just @noindent does not generate a blank line, and neither does an @end line for an environment.

Do not put braces after an @noindent command; they are not used, since @noindent is a command used outside of paragraphs (see Section A.1 [Command Syntax], page 256).

10.15 @indent: Forcing Indentation

To complement the @noindent command (see the previous section), Texinfo provides the @indent command to force a paragraph to be indented. For instance, this paragraph (the first in this section) is indented using an @indent command.

And indeed, the first paragraph of a section is the most likely place to use @indent, to override the normal behavior of no indentation there (see Section 3.7.4 [@paragraphindent], page 43). It can either be followed by text or be on a line by itself.

As a special case, when @indent is used in an environment where text is not filled, it produces a paragraph indentation space in the TeX output. (These environments are where a line of input produces a line of output, such as @example and @display; for a summary of all environments, see Section 10.1 [Block Enclosing Commands], page 89.)

Do not put braces after an @indent command; they are not used, since @indent is a command used outside of paragraphs (see Section A.1 [Command Syntax], page 256).

10.16 @cartouche: Rounded Rectangles

In a printed manual, the @cartouche command draws a box with rounded corners around its contents. In HTML, a normal rectangle is drawn. @cartouche has no effect in Info output.

You can use this command to further highlight an example or quotation. For instance, you could write a manual in which one type of example is surrounded by a cartouche for emphasis.

For example,

```
@cartouche
@example
% pwd
/usr/local/share/emacs
@end example
@end cartouche
```

surrounds the two-line example with a box with rounded corners, in the printed manual.

The output from the example looks like this (if you're reading this in Info, you'll see the @cartouche had no effect):

```
% pwd
/usr/local/info
```

@cartouche also implies @group (see Section 15.9 [@group], page 137).

11 Lists and Tables

Texinfo has several ways of making lists and tables. Lists can be bulleted or numbered; two-column tables can highlight the items in the first column; multi-column tables are also supported.

11.1 Introducing Lists

Texinfo automatically indents the text in lists or tables, and numbers an enumerated list. This last feature is useful if you modify the list, since you do not need to renumber it yourself.

Numbered lists and tables begin with the appropriate @-command at the beginning of a line, and end with the corresponding `@end` command on a line by itself. The table and itemized-list commands also require that you write formatting information on the same line as the beginning @-command.

Begin an enumerated list, for example, with an `@enumerate` command and end the list with an `@end enumerate` command. Begin an itemized list with an `@itemize` command, followed on the same line by a formatting command such as `@bullet`, and end the list with an `@end itemize` command.

Precede each element of a list with an `@item` or `@itemx` command.

Here is an itemized list of the different kinds of table and lists:

- Itemized lists with and without bullets.
- Enumerated lists, using numbers or letters.
- Two-column tables with highlighting.

Here is an enumerated list with the same items:

1. Itemized lists with and without bullets.
2. Enumerated lists, using numbers or letters.
3. Two-column tables with highlighting.

And here is a two-column table with the same items and their @-commands:

`@itemize`   Itemized lists with and without bullets.

`@enumerate`
              Enumerated lists, using numbers or letters.

`@table`
`@ftable`
`@vtable`   Two-column tables, optionally with indexing.

11.2 `@itemize`: Making an Itemized List

The `@itemize` command produces a sequence of "items", each starting with a bullet or other mark inside the left margin, and generally indented.

Begin an itemized list by writing `@itemize` at the beginning of a line. Follow the command, on the same line, with a character or a Texinfo command that generates a mark. Usually, you will use `@bullet` after `@itemize`, but you can use `@minus`, or any command or character that results in a single character in the Info file. (When you write the mark command such as `@bullet` after an `@itemize` command, you may omit the '`{}`'.) If you don't specify a mark command, the default is `@bullet`. If you don't want any mark at all, but still want logical items, use `@w{}` (in this case the braces are required).

After the `@itemize`, write your items, each starting with `@item`. Text can follow on the same line as the `@item`. The text of an item can continue for more than one paragraph.

There should be at least one `@item` inside the `@itemize` environment. If none are present, `makeinfo` gives a warning. If you just want indented text and not a list of items, use `@indentedblock`; see Section 10.3 [`@indentedblock`], page 91.

Index entries and comments that are given before an `@item` including the first, are automatically moved (internally) to after the `@item`, so the output is as expected. Historically this has been a common practice.

Usually, you should put a blank line between items. This puts a blank line in the Info file. (TEX inserts the proper vertical space in any case.) Except when the entries are very brief, these blank lines make the list look better.

Here is an example of the use of `@itemize`, followed by the output it produces. `@bullet` produces an '`*`' in Info and a round dot in other output formats.

```
@itemize @bullet
@item
Some text for foo.

@item
Some text
for bar.
@end itemize
```

This produces:

- Some text for foo.

- Some text for bar.

Itemized lists may be embedded within other itemized lists. Here is a list marked with dashes embedded in a list marked with bullets:

```
@itemize @bullet
@item
First item.

@itemize @minus
@item
Inner item.

@item
Second inner item.
@end itemize

@item
Second outer item.
@end itemize
```

This produces:

- First item.
  - Inner item.
  - Second inner item.
- Second outer item.

11.3 @enumerate: Making a Numbered or Lettered List

@enumerate is like @itemize (see Section 11.2 [@itemize], page 100), except that the labels on the items are successive integers or letters instead of bullets.

Write the @enumerate command at the beginning of a line. The command does not require an argument, but accepts either a number or a letter as an option. Without an argument, @enumerate starts the list with the number '1'. With a numeric argument, such as '3', the command starts the list with that number. With an upper- or lowercase letter, such as 'a' or 'A', the command starts the list with that letter.

Write the text of the enumerated list in the same way as an itemized list: write a line starting with @item at the beginning of each item in the enumeration. It is ok to have text following the @item, and the text for an item can continue for several paragraphs.

You should put a blank line between entries in the list. This generally makes it easier to read the Info file.

Here is an example of @enumerate without an argument:

```
@enumerate
@item
Underlying causes.

@item
Proximate causes.
@end enumerate
```

This produces:

1. Underlying causes.

2. Proximate causes.

   Here is an example with an argument of *3*:

   ```
   @enumerate 3
   @item
   Predisposing causes.

   @item
   Precipitating causes.

   @item
   Perpetuating causes.
   @end enumerate
   ```

This produces:

3. Predisposing causes.

4. Precipitating causes.

5. Perpetuating causes.

Here is a brief summary of the alternatives. The summary is constructed using @enumerate with an argument of a.

a. @enumerate

   Without an argument, produce a numbered list, starting with the number 1.

b. @enumerate *positive-integer*

   With a (positive) numeric argument, start a numbered list with that number. You can use this to continue a list that you interrupted with other text.

c. @enumerate *upper-case-letter*

   With an uppercase letter as argument, start a list in which each item is marked by a letter, beginning with that uppercase letter.

d. @enumerate *lower-case-letter*

   With a lowercase letter as argument, start a list in which each item is marked by a letter, beginning with that lowercase letter.

   You can also nest enumerated lists, as in an outline.

11.4 Making a Two-column Table

@table is similar to @itemize (see Section 11.2 [@itemize], page 100), but allows you to specify a name or heading line for each item. The @table command is used to produce two-column tables, and is especially useful for glossaries, explanatory exhibits, and command-line option summaries.

11.4.1 Using the `@table` Command

Use the `@table` command to produce two-column tables. It is typically used when you have a list of items and a brief text with each one, such as "definition lists".

Write the `@table` command at the beginning of a line, after a blank line, and follow it on the same line with an argument that is a Texinfo "indicating" command such as `@code`, `@samp`, `@var`, `@option`, or `@kbd` (see Section 9.1 [Indicating], page 78).

This command will be applied to the text that goes into the first column of each item and thus determines how it will be highlighted. For example, `@table @code` will cause the text in the first column to be output as if it had been the argument to an `@code` command.

You may also use the `@asis` command as an argument to `@table`. `@asis` is a command that does nothing; if you use this command after `@table`, the first column entries are output without added highlighting ("as is").

The `@table` command works with other commands besides those explicitly mentioned here. However, you can only use predefined Texinfo commands that normally take an argument in braces. You cannot reliably use a new command defined with `@macro`, but an `@alias` (for a suitable predefined command) is acceptable. See Chapter 19 [Defining New Texinfo Commands], page 165.

Begin each table entry with an `@item` command at the beginning of a line. Write the first column text on the same line as the `@item` command. Write the second column text on the line following the `@item` line and on subsequent lines. (You do not need to type anything for an empty second column entry.) You may write as many lines of supporting text as you wish, even several paragraphs. But only the text on the same line as the `@item` will be placed in the first column (including any footnotes).

Normally, you should put a blank line before an `@item` line (except the first one). This puts a blank line in the Info file. Except when the entries are very brief, a blank line looks better.

End the table with a line consisting of `@end table`, followed by a blank line. TEX will always start a new paragraph after the table, so the blank line is needed for the Info output to be analogous.

The following table, for example, highlights the text in the first column with an `@samp` command:

```
@table @samp
@item foo
This is the text for
@samp{foo}.

@item bar
Text for @samp{bar}.
@end table
```

This produces:

'foo'   This is the text for 'foo'.

'bar'   Text for 'bar'.

If you want to list two or more named items with a single block of text, use the `@itemx` command. (See Section 11.4.3 [`@itemx`], page 104.)

11.4.2 @ftable and @vtable

The @ftable and @vtable commands are the same as the @table command except that @ftable automatically enters each of the items in the first column of the table into the index of functions and @vtable automatically enters each of the items in the first column of the table into the index of variables. This simplifies the task of creating indices. Only the items on the same line as the @item commands are indexed, and they are indexed in exactly the form that they appear on that line. See Chapter 13 [Indices], page 114, for more information about indices.

Begin a two-column table using @ftable or @vtable by writing the @-command at the beginning of a line, followed on the same line by an argument that is a Texinfo command such as @code, exactly as you would for an @table command; and end the table with an @end ftable or @end vtable command on a line by itself.

See the example for @table in the previous section.

11.4.3 @itemx: Second and Subsequent Items

Use the @itemx command inside a table when you have two or more first column entries for the same item, each of which should appear on a line of its own.

Use @item for the first entry, and @itemx for all subsequent entries; @itemx must always follow an @item command, with no blank line intervening.

The @itemx command works exactly like @item except that it does not generate extra vertical space above the first column text. If you have multiple consecutive @itemx commands, do not insert any blank lines between them.

For example,

```
@table @code
@item upcase
@itemx downcase
These two functions accept a character or a string as
argument, and return the corresponding uppercase (lowercase)
character or string.
@end table
```

This produces:

upcase
downcase   These two functions accept a character or a string as argument, and return the
             corresponding uppercase (lowercase) character or string.

(Note also that this example illustrates multi-line supporting text in a two-column table.)

11.5 @multitable: Multi-column Tables

@multitable allows you to construct tables with any number of columns, with each column having any width you like.

You define the column widths on the @multitable line itself, and write each row of the actual table following an @item command, with columns separated by an @tab command. Finally, @end multitable completes the table. Details in the sections below.

11.5.1 Multitable Column Widths

You can define the column widths for a multitable in two ways: as fractions of the line length; or with a prototype row. Mixing the two methods is not supported. In either case, the widths are defined entirely on the same line as the @multitable command.

1. To specify column widths as fractions of the line length, write @columnfractions and the decimal numbers (presumably less than 1; a leading zero is allowed and ignored) after the @multitable command, as in:

```
@multitable @columnfractions .33 .33 .33
```

The fractions need not add up exactly to 1.0, as these do not. This allows you to produce tables that do not need the full line length.

2. To specify a prototype row, write the longest entry for each column enclosed in braces after the @multitable command. For example:

```
@multitable {some text for column one} {for column two}
```

The first column will then have the width of the typeset 'some text for column one', and the second column the width of 'for column two'.

The prototype entries need not appear in the table itself.

Although we used simple text in this example, the prototype entries can contain Texinfo commands; markup commands such as @code are particularly likely to be useful.

11.5.2 Multitable Rows

After the @multitable command defining the column widths (see the previous section), you begin each row in the body of a multitable with @item, and separate the column entries with @tab. Line breaks are not special within the table body, and you may break input lines in your source file as necessary.

You can also use @headitem instead of @item to produce a *heading row*. The TeX output for such a row is in bold, and the HTML and Docbook output uses the <thead> tag. In Info, the heading row is followed by a separator line made of dashes ('-' characters).

The command @headitemfont can be used in templates when the entries in an @headitem row need to be used in a template. It is a synonym for @b, but using @headitemfont avoids any dependency on that particular font style, in case we provide a way to change it in the future.

Here is a complete example of a multi-column table (the text is from *The GNU Emacs Manual*, see Section "Splitting Windows" in *The GNU Emacs Manual*):

```
@multitable @columnfractions .15 .45 .4
@headitem Key @tab Command @tab Description
@item C-x 2
@tab @code{split-window-vertically}
@tab Split the selected window into two windows,
with one above the other.
@item C-x 3
@tab @code{split-window-horizontally}
@tab Split the selected window into two windows
positioned side by side.
@item C-Mouse-2
```

```
@tab
@tab In the mode line or scroll bar of a window,
split that window.
@end multitable
```

produces:

Key	Command	Description
C-x 2	`split-window-vertically`	Split the selected window into two windows, with one above the other.
C-x 3	`split-window-horizontally`	Split the selected window into two windows positioned side by side.
C-Mouse-2		In the mode line or scroll bar of a window, split that window.

12 Special Displays

The commands in this chapter allow you to write text that is specially displayed (output format permitting), outside of the normal document flow.

One set of such commands is for creating "floats", that is, figures, tables, and the like, set off from the main text, possibly numbered, captioned, and/or referred to from elsewhere in the document. Images are often included in these displays.

Another group of commands is for creating footnotes in Texinfo.

12.1 Floats

A *float* is a display which is set off from the main text. It is typically labeled as being a "Figure", "Table", "Example", or some similar type.

A float is so-named because, in principle, it can be moved to the bottom or top of the current page, or to a following page, in the printed output. (Floating does not make sense in other output formats.) In the present version of Texinfo, however, this floating is unfortunately not yet implemented. Instead, the floating material is simply output at the current location, more or less as if it were an `@group` (see Section 15.9 [`@group`], page 137).

12.1.1 `@float` [*type*][,*label*]: Floating Material

To produce floating material, enclose the material you want to be displayed separate between `@float` and `@end float` commands, on lines by themselves.

Floating material often uses `@image` to display an already-existing graphic (see Section 12.2 [Images], page 109), or `@multitable` to display a table (see Section 11.5 [Multi-column Tables], page 104). However, the contents of the float can be anything. Here's an example with simple text:

```
@float Figure,fig:ex1
This is an example float.
@end float
```

And the output:

This is an example float.

Figure 12.1

As shown in the example, `@float` takes two arguments (separated by a comma), *type* and *label*. Both are optional.

type   Specifies the sort of float this is; typically a word such as "Figure", "Table", etc. If this is not given, and *label* is, any cross referencing will simply use a bare number.

label   Specifies a cross reference label for this float. If given, this float is automatically given a number, and will appear in any `@listoffloats` output (see Section 12.1.3 [`@listoffloats`], page 108). Cross references to *label* are allowed.

On the other hand, if *label* is not given, then the float will not be numbered and consequently will not appear in the `@listoffloats` output or be cross-referenceable.

Ordinarily, you specify both *type* and *label*, to get a labeled and numbered float.

In Texinfo, all floats are numbered in the same way: with the chapter number (or appendix letter), a period, and the float number, which simply counts 1, 2, 3, ..., and is reset at each chapter. Each float type is counted independently.

Floats within an @unnumbered, or outside of any chapter, are simply numbered consecutively from 1.

These numbering conventions are not, at present, changeable.

12.1.2 @caption & @shortcaption

You may write an @caption anywhere within an @float environment, to define a caption for the float. It is not allowed in any other context. @caption takes a single argument, enclosed in braces. Here's an example:

```
@float
An example float, with caption.
@caption{Caption for example float.}
@end float
```

The output is:

An example float, with caption.

Caption for example float.

@caption can appear anywhere within the float; it is not processed until the @end float. The caption text is usually a sentence or two, but may consist of several paragraphs if necessary.

In the output, the caption always appears below the float; this is not currently changeable. It is preceded by the float type and/or number, as specified to the @float command (see the previous section).

The @shortcaption command likewise may be used only within @float, and takes a single argument in braces. The short caption text is used instead of the caption text in a list of floats (see the next section). Thus, you can write a long caption for the main document, and a short title to appear in the list of floats. For example:

```
@float
... as above ...
@shortcaption{Text for list of floats.}
@end float
```

The text for @shortcaption may not contain comments (@c), verbatim text (@verb), environments such as @example, footnotes (@footnote) or other complex constructs. The same constraints apply to @caption unless there is an @shortcaption.

12.1.3 @listoffloats: Tables of Contents for Floats

You can write an @listoffloats command to generate a list of floats for a given float type (see Section 12.1.1 [@float], page 107), analogous to the document's overall table of contents. Typically, it is written in its own @unnumbered node to provide a heading and structure, rather like @printindex (see Section 4.1 [Printing Indices & Menus], page 45).

@listoffloats takes one optional argument, the float type. Here's an example:

```
@node List of Figures
@unnumbered List of Figures
@listoffloats Figure
```

And here's what the output from `@listoffloats` looks like, given the example figure earlier in this chapter (the Info output is formatted as a menu):

Figure 12.1 107

Without any argument, `@listoffloats` generates a list of floats for which no float type was specified, i.e., no first argument to the `@float` command (see Section 12.1.1 [`@float`], page 107).

Each line in the list of floats contains the float type (if any), the float number, and the caption, if any—the `@shortcaption` argument, if it was specified, else the `@caption` argument. In Info, the result is a menu where each float can be selected. In HTML, each line is a link to the float. In printed output, the page number is included.

Unnumbered floats (those without cross reference labels) are omitted from the list of floats.

12.2 Inserting Images

You can insert an image given in an external file with the `@image` command. Although images can be used anywhere, including the middle of a paragraph, we describe them in this chapter since they are most often part of a displayed figure or example.

12.2.1 Image Syntax

Here is the synopsis of the `@image` command:

```
@image{filename[, width[, height[, alttext[, extension]]]]}
```

The *filename* argument is mandatory, and must not have an extension, because the different processors support different formats:

- TEX (DVI output) reads the file *filename*.eps (Encapsulated PostScript format).

- pdfTEX reads *filename*.pdf, *filename*.png, *filename*.jpg, or *filename*.jpeg (in that order). It also tries uppercase versions of the extensions. The PDF format does not support EPS images, so such must be converted first.

- For Info, `makeinfo` includes *filename*.txt verbatim (more or less as if it were in `@verbatim`). The Info output may also include a reference to *filename*.png or *filename*.jpg. (See below.)

- For HTML, `makeinfo` outputs a reference to *filename*.png, *filename*.jpg, *filename*.jpeg or *filename*.gif (in that order). If none of those exist, it gives an error, and outputs a reference to *filename*.jpg anyway.

- For Docbook, `makeinfo` outputs references to *filename*.eps, *filename*.gif *filename*.jpeg, *filename*.jpg, *filename*.pdf, *filename*.png and *filename*.svg, for every file found. Also, *filename*.txt is included verbatim, if present. (The subsequent Docbook processor is supposed to choose the appropriate one.)

- For Info and HTML output, `makeinfo` uses the optional fifth argument *extension* to `@image` for the filename extension, if it is specified and the file is found. Any leading period should be included in *extension*. For example:

  ```
  @image{foo,,,,.xpm}
  ```

If you want to install image files for use by Info readers too, we recommend putting them in a subdirectory like '*foo*-figures' for a package *foo*. Copying the files into `$(infodir)/`*foo*-figures/ should be done in your `Makefile`.

The *width* and *height* arguments are described in the next section.

For TEX output, if an image is the only thing in a paragraph it will ordinarily be displayed on a line by itself, respecting the current environment indentation, but without the normal paragraph indentation. If you want it centered, use `@center` (see Section 3.4.2 [`@titlefont @center @sp`], page 35).

For HTML output, `makeinfo` sets the *alt attribute* for inline images to the optional *alttext* (fourth) argument to `@image`, if supplied. If not supplied, `makeinfo` uses the full file name of the image being displayed. The *alttext* is processed as Texinfo text, so special characters such as '"' and '<' and '&' are escaped in the HTML output; also, you can get an empty `alt` string with `@-` (a command that produces no output; see Section 15.3 [`@-` `@hyphenation`], page 136).

For Info output, the `alt` string is also processed as Texinfo text and output. In this case, '\' is escaped as '\\' and '"' as '\"'; no other escapes are done.

In Info output, `makeinfo` writes a reference to the binary image file (trying *filename* suffixed with *extension*, `.extension`, `.png`, or `.jpg`, in that order) if one exists. It also literally includes the `.txt` file if one exists. This way, Info readers which can display images (such as the Emacs Info browser, running under X) can do so, whereas Info readers which can only use text (such as the standalone Info reader) can display the textual version.

The implementation of this is to put the following construct into the Info output:

```
^@^H[image src="binaryfile" text="txtfile"
          alt="alttext ... ^@^H]
```

where '^@' and '^H' stand for the actual null and backspace control characters. If one of the files is not present, the corresponding argument is omitted.

The reason for mentioning this here is that older Info browsers (this feature was introduced in Texinfo version 4.6) will display the above literally, which, although not pretty, should not be harmful.

12.2.2 Image Scaling

The optional *width* and *height* arguments to the `@image` command (see the previous section) specify the size to which to scale the image. They are only taken into account in TEX. If neither is specified, the image is presented in its natural size (given in the file); if only one is specified, the other is scaled proportionately; and if both are specified, both are respected, thus likely distorting the original image by changing its aspect ratio.

The *width* and *height* may be specified using any valid TEX dimension, namely:

pt   point (72.27pt = 1in)

pc   pica (1pc = 12pt)

bp	big point (72bp = 1in)
in	inch
cm	centimeter (2.54cm = 1in)
mm	millimeter (10mm = 1cm)
dd	didôt point (1157dd = 1238pt)
cc	cicero (1cc = 12dd)
sp	scaled point (65536sp = 1pt)

For example, the following will scale a file `ridt.eps` to one inch vertically, with the width scaled proportionately:

```
@image{ridt,,1in}
```

For `@image` to work with TEX, the file `epsf.tex` must be installed somewhere that TEX can find it. (The standard location is *texmf*/tex/generic/dvips/epsf.tex, where *texmf* is a root of your TEX directory tree.) This file is included in the Texinfo distribution and is also available from `ftp://tug.org/tex/epsf.tex`, among other places.

`@image` can be used within a line as well as for displayed figures. Therefore, if you intend it to be displayed, be sure to leave a blank line before the command, or the output will run into the preceding text.

Image scaling is presently implemented only in TEX, not in HTML or any other sort of output.

12.3 Footnotes

A *footnote* is for a reference that documents or elucidates the primary text.[1]

Footnotes are distracting; use them sparingly at most, and it is best to avoid them completely. Standard bibliographical references are usually better placed in a bibliography at the end of a document instead of in footnotes throughout.

12.3.1 Footnote Commands

In Texinfo, footnotes are created with the `@footnote` command. This command is followed immediately by a left brace, then by the text of the footnote, and then by a terminating right brace. Footnotes may be of any length (they will be broken across pages if necessary), but are usually short. The template is:

```
ordinary text@footnote{text of footnote}
```

As shown here, the `@footnote` command should come right after the text being footnoted, with no intervening space; otherwise, the footnote marker might end up starting a line.

For example, this clause is followed by a sample footnote[2]; in the Texinfo source, it looks like this:

---

[1] A footnote should complement or expand upon the primary text, but a reader should not need to read a footnote to understand the primary text. For a thorough discussion of footnotes, see *The Chicago Manual of Style*, which is published by the University of Chicago Press.

[2] Here is the sample footnote.

```
...a sample footnote@footnote{Here is the sample
footnote.}; in the Texinfo source...
```

As you can see, this source includes two punctuation marks next to each other; in this case, '.};' is the sequence. This is normal (the first ends the footnote and the second belongs to the sentence being footnoted), so don't worry that it looks odd. (Another style, perfectly acceptable, is to put the footnote after punctuation belonging to the sentence, as in ';@footnote{...'.)

In a printed manual or book, the reference mark for a footnote is a small, superscripted number; the text of the footnote appears at the bottom of the page, below a horizontal line.

In Info, the reference mark for a footnote is a pair of parentheses with the footnote number between them, like this: '(1)'. The reference mark is followed by a cross reference link to the footnote text if footnotes are put in separate nodes (see Section 12.3.2 [Footnote Styles], page 112).

In the HTML output, footnote references are generally marked with a small, superscripted number which is rendered as a hypertext link to the footnote text.

Footnotes cannot be nested, and cannot appear in section headings of any kind or other "unusual" places.

A final tip: footnotes in the argument of an @item command for an @table must be entirely on the same line as the @item (as usual). See Section 11.4 [Two-column Tables], page 102.

12.3.2 Footnote Styles

Info has two footnote styles, which determine where the text of the footnote is located:

- In the 'End' node style, all the footnotes for a single node are placed at the end of that node. The footnotes are separated from the rest of the node by a line of dashes with the word 'Footnotes' within it. Each footnote begins with an '(n)' reference mark.

  Here is an example of the Info output for a single footnote in the end-of-node style:

  ```
  --------- Footnotes ---------


  (1)  Here is a sample footnote.
  ```

- In the 'Separate' node style, all the footnotes for a single node are placed in an automatically constructed node of their own. In this style, a "footnote reference" follows each '(n)' reference mark in the body of the node. The footnote reference is actually a cross reference which you use to reach the footnote node.

  The name of the node with the footnotes is constructed by appending '-Footnotes' to the name of the node that contains the footnotes. (Consequently, the footnotes' node for the Footnotes node is Footnotes-Footnotes!) The footnotes' node has an 'Up' node pointer that leads back to its parent node.

  Here is how the first footnote in this manual looks after being formatted for Info in the separate node style:

  ```
  File: texinfo.info  Node: Overview-Footnotes, Up: Overview

  (1) The first syllable of "Texinfo" is pronounced like "speck", not
  "hex". ...
  ```

Unless your document has long and important footnotes (as in, say, Gibbon's *Decline and Fall* . . .), we recommend the 'end' style, as it is simpler for readers to follow.

Use the `@footnotestyle` command to specify an Info file's footnote style. Write this command at the beginning of a line followed by an argument, either 'end' for the end node style or 'separate' for the separate node style.

For example,

```
@footnotestyle end
```

or

```
@footnotestyle separate
```

Write an `@footnotestyle` command before or shortly after the end-of-header line at the beginning of a Texinfo file. (You should include any `@footnotestyle` command between the start-of-header and end-of-header lines, so the region formatting commands will format footnotes as specified.)

In HTML, when the footnote style is 'end', or if the output is not split, footnotes are put at the end of the output. If set to 'separate', and the output is split, they are placed in a separate file.

13 Indices

Using Texinfo, you can generate indices without having to sort and collate entries manually. In an index, the entries are listed in alphabetical order, together with information on how to find the discussion of each entry. In a printed manual, this information consists of page numbers. In an Info file, this information is a menu entry leading to the first node referenced.

Texinfo provides several predefined kinds of index: an index for functions, an index for variables, an index for concepts, and so on. You can combine indices or use them for other than their canonical purpose. Lastly, you can define your own new indices.

See Section 4.1 [Printing Indices & Menus], page 45, for information on how to print indices.

13.1 Making Index Entries

When you are making index entries, it is good practice to think of the different ways people may look for something. Different people *do not* think of the same words when they look something up. A helpful index will have items indexed under all the different words that people may use. For example, one reader may think it obvious that the two-letter names for indices should be listed under "Indices, two-letter names, since "Indices" are the general concept. But another reader may remember the specific concept of two-letter names and search for the entry listed as "Two letter names for indices". A good index will have both entries and will help both readers.

Like typesetting, the construction of an index is a skilled art, the subtleties of which may not be appreciated until you need to do it yourself.

See Section 4.1 [Printing Indices & Menus], page 45, for information about printing an index at the end of a book or creating an index menu in an Info file.

13.2 Predefined Indices

Texinfo provides six predefined indices. Here are their nominal meanings, abbreviations, and the corresponding index entry commands:

'cp'   (@cindex) concept index, for general concepts.

'fn'   (@findex) function index, for function and function-like names (such as entry points of libraries).

'ky'   (@kindex) keystroke index, for keyboard commands.

'pg'   (@pindex) program index, for names of programs.

'tp'   (@tindex) data type index, for type names (such as structures defined in header files).

'vr'   (@vindex) variable index, for variable names (such as global variables of libraries).

Not every manual needs all of these, and most manuals use only two or three at most. The present manual, for example, has two indices: a concept index and an @-command index (that is actually the function index but is called a command index in the chapter heading).

You are not required to use the predefined indices strictly for their canonical purposes. For example, suppose you wish to index some C preprocessor macros. You could put them in the function index along with actual functions, just by writing `@findex` commands for them; then, when you print the "Function Index" as an unnumbered chapter, you could give it the title 'Function and Macro Index' and all will be consistent for the reader.

On the other hand, it is best not to stray too far from the meaning of the predefined indices. Otherwise, in the event that your text is combined with other text from other manuals, the index entries will not match up. Instead, define your own new index (see Section 13.5 [New Indices], page 117).

We recommend having a single index in the final document whenever possible, however many source indices you use, since then readers have only one place to look. Two or more source indices can be combined into one output index using the `@synindex` or `@syncodeindex` commands (see Section 13.4 [Combining Indices], page 116).

13.3 Defining the Entries of an Index

The data to make an index come from many individual indexing commands scattered throughout the Texinfo source file. Each command says to add one entry to a particular index; after formatting, the index will give the current page number or node name as the reference.

An index entry consists of an indexing command at the beginning of a line followed, on the rest of the line, by the entry.

For example, this section begins with the following five entries for the concept index:

```
@cindex Defining indexing entries
@cindex Index entries, defining
@cindex Entries for an index
@cindex Specifying index entries
@cindex Creating index entries
```

Each predefined index has its own indexing command—`@cindex` for the concept index, `@findex` for the function index, and so on, as listed in the previous section.

Concept index entries consist of text. The best way to write an index is to devise entries which are terse yet clear. If you can do this, the index usually looks better if the entries are written just as they would appear in the middle of a sentence, that is, capitalizing only proper names and acronyms that always call for uppercase letters. This is the case convention we use in most GNU manuals' indices.

If you don't see how to make an entry terse yet clear, make it longer and clear—not terse and confusing. If many of the entries are several words long, the index may look better if you use a different convention: to capitalize the first word of each entry. Whichever case convention you use, use it consistently.

In any event, do not ever capitalize a case-sensitive name such as a C or Lisp function name or a shell command; that would be a spelling error. Entries in indices other than the concept index are symbol names in programming languages, or program names; these names are usually case-sensitive, so likewise use upper- and lowercase as required.

It is a good idea to make index entries unique wherever feasible. That way, people using the printed output or online completion of index entries don't see undifferentiated lists.

Consider this an opportunity to make otherwise-identical index entries be more specific, so readers can more easily find the exact place they are looking for.

Index entries should precede the visible material that is being indexed. For instance:

```
@cindex hello
Hello, there!
```

Among other reasons, that way following indexing links (in whatever context) ends up before the material, where readers want to be, instead of after.

By default, entries for a concept index are printed in a small roman font and entries for the other indices are printed in a small `@code` font. You may change the way part of an entry is printed with the usual Texinfo commands, such as `@file` for file names (see Chapter 9 [Marking Text], page 78), and `@r` for the normal roman font (see Section 9.2.3 [Fonts], page 87).

> **Caution:** Do not use a colon in an index entry. In Info, a colon separates the menu entry name from the node name, so a colon in the entry itself confuses Info. See Section 7.3 [Menu Parts], page 63, for more information about the structure of a menu entry.

13.4 Combining Indices

Sometimes you will want to combine two disparate indices such as functions and concepts, perhaps because you have few enough entries that a separate index would look silly.

You could put functions into the concept index by writing `@cindex` commands for them instead of `@findex` commands, and produce a consistent manual by printing the concept index with the title 'Function and Concept Index' and not printing the 'Function Index' at all; but this is not a robust procedure. It works only if your document is never included as part of another document that is designed to have a separate function index; if your document were to be included with such a document, the functions from your document and those from the other would not end up together. Also, to make your function names appear in the right font in the concept index, you would need to enclose every one of them between the braces of `@code`.

13.4.1 `@syncodeindex`: Combining indices using `@code`

When you want to combine functions and concepts into one index, you should index the functions with `@findex` and index the concepts with `@cindex`, and use the `@syncodeindex` command to redirect the function index entries into the concept index.

The `@syncodeindex` command takes two arguments; they are the name of the index to redirect, and the name of the index to redirect it to. The template looks like this:

```
@syncodeindex from to
```

For this purpose, the indices are given two-letter names:

'cp'   concept index

'fn'   function index

'vr'   variable index

'ky'   key index

'pg'   program index

'tp'   data type index

Write an `@syncodeindex` command before or shortly after the end-of-header line at the beginning of a Texinfo file. For example, to merge a function index with a concept index, write the following:

```
@syncodeindex fn cp
```

This will cause all entries designated for the function index to merge in with the concept index instead.

To merge both a variables index and a function index into a concept index, write the following:

```
@syncodeindex vr cp
@syncodeindex fn cp
```

The `@syncodeindex` command puts all the entries from the 'from' index (the redirected index) into the `@code` font, overriding whatever default font is used by the index to which the entries are now directed. This way, if you direct function names from a function index into a concept index, all the function names are printed in the `@code` font as you would expect.

13.4.2 `@synindex`: Combining indices

The `@synindex` command is nearly the same as the `@syncodeindex` command, except that it does not put the 'from' index entries into the `@code` font; rather it puts them in the roman font. Thus, you use `@synindex` when you merge a concept index into a function index.

See Section 4.1 [Printing Indices & Menus], page 45, for information about printing an index at the end of a book or creating an index menu in an Info file.

13.5 Defining New Indices

In addition to the predefined indices (see Section 13.2 [Predefined Indices], page 114), you may use the `@defindex` and `@defcodeindex` commands to define new indices. These commands create new indexing @-commands with which you mark index entries. The `@defindex` command is used like this:

```
@defindex name
```

New index names are usually two-letter words, such as 'au'. For example:

```
@defindex au
```

This defines a new index, called the 'au' index. At the same time, it creates a new indexing command, `@auindex`, that you can use to make index entries. Use this new indexing command just as you would use a predefined indexing command.

For example, here is a section heading followed by a concept index entry and two 'au' index entries.

```
@section Cognitive Semantics
@cindex kinesthetic image schemas
@auindex Johnson, Mark
@auindex Lakoff, George
```

(Evidently, 'au' serves here as an abbreviation for "author".)

Texinfo constructs the new indexing command by concatenating the name of the index with 'index'; thus, defining an 'xy' index leads to the automatic creation of an @xyindex command.

Use the @printindex command to print the index, as you do with the predefined indices. For example:

```
@node Author Index
@unnumbered Author Index


@printindex au
```

The @defcodeindex is like the @defindex command, except that, in the printed output, it prints entries in an @code font by default instead of a roman font.

You should define new indices before the end-of-header line of a Texinfo file, and (of course) before any @synindex or @syncodeindex commands (see Section 3.2 [Texinfo File Header], page 30).

As mentioned earlier (see Section 13.2 [Predefined Indices], page 114), we recommend having a single index in the final document whenever possible, however many source indices you use, since then readers have only one place to look.

When creating an index, TeX creates a file whose extension is the name of the index (see [Names of index files], page 178). Therefore you should avoid using index names that collide with extensions used for other purposes, such as '.aux' or '.xml'. makeinfo already reports an error if a new index conflicts well-known extension name.

14 Special Insertions

Texinfo provides several commands for inserting characters that have special meaning in Texinfo, such as braces, and for other graphic elements that do not correspond to simple characters you can type.

These are:

- The Texinfo special characters: '@ {} , \ #'.
- Whitespace within and around a sentence.
- Accents.
- Dots and bullets.
- The TeX logo and the copyright symbol.
- The euro and pounds currency symbols.
- The degrees symbol.
- The minus sign.
- Mathematical expressions.
- Glyphs for examples of programming: evaluation, macros, errors, etc.
- Footnotes.

14.1 Special Characters: Inserting @ {} , \

'@' and curly braces are the basic special characters in Texinfo. To insert these characters so they appear in text, you must put an '@' in front of these characters to prevent Texinfo from misinterpreting them. Alphabetic commands are also provided.

The other characters (comma, backslash, hash) are special only in restricted contexts, as explained in the respective sections.

14.1.1 Inserting '@' with @@ and @atchar{}

@@ produces a single '@' character in the output. Do not put braces after an @@ command.

@atchar{} also produces a single '@' character in the output. It does need following braces, as usual for alphabetic commands. In inline conditionals (see Section 18.4 [Inline Conditionals], page 158), it can be necessary to avoid using the literal '@' character in the source (and may be clearer in other contexts).

14.1.2 Inserting '{ '}' with @{ @} and @l rbracechar{}

@{ produces a single '{' in the output, and @} produces a single '}'. Do not put braces after either an @{ or an @} command.

@lbracechar{} and @rbracechar{} also produce single '{' and '}' characters in the output. They do need following braces, as usual for alphabetic commands. In inline conditionals (see Section 18.4 [Inline Conditionals], page 158), it can be necessary to avoid using literal brace characters in the source (and may be clearer in other contexts).

14.1.3 Inserting ',' with `@comma{}`

Ordinarily, a comma ',' is a normal character that can be simply typed in your input where you need it.

However, Texinfo uses the comma as a special character only in one context: to separate arguments to those Texinfo commands, such as `@acronym` (see Section 9.1.14 [`@acronym`], page 85) and `@xref` (see Chapter 8 [Cross References], page 66), as well as user-defined macros (see Section 19.1 [Defining Macros], page 165), which take more than one argument.

Since a comma character would confuse Texinfo's parsing for these commands, you must use the command '`@comma{}`' instead if you want to pass an actual comma. Here are some examples:

```
@acronym{ABC, A Bizarre @comma{}}
@xref{Comma,, The @comma{} symbol}
@mymac{One argument@comma{} containing a comma}
```

Although '`@comma{}`' can be used nearly anywhere, there is no need for it anywhere except in this unusual case.

(Incidentally, the name '`@comma`' lacks the '`char`' suffix used in its companion commands only for historical reasons. It didn't seem important enough to define a synonym.)

14.1.4 Inserting '\' with `@backslashchar{}`

Ordinarily, a backslash '\' is a normal character in Texinfo that can be simply typed in your input where you need it. The result is to typeset the backslash from the typewriter font.

However, Texinfo uses the backslash as a special character in one restricted context: to delimit formal arguments in the bodies of user-defined macros (see Section 19.1 [Defining Macros], page 165).

Due to the vagaries of macro argument parsing, it is more reliable to pass an alphabetic command that produces a backslash instead of using a literal \. Hence `@backslashchar{}`. Here is an example macro call:

```
@mymac{One argument@backslashchar{} with a backslash}
```

Texinfo documents may also use \ as a command character inside `@math` (see Section 14.7 [Inserting Math], page 127). In this case, `@\` or `\backslash` produces a "math" backslash (from the math symbol font), while `@backslashchar{}` produces a typewriter backslash as usual.

Although '`@backslashchar{}`' can be used nearly anywhere, there is no need for it except in these unusual cases.

14.1.5 Inserting '#' with `@hashchar{}`

Ordinarily, a hash '#' is a normal character in Texinfo that can be simply typed in your input where you need it. The result is to typeset the hash character from the current font.

This character has many other names, varying by locale, such as "number sign", "pound", and "octothorp". It is also sometimes called "sharp" or "sharp sign" since it vaguely resembles the musical symbol by that name. In situations where Texinfo is used, "hash" is the most common in our experience.

However, Texinfo uses the hash character as a special character in one restricted context: to introduce the so-called `#line` directive and variants (see Section 19.6 [External Macro Processors], page 172).

So, in order to typeset an actual hash character in such a place (for example, in a program that needs documentation about `#line`), it's necessary to use `@hashchar{}` or some other construct. Here's an example:

```
@hashchar{} 10 "example.c"
```

Although '`@hashchar{}`' can be used nearly anywhere, there is no need for it anywhere except this unusual case.

14.2 Inserting Quote Characters

As explained in the early section on general Texinfo input conventions (see Section 1.9 [Conventions], page 9), Texinfo source files use the ASCII character ` (96 decimal) to produce a left quote ('), and ASCII ' (39 decimal) to produce a right quote ('). Doubling these input characters (`` and '') produces double quotes (" and "). These are the conventions used by TEX.

This works all right for text. However, in examples of computer code, readers are especially likely to cut and paste the text verbatim—and, unfortunately, some document viewers will mangle these characters. (The free PDF reader `xpdf` works fine, but other PDF readers, both free and nonfree, have problems.)

If this is a concern for you, Texinfo provides these two commands:

`@codequoteundirected` *on-off*

> causes the output for the ' character in code environments to be the undirected single quote, like this: '.

`@codequotebacktick` *on-off*

> causes the output for the ` character in code environments to be the backtick character (standalone grave accent), like this: `.

If you want these settings for only part of the document, `@codequote... off` will restore the normal behavior, as in `@codequoteundirected off`.

These settings affect `@code`, `@example`, `@kbd`, `@samp`, `@verb`, and `@verbatim`. See Section 9.1.1 [Useful Highlighting], page 78.

This feature used to be controlled by using `@set` to change the values of the corresponding variables `txicodequoteundirected` and `txicodequotebacktick`; they are still supported, but the command interface is preferred.

14.3 Inserting Space

The following sections describe commands that control spacing of various kinds within and after sentences.

14.3.1 Multiple Spaces

Ordinarily, multiple whitespace characters (space, tab, and newline) are collapsed into a single space.

Occasionally, you may want to produce several consecutive spaces, either for purposes of example (e.g., what your program does with multiple spaces as input), or merely for purposes of appearance in headings or lists. Texinfo supports three commands: `@SPACE`, `@TAB`, and `@NL`, all of which insert a single space into the output. (Here, `@SPACE` represents an '`@`' character followed by a space, i.e., '`@ `', `TAB` represents an actual tab character, and `@NL` represents an '`@`' character and end-of-line, i.e., when '`@`' is the last character on a line.)

For example,

```
Spacey@ @ @ @
example.
```

produces

```
Spacey      example.
```

Other possible uses of `@SPACE` have been subsumed by `@multitable` (see Section 11.5 [Multi-column Tables], page 104).

Do not follow any of these commands with braces.

To produce a non-breakable space, see Section 15.6 [`@tie`], page 137.

14.3.2 Not Ending a Sentence

Depending on whether a period or exclamation point or question mark is inside or at the end of a sentence, slightly less or more space is inserted after a period in a typeset manual. Since it is not always possible to determine automatically when a period ends a sentence, special commands are needed in some circumstances. Usually, Texinfo can guess how to handle periods, so you do not need to use the special commands; you just enter a period as you would if you were using a typewriter: put two spaces after the period, question mark, or exclamation mark that ends a sentence.

Use the `@:` command after a period, question mark, exclamation mark, or colon that should not be followed by extra space. For example, use `@:` after periods that end (lowercase) abbreviations which are not at the ends of sentences.

Also, when a parenthetical remark in the middle of a sentence (like this one!) ends with a period, exclamation point, or question mark, `@:` should be used after the right parenthesis. Similarly for right brackets and right quotes (both single and double).

For example,

```
foo vs.@: bar (or?)@: baz
foo vs. bar (or?) baz
```

produces the following. If you look carefully at this printed output, you will see a bit of extraneous space after the '`vs.`' and '`(or?)`' in the second line.

foo vs. bar (or?) baz
foo vs. bar (or?) baz

`@:` has no effect on the HTML or Docbook output.

Do not put braces after `@:` (or any non-alphabetic command).

A few Texinfo commands force normal interword spacing, so that you don't have to insert `@:` where you otherwise would. These are the code-like highlighting commands, `@var`, `@abbr`, and `@acronym` (see Section 9.1.1 [Useful Highlighting], page 78). For example, in '`@code{foo. bar}`' the period is not considered the end of a sentence, and no extra space is inserted.

14.3.3 Ending a Sentence

As mentioned above, Texinfo normally inserts additional space after the end of a sentence. It uses the same heuristic for this as TeX: a sentence ends with a period, exclamation point, or question mark, either preceded or followed by optional closing punctuation, and then whitespace, and *not* preceded by a capital letter.

Use `@.` instead of a period, `@!` instead of an exclamation point, and `@?` instead of a question mark at the end of a sentence that does end with a capital letter. Do not put braces after any of these commands. For example:

```
Give it to M.I.B. and to M.E.W@.  Also, give it to R.J.C@.
Give it to M.I.B. and to M.E.W.  Also, give it to R.J.C.
```

The output follows. In printed output and Info, you can see the desired extra whitespace after the 'W' in the first line.

> Give it to M.I.B. and to M.E.W. Also, give it to R.J.C.
> Give it to M.I.B. and to M.E.W. Also, give it to R.J.C.

In the HTML output, `@.` is equivalent to a simple '.'; likewise for `@!` and `@?`.

The "closing punctuation" mentioned above is defined as a right parenthesis (')', right bracket (']'), or right quote, either single or double ('' and '''; the many possible additional Unicode right quotes are not included). These characters can be thought of as invisible with respect to whether a given period ends a sentence. (This is the same rule as TeX.) For instance, the periods in 'foo.) Bar' and 'foo.'' Bar' do end sentences.

The meanings of `@:` and `@.`, etc. in Texinfo are designed to work well with the Emacs sentence motion commands (see Section "Sentences" in *The GNU Emacs Manual*).

A few Texinfo commands are not considered as being an abbreviation, even though they may end with a capital letter when expanded, so that you don't have to insert `@.` and companions. Notably, this is the case for code-like highlighting commands, `@var` arguments ending with a capital letter, `@LaTeX`, and `@TeX`. For example, that sentence ended with '... `@code{@@TeX}`.'; `@.` was not needed. Similarly, in ... `@var{VARNAME}`. Text the period after *VARNAME* ends the sentence; there is no need to use `@.`.

14.3.4 `@frenchspacing` *val*: Control Sentence Spacing

In American typography, it is traditional and correct to put extra space at the end of a sentence. This is the default in Texinfo (implemented in Info and printed output; for HTML, we don't try to override the browser). In French typography (and others), this extra space is wrong; all spaces are uniform.

Therefore Texinfo provides the `@frenchspacing` command to control the spacing after punctuation. It reads the rest of the line as its argument, which must be the single word 'on' or 'off' (always these words, regardless of the language of the document). Here is an example:

```
@frenchspacing on
This is text. Two sentences. Three sentences. French spacing.

@frenchspacing off
This is text. Two sentences. Three sentences. Non-French spacing.
```

produces:

This is text. Two sentences. Three sentences. French spacing.

This is text. Two sentences. Three sentences. Non-French spacing.

`@frenchspacing` also affects the output after `@.`, `@!`, and `@?` (see Section 14.3.3 [Ending a Sentence], page 123).

`@frenchspacing` has no effect on the HTML or Docbook output; for XML, it outputs a transliteration of itself (see Section 1.3 [Output Formats], page 4).

14.3.5 `@dmn{`*dimension*`}`: Format a Dimension

You can use the `@dmn` command to format a dimension with a little extra space in the printed output. That is, on seeing `@dmn`, TeX inserts just enough space for proper typesetting; in other output formats, the formatting commands insert no space at all.

To use the `@dmn` command, write the number and then follow it immediately, with no intervening space, by `@dmn`, and then by the dimension within braces. For example,

```
A4 paper is 8.27@dmn{in} wide.
```

produces

A4 paper is 8.27 in wide.

Not everyone uses this style. Some people prefer '8.27 in.' or '8.27 inches'. In these cases, however, you need to use `@tie` (see Section 15.6 [@tie], page 137) or `@w` (see Section 15.5 [@w], page 136) so that no line break can occur between the number and the dimension. Also, if you write a period after an abbreviation within a sentence (as with the 'in.' above), you should write '`@:`' after the period to prevent TeX from inserting extra whitespace, as shown here. See Section 14.3.2 [Not Ending a Sentence], page 122.

14.4 Inserting Accents

Here is a table with the commands Texinfo provides for inserting floating accents. They all need an argument, the character to accent, which can either be given in braces as usual (`@'{e}`), or, as a special case, the braces can be omitted, in which case the argument is the next character (`@'e`). This is to make the source as convenient as possible to type and read, since accented characters are very common in some languages.

If the command is alphabetic, such as `@dotaccent`, then there must be a space between the command name and argument if braces are not used. If the command is non-alphabetic, such as `@'`, then there must *not* be a space; the argument is the very next character.

Exception: the argument to `@tieaccent` must be enclosed in braces (since it is two characters instead of one).

To get the true accented characters output in Info, not just the ASCII transliterations, it is necessary to specify `@documentencoding` with an encoding which supports the required characters (see Section 17.2 [@documentencoding], page 153). In this case, you can also use non-ASCII (e.g., pre-accented) characters in the source file.

Command	Output	What
`@"o`	ö	umlaut accent
`@'o`	ó	acute accent
`@,{c}`	ç	cedilla accent

`@=o`	ō	macron/overbar accent
`@^o`	ô	circumflex accent
`@'o`	ò	grave accent
`@~o`	õ	tilde accent
`@dotaccent{o}`	ȯ	overdot accent
`@H{o}`	ő	long Hungarian umlaut
`@ogonek{a}`	ą	ogonek
`@ringaccent{o}`	å	ring accent
`@tieaccent{oo}`	o͡o	tie-after accent
`@u{o}`	ŏ	breve accent
`@ubaraccent{o}`	o̲	underbar accent
`@udotaccent{o}`	ọ	underdot accent
`@v{o}`	ŏ	caron/hacek/check accent

This table lists the Texinfo commands for inserting other characters commonly used in languages other than English.

`@exclamdown{}`	¡	upside-down !
`@questiondown{}`	¿	upside-down ?
`@aa{} @AA{}`	å Å	a,A with circle
`@ae{} @AE{}`	æ Æ	ae,AE ligatures
`@dh{} @DH{}`	ð Ð	Icelandic eth
`@dotless{i}`	ı	dotless i
`@dotless{j}`	ȷ	dotless j
`@l{} @L{}`	ł Ł	suppressed-L,l
`@o{} @O{}`	ø Ø	O,o with slash
`@oe{} @OE{}`	œ Œ	oe,OE ligatures
`@ordf{} @ordm{}`	ª º	Spanish ordinals
`@ss{}`	ß	es-zet or sharp S
`@th{} @TH{}`	þ Þ	Icelandic thorn

14.5 Inserting Quotation Marks

Use doubled single-quote characters to begin and end quotations: ''...''. TeX converts two single quotes to left- and right-hand doubled quotation marks, "like this", and Info converts doubled single-quote characters to ASCII double-quotes: ''...'' becomes "...".

You may occasionally need to produce two consecutive single quotes; for example, in documenting a computer language such as Maxima where '' is a valid command. You can do this with the input `'@w{}'`; the empty `@w` command stops the combination into the double-quote characters.

The left quote character (`, ASCII code 96) used in Texinfo is a grave accent in ANSI and ISO character set standards. We use it as a quote character because that is how TeX is set up, by default.

Texinfo supports several other quotation marks used in languages other than English. Below is a table with the commands Texinfo provides for inserting quotation marks.

In order to get the symbols for the quotation marks in encoded Info output, it is necessary to specify `@documentencoding UTF-8`. (See Section 17.2 [`@documentencoding`], page 153.) Double guillemets are also present in ISO 8859-1 (aka Latin 1) and ISO 8859-15 (aka Latin 9).

The standard TEX fonts support the usual quotation marks used in English (the ones produced with single and doubled ASCII single-quotes). For the other quotation marks, TEX uses European Computer Modern (EC) fonts (`ecrm1000` and other variants). These fonts are freely available, of course; you can download them from `http://ctan.org/pkg/ec`, among other places.

The free EC fonts are bitmap fonts created with Metafont. Especially for on-line viewing, Type 1 (vector) versions of the fonts are preferable; these are available in the CM-Super font package (`http://ctan.org/pkg/cm-super`).

Both distributions include installation instructions.

Command	Glyph	Unicode name (point)
`@quotedblleft{}` `` `` ``	"	Left double quotation mark (U+201C)
`@quotedblright{}` `''`	"	Right double quotation mark (U+201D)
`@quoteleft{}` `` ` ``	'	Left single quotation mark (U+2018)
`@quoteright{}` `'`	'	Right single quotation mark (U+2019)
`@quotedblbase{}`	„	Double low-9 quotation mark (U+201E)
`@quotesinglbase{}`	‚	Single low-9 quotation mark (U+201A)
`@guillemetleft{}`	«	Left-pointing double angle quotation mark (U+00AB)
`@guillemetright{}`	»	Right-pointing double angle quotation mark (U+00BB)
`@guilsinglleft{}`	‹	Single left-pointing angle quotation mark (U+2039)
`@guilsinglright{}`	›	Single right-pointing angle quotation mark (U+203A)

For the double angle quotation marks, Adobe and LATEX glyph names are also supported: `@guillemotleft` and `@guillemotright`. These names are incorrect; a "guillemot" is a bird species (a type of auk).

Traditions for quotation mark usage vary to a great extent between languages (`http://en.wikipedia.org/wiki/Quotation_mark`). Texinfo does not provide commands or configurations for typesetting quotation marks according to the numerous traditions. Therefore, you have to choose the commands appropriate for the language of your manual. Sometimes aliases (see Section 19.4 [`@alias`], page 170) can simplify the usage and make the source code more readable. For example, in German, `@quotedblbase` is used for the left double quote, and the right double quote is the glyph produced by `@quotedblleft`, which is counter-intuitive. Thus, in this case the following aliases would be convenient:

```
@alias lgqq = quotedblbase
@alias rgqq = quotedblleft
```

14.6 @sub and @sup: Inserting Subscripts and Superscripts

You can insert subscripts and superscripts, in either text or math, with the `@sub` and `@sup` commands. (For other mathematical expressions, see the next section.) For example, here is a purely textual subscript and superscript:

```
here@sub{below}@sup{above}
```

produces:

here$_{below}$^{above}

Inside `@math`, `@sub` and `@sup` produce mathematical subscripts and superscripts. This uses a different font in the TeX output (math italic instead of text italic); it makes no difference in the other output formats. Here's an example:

    @math{e@sup{x}}

produces:

e^x

In Info and plain text, regardless of being used inside `@math`, `@sub{text}` is output as '`_{text}`' and `@sup{text}` as '`^{text}`', including the literal braces (to mark the beginning and end of the "script" text to the reader).

When the output format (and display program) permit (TeX math, HTML), the superscript is set above the subscript when both commands are given consecutively.

14.7 `@math`: Inserting Mathematical Expressions

You can write a short mathematical expression with the `@math` command. Write the mathematical expression between braces, like this:

    @math{(a + b) = (b + a)}

This produces the following in TeX:

$(a + b) = (b + a)$

and the following in other formats:

    (a + b) = (b + a)

The `@math` command has no special effect on the Info and HTML output. `makeinfo` expands any @-commands as usual, but it does not try to use produce good mathematical formatting in any way (no use of MathML, etc.). The HTML output is enclosed by `<em>...</em>`, but nothing more.

However, as far as the TeX output is concerned, plain TeX mathematical commands are allowed in `@math`, starting with '`\`'. In essence, `@math` switches into plain TeX math mode. (Exception: the plain TeX command `\sup`, which typesets the mathematical operator name 'sup', must be accessed as `\mathopsup`, due to the conflict with Texinfo's `@sup` command.)

This allows you to use all the plain TeX math control sequences for symbols, functions, and so on, and thus get proper formatting in the TeX output, at least.

The `@sub` and `@sup` commands described in the previous section produce subscripts and superscripts in HTML output as well as TeX; the plain TeX characters `_` and `^` for subscripts and superscripts are recognized by TeX inside `@math`, but do nothing special in HTML or other output formats.

It's best to use '`\`' instead of '`@`' for any such mathematical commands; otherwise, `makeinfo` will complain. On the other hand, `makeinfo` does allow input with matching (but unescaped) braces, such as '`k_{75}`'; it complains about such bare braces in regular input.

Here's an example:

    @math{\sin 2\pi \equiv \cos 3\pi}

which looks like this in TeX:

$$\sin 2\pi \equiv \cos 3\pi$$

but which looks like the input in Info and HTML:

```
\sin 2\pi \equiv \cos 3\pi
```

Since '\' is an escape character inside `@math`, you can use `@\` to get a literal backslash (\\ will work in TeX, but you'd get the literal two characters '\\' in Info). `@\` is not defined outside of `@math`, since a '\' ordinarily produces a literal (typewriter) '\'. You can also use `@backslashchar{}` in any mode to get a typewriter backslash. See Section 14.1.4 [Inserting a Backslash], page 120.

For displayed equations, you must at present use TeX directly (see Section 18.3 [Raw Formatter Commands], page 157).

14.8 Glyphs for Text

Texinfo has support for a few additional glyphs that are commonly used in printed text but not available in ASCII. Of course, there are many thousands more. It is possible to use Unicode characters as-is as far as `makeinfo` is concerned, but TeX is not so lucky.

14.8.1 @TeX{} (TeX) and @LaTeX{} (LaTeX)

Use the `@TeX{}` command to generate 'TeX'. In a printed manual, this is a special logo that is different from three ordinary letters. In Info, it just looks like 'TeX'.

Similarly, use the `@LaTeX{}` command to generate 'LaTeX', which is even more special in printed manuals (and different from the incorrect `La@TeX{}`. In Info, the result is just 'LaTeX'. (LaTeX is another macro package built on top of TeX, very loosely analogous to Texinfo in that it emphasizes logical structure, but much (much) larger.)

The spelling of these commands are unusual for Texinfo, in that they use both uppercase and lowercase letters.

14.8.2 @copyright{} (©)

Use the `@copyright{}` command to generate the copyright symbol, '©'. Where possible, this is a 'c' inside a circle; in Info, this is '(C)'.

Legally, it's not necessary to use the copyright symbol; the English word 'Copyright' suffices, according to international treaty.

14.8.3 @registeredsymbol{} (®)

Use the `@registeredsymbol{}` command to generate the registered symbol, '®'. Where possible, this is an 'R' inside a circle; in Info, this is '(R)'.

14.8.4 @dots (...) and @enddots (...)

An *ellipsis* (a sequence of dots) would be spaced wrong when typeset as a string of periods, so a special command is used in Texinfo: use the `@dots{}` command to generate a normal ellipsis, which is three dots in a row, appropriately spaced ... like so. To emphasize: do not simply write three periods in the input file; that would work for the Info file output, but would produce the wrong amount of space between the periods in the printed manual.

The `@enddots{}` command generates an end-of-sentence ellipsis, which also has three dots, but with different spacing afterwards, ... Look closely to see the difference.

Here is an ellipsis: . . . Here are three periods in a row: ...

In printed (and usually HTML) output, the three periods in a row are much closer together than the dots in the ellipsis.

14.8.5 @bullet (•)

Use the `@bullet{}` command to generate a large round dot, or the closest possible thing to one. In Info, an asterisk is used. Here is a bullet: •

When you use `@bullet` in `@itemize`, you do not need to type the braces, because `@itemize` supplies them. (see Section 11.2 [`@itemize`], page 100).

14.8.6 @euro (€): Euro Currency Symbol

Use the `@euro{}` command to generate '€'. Where possible, this is the symbol for the Euro currency. Otherwise, the word 'Euro' is used.

Texinfo cannot magically synthesize support for the Euro symbol where the underlying system (fonts, software, whatever) does not support it. Therefore, you may find it preferable to use the word "Euro". (In banking contexts, the abbreviation for the Euro is EUR.)

In order to get the Euro symbol in encoded Info output, for example, it is necessary to specify `@documentencoding ISO-8859-15` or `@documentencoding UTF-8` (See Section 17.2 [`@documentencoding`], page 153.) The Euro symbol is in ISO 8859-15 (aka Latin 9), and is *not* in the more widely-used ISO 8859-1 (Latin 1).

The Euro symbol does not exist in the standard TEX fonts (which were designed before the Euro was legislated into existence). Therefore, TEX uses an additional font, named `feymr10` (along with other variables). It is freely available, of course; you can download it from `http://ctan.org/pkg/eurosym`, among other places. The distribution includes installation instructions.

14.8.7 @pounds (£): Pounds Sterling

Use the `@pounds{}` command to generate '£'. Where possible, this is the symbol for the pounds sterling British currency. Otherwise, it is '#'.

14.8.8 @textdegree (°): Degrees Symbol

Use the `@textdegree{}` command to generate '°'. Where possible, this is the normal symbol for degrees. Otherwise, it is an 'o'.

14.8.9 @minus (−): Inserting a Minus Sign

Use the `@minus{}` command to generate a minus sign. In a fixed-width font, this is a single hyphen, but in a proportional font, the symbol is the customary length for a minus sign—a little longer than a hyphen, shorter than an em-dash:

'−' is a minus sign generated with '`@minus{}`',

'-' is a hyphen generated with the character '-',

'—' is an em-dash for text.

In the fixed-width font used by Info, `@minus{}` is the same as a hyphen.

You should not use @minus{} inside @code or @example because the width distinction is not made in the fixed-width font they use.

When you use @minus to specify the mark beginning each entry in an itemized list, you do not need to type the braces (see Section 11.2 [@itemize], page 100).

If you actually want to typeset some math that does a subtraction, it is better to use @math. Then the regular '-' character produces a minus sign, as in @math{a-b} (see Section 14.7 [Inserting Math], page 127).

14.8.10 @geq (≥) and @leq (≤): Inserting Relations

Use the @geq{} and @leq{} commands to generate greater-than-or-equal and less-than-equal-signs, '≥' and '≤'. When those symbols are not available, the ASCII sequences '>=' and '<=' are output.

14.9 Glyphs for Programming

In Texinfo, code is often illustrated in examples that are delimited by @example and @end example, or by @lisp and @end lisp. In such examples, you can indicate the results of evaluation or an expansion using '⇒' or '↦'. Likewise, there are commands to insert glyphs to indicate printed output, error messages, equivalence of expressions, the location of point in an editor, and GUI operation sequences.

The glyph-insertion commands do not need to be used within an example, but most often they are. All glyph-insertion commands are followed by empty braces.

14.9.1 Glyphs Summary

Here is a summary of the glyph commands:

⇒   @result{} indicates the result of an expression.

↦   @expansion{} indicates the results of a macro expansion.

⊣   @print{} indicates printed output.

error   @error{} indicates the following text is an error message.

≡   @equiv{} indicates the exact equivalence of two forms.

⋆   @point{} shows the location of point.

A → B   @clicksequence{A @click{} B indicates a GUI operation sequence: first A, then clicking B, or choosing B from a menu, or otherwise selecting it.

14.9.2 @result{} (⇒): Result of an Expression

Use the @result{} command to indicate the result of evaluating an expression.

The @result{} command is displayed as '⇒', either a double stemmed arrow or (when that is not available) the ASCII sequence '=>'.

Thus, the following,

```
(cdr '(1 2 3))
     ⇒ (2 3)
```

may be read as "(cdr '(1 2 3)) evaluates to (2 3)".

14.9.3 @expansion{} (↦): Indicating an Expansion

When an expression is a macro call, it expands into a new expression. You can indicate the result of the expansion with the @expansion{} command.

The @expansion{} command is displayed as '↦', either a long arrow with a flat base or (when that is not available) the ASCII sequence '==>'.

For example, the following

```
@lisp
(third '(a b c))
    @expansion{} (car (cdr (cdr '(a b c))))
    @result{} c
@end lisp
```

produces

```
(third '(a b c))
    ↦ (car (cdr (cdr '(a b c))))
    ⇒ c
```

which may be read as:

> (third '(a b c)) expands to (car (cdr (cdr '(a b c)))); the result of evaluating the expression is c.

Often, as in this case, an example looks better if the @expansion{} and @result{} commands are indented.

14.9.4 @print{} (⊣): Indicating Generated Output

Sometimes an expression will generate output during its execution. You can indicate such displayed output with the @print{} command.

The @print{} command is displayed as '⊣', either a horizontal dash butting against a vertical bar or (when that is not available) the ASCII sequence '-|'.

In the following example, the printed text is indicated with '⊣', and the value of the expression follows on the last line.

```
(progn (print 'foo) (print 'bar))
    ⊣ foo
    ⊣ bar
    ⇒ bar
```

In a Texinfo source file, this example is written as follows:

```
@lisp
(progn (print 'foo) (print 'bar))
    @print{} foo
    @print{} bar
    @result{} bar
@end lisp
```

14.9.5 @error{} (error): Indicating an Error Message

A piece of code may cause an error when you evaluate it. You can designate the error message with the @error{} command.

The @error{} command is displayed as ' `error` ', either the word 'error' in a box in the printed output, the word error followed by an arrow in other formats or (when no arrow is available) 'error-->'.

Thus,

```
@lisp
(+ 23 'x)
@error{} Wrong type argument: integer-or-marker-p, x
@end lisp
```

produces

```
(+ 23 'x)
```
`error` `Wrong type argument: integer-or-marker-p, x`

This indicates that the following error message is printed when you evaluate the expression:

```
Wrong type argument: integer-or-marker-p, x
```

The word ' `error` ' itself is not part of the error message.

14.9.6 @equiv{} ($\equiv$): Indicating Equivalence

Sometimes two expressions produce identical results. You can indicate the exact equivalence of two forms with the @equiv{} command. The @equiv{} command is displayed as '$\equiv$', either a standard mathematical equivalence sign (three parallel horizontal lines) or (when that is not available) as the ASCII sequence '=='.

Thus,

```
@lisp
(make-sparse-keymap) @equiv{} (list 'keymap)
@end lisp
```

produces

```
(make-sparse-keymap) ≡ (list 'keymap)
```

This indicates that evaluating (make-sparse-keymap) produces identical results to evaluating (list 'keymap).

14.9.7 @point{} ($\star$): Indicating Point in a Buffer

Sometimes you need to show an example of text in an Emacs buffer. In such examples, the convention is to include the entire contents of the buffer in question between two lines of dashes containing the buffer name.

You can use the '@point{}' command to show the location of point in the text in the buffer. (The symbol for point, of course, is not part of the text in the buffer; it indicates the place *between* two characters where point is located.)

The @point{} command is displayed as '$\star$', either a pointed star or (when that is not available) the ASCII sequence '-!-'.

The following example shows the contents of buffer foo before and after evaluating a Lisp command to insert the word changed.

```
---------- Buffer: foo ----------
This is the *contents of foo.
---------- Buffer: foo ----------
```

```
(insert "changed ")
     ⇒ nil
---------- Buffer: foo ----------
This is the changed ⋆contents of foo.
---------- Buffer: foo ----------
```

In a Texinfo source file, the example is written like this:

```
@example
---------- Buffer: foo ----------
This is the @point{}contents of foo.
---------- Buffer: foo ----------

(insert "changed ")
     @result{} nil
---------- Buffer: foo ----------
This is the changed @point{}contents of foo.
---------- Buffer: foo ----------
@end example
```

14.9.8 Click Sequences

When documenting graphical interfaces, it is necessary to describe sequences such as 'Click on 'File', then choose 'Open', then ...'. Texinfo offers commands @clicksequence and click to represent this, typically used like this:

```
... @clicksequence{File @click{} Open} ...
```

which produces:

> ... File → Open ...

The @click command produces a right arrow by default; this glyph is also available independently via the command @arrow{}.

You can change the glyph produced by @click with the command @clickstyle, which takes a command name as its single argument on the rest of the line, much like @itemize and friends (see Section 11.2 [@itemize], page 100). The command should produce a glyph, and the usual empty braces '{}' are omitted. Here's an example:

```
@clickstyle @result
... @clicksequence{File @click{} Open} ...
```

now produces:

> ... File ⇒ Open ...

14.10 Inserting Unicode: @U

The command @U{hex} inserts a representation of the Unicode character U+hex. For example, @U{0132} inserts the Dutch 'IJ' ligature (poorly shown here as simply the two letters 'I' and 'J').

The hex value should be at least four hex digits; leading zeros are *not* added. In general, hex must specify a valid normal Unicode character; e.g., U+10FFFF (the very last code point) is invalid by definition, and thus cannot be inserted this way.

@U is useful for inserting occasional glyphs for which Texinfo has no dedicated command, while allowing the Texinfo source to remain purely 7-bit ASCII for maximum portability.

This command has many limitations—the same limitations as inserting Unicode characters in UTF-8 or another binary form. First and most importantly, TEX knows nothing about most of Unicode. Supporting specific additional glyphs upon request is possible, but it's not viable for `texinfo.tex` to support whole additional scripts (Japanese, Urdu, ...). The @U command does nothing to change this. If the specified character is not supported in TEX, an error is given. (See Section 17.2 [@documentencoding], page 153.)

In HTML, XML, and Docbook, the output from @U is always an entity reference of the form '&#x*hex*;', as in 'Ĳ' for the example above. This should work even when an HTML document uses some other encoding (say, Latin 1) and the given character is not supported in that encoding.

In Info and plain text, if the document encoding is specified explicitly to be UTF-8, the output will be the UTF-8 representation of the character U+*hex* (presuming it's a valid character). In all other cases, the output is the ASCII sequence 'U+*hex*', as in the six ASCII characters 'U+0132' for the example above.

That's all. No magic!

15 Forcing and Preventing Breaks

Line and page breaks can sometimes occur in the 'wrong' place in one or another form of output. It's up to you to ensure that text looks right in all the output formats.

For example, in a printed manual, page breaks may occur awkwardly in the middle of an example; to prevent this, you can hold text together using a grouping command that keeps the text from being split across two pages. Conversely, you may want to force a page break where none would occur normally.

You can use the break, break prevention, or pagination commands to fix problematic line and page breaks.

15.1 Break Commands

The break commands create or allow line and paragraph breaks:

@*   Force a line break.

@sp *n*   Skip *n* blank lines.

@-   Insert a discretionary hyphen.

@hyphenation{hy-phen-a-ted words}
                Define hyphen points in *hy-phen-a-ted words*.

These commands hold text together on a single line:

@w{text}   Prevent *text* from being split and hyphenated across two lines.

@tie{}   Insert a normal interword space at which a line break may not occur.

The pagination commands apply only to printed output, since other output formats do not have pages.

@page   Start a new page.

@group   Hold text together that must appear on one page.

@need *mils*
                Start a new page if not enough space on this one.

15.2 @* and @/: Generate and Allow Line Breaks

The @* command forces a line break in all output formats. The @/ command allows a line break (printed manual only).

Here is an example with @*:

    This sentence is broken @*into two lines.

produces

    This sentence is broken
    into two lines.

The @/ command can be useful within long urls or other identifiers where TeX can't find a good place to break. TeX will automatically break urls at the natural places (see Section 8.9.2 [URL Line Breaking], page 76), so only use @/ if you need it. @/ has no effect in the other output format.

15.3 @- and @hyphenation: Helping TEX Hyphenate

Although TEX's hyphenation algorithm is generally pretty good, it does miss useful hyphenation points from time to time. (Or, far more rarely, insert an incorrect hyphenation.) So, for documents with an unusual vocabulary or when fine-tuning for a printed edition, you may wish to help TEX out. Texinfo supports two commands for this:

@-   Insert a discretionary hyphen, i.e., a place where TEX can (but does not have to) hyphenate. This is especially useful when you notice an overfull hbox is due to TEX missing a hyphenation (see Section 21.10 [Overfull hboxes], page 185). TEX will not insert any hyphenation points itself into a word containing @-.

@hyphenation{*hy-phen-a-ted words*}
           Tell TEX how to hyphenate *hy-phen-a-ted words*. As shown, you put a '-' at each hyphenation point. For example:

               @hyphenation{man-u-script man-u-scripts}

           TEX only uses the specified hyphenation points when the words match exactly, so give all necessary variants, such as plurals.

Info, HTML, and other non-TEX output is not hyphenated, so none of these commands have any effect there.

15.4 @allowcodebreaks: Control Line Breaks in @code

Ordinarily, TEX considers breaking lines at '-' and '_' characters within @code and related commands (see Section 9.1.2 [@code], page 79), more or less as if they were "empty" hyphenation points.

This is necessary since many manuals, especially for Lisp-family languages, must document very long identifiers. On the other hand, some manuals don't have this problems, and you may not wish to allow a line break at the underscore in, for example, SIZE_MAX, or even worse, after any of the four underscores in __typeof__.

So Texinfo provides this command:

    @allowcodebreaks false

to prevent from breaking at '-' or '_' within @code. You can go back to allowing such breaks with @allowcodebreaks true. Write these commands on lines by themselves.

These commands can be given anywhere in the document. For example, you may have just one problematic paragraph where you need to turn off the breaks, but want them in general, or vice versa.

This command has no effect except in HTML and TEX output.

15.5 @w{*text*}: Prevent Line Breaks

@w{*text*} outputs *text*, while prohibiting line breaks within *text*.

Thus, you can use @w to produce a non-breakable space, fixed at the width of a normal interword space:

    @w{ } @w{ } @w{ } indentation.

produces:

indentation.

The space from `@w{ }`, as well as being non-breakable, also will not stretch or shrink. Sometimes that is what you want, for instance if you're doing manual indenting. However, usually you want a normal interword space that does stretch and shrink (in the printed output); for that, see the `@tie` command in the next section.

You can also use the `@w` command to prevent TeX from automatically hyphenating a long name or phrase that happens to fall near the end of a line. `makeinfo` does not ever hyphenate words.

You can also use `@w` to avoid unwanted keyword expansion in source control systems. For example, to literally write `$Id$` in your document, use `@w{$}Id$`. This trick isn't effective in Info or plain text output, though.

15.6 `@tie{}`: Inserting an Unbreakable Space

The `@tie{}` command produces a normal interword space at which a line break may not occur. Always write it with following (empty) braces, as usual for commands used within a paragraph. Here's an example:

```
@TeX{} was written by Donald E.@tie{}Knuth.
```

produces:

TeX was written by Donald E. Knuth.

There are two important differences between `@tie{}` and `@w{ }`:

- The space produced by `@tie{}` will stretch and shrink slightly along with the normal interword spaces in the paragraph; the space produced by `@w{ }` will not vary.
- `@tie{}` allows hyphenation of the surrounding words, while `@w{ }` inhibits hyphenation of those words (for TeXnical reasons, namely that it produces an '\hbox').

15.7 `@sp` *n*: Insert Blank Lines

A line beginning with and containing only `@sp n` generates *n* blank lines of space in both the printed manual and the Info file. `@sp` also forces a paragraph break. For example,

```
@sp 2
```

generates two blank lines.

The `@sp` command is most often used in the title page.

15.8 `@page`: Start a New Page

A line containing only `@page` starts a new page in a printed manual. In other formats, without the concept of pages, it starts a new paragraph. An `@page` command is often used in the `@titlepage` section of a Texinfo file to start the copyright page.

15.9 `@group`: Prevent Page Breaks

The `@group` command (on a line by itself) is used inside an `@example` or similar construct to begin an unsplittable vertical group, which will appear entirely on one page in the printed output. The group is terminated by a line containing only `@end group`. These two lines produce no output of their own, and in the Info file output they have no effect at all.

Although `@group` would make sense conceptually in a wide variety of contexts, its current implementation works reliably only within `@example` and variants, and within `@display`, `@format`, `@flushleft` and `@flushright`. See Chapter 10 [Quotations and Examples], page 89. (What all these commands have in common is that each line of input produces a line of output.) In other contexts, `@group` can cause anomalous vertical spacing.

This formatting requirement means that you should write:

```
@example
@group
...
@end group
@end example
```

with the `@group` and `@end group` commands inside the `@example` and `@end example` commands.

The `@group` command is most often used to hold an example together on one page. In this Texinfo manual, more than 100 examples contain text that is enclosed between `@group` and `@end group`.

If you forget to end a group, you may get strange and unfathomable error messages when you run TeX. This is because TeX keeps trying to put the rest of the Texinfo file onto the one page and does not start to generate error messages until it has processed considerable text. It is a good rule of thumb to look for a missing `@end group` if you get incomprehensible error messages in TeX.

15.10 `@need mils`: Prevent Page Breaks

A line containing only `@need n` starts a new page in a printed manual if fewer than n mils (thousandths of an inch) remain on the current page. Do not use braces around the argument n. The `@need` command has no effect on other output formats since they are not paginated.

This paragraph is preceded by an `@need` command that tells TeX to start a new page if fewer than 800 mils (eight-tenths inch) remain on the page. It looks like this:

```
@need 800
This paragraph is preceded by ...
```

The `@need` command is useful for preventing orphans: single lines at the bottoms of printed pages.

16 Definition Commands

The `@deffn` command and the other *definition commands* enable you to describe functions, variables, macros, commands, user options, special forms and other such artifacts in a uniform format.

In the Info file, a definition causes the entity category—'Function', 'Variable', or whatever—to appear at the beginning of the first line of the definition, followed by the entity's name and arguments. In the printed manual, the command causes TEX to print the entity's name and its arguments on the left margin and print the category next to the right margin. In both output formats, the body of the definition is indented. Also, the name of the entity is entered into the appropriate index: `@deffn` enters the name into the index of functions, `@defvr` enters it into the index of variables, and so on (see Section 13.2 [Predefined Indices], page 114).

A manual need not and should not contain more than one definition for a given name. An appendix containing a summary should use `@table` rather than the definition commands.

16.1 The Template for a Definition

The `@deffn` command is used for definitions of entities that resemble functions. To write a definition using the `@deffn` command, write the `@deffn` command at the beginning of a line and follow it on the same line by the category of the entity, the name of the entity itself, and its arguments (if any). Then write the body of the definition on succeeding lines. (You may embed examples in the body.) Finally, end the definition with an `@end deffn` command written on a line of its own.

The other definition commands follow the same format: a line with the `@def...` command and whatever arguments are appropriate for that command; the body of the definition; and a corresponding `@end` line.

The template for a definition looks like this:

```
@deffn category name arguments...
body-of-definition
@end deffn
```

For example,

```
@deffn Command forward-word count
This command moves point forward @var{count} words
(or backward if @var{count} is negative). ...
@end deffn
```

produces

forward-word *count*   [Command]
> This command moves point forward *count* words (or backward if *count* is negative). ...

Capitalize the category name like a title. If the name of the category contains spaces, as in the phrase 'Interactive Command', enclose it in braces. For example:

```
@deffn {Interactive Command} isearch-forward
...
@end deffn
```

Otherwise, the second word will be mistaken for the name of the entity. As a general rule, when any of the arguments in the heading line *except* the last one are more than one word, you need to enclose them in braces. This may also be necessary if the text contains commands, for example, '{declaraci@'on}' if you are writing in Spanish.

Some of the definition commands are more general than others. The `@deffn` command, for example, is the general definition command for functions and the like—for entities that may take arguments. When you use this command, you specify the category to which the entity belongs. Three predefined, specialized variations (`@defun`, `@defmac`, and `@defspec`) specify the category for you: "Function", "Macro", and "Special Form" respectively. (In Lisp, a special form is an entity much like a function.) Similarly, the general `@defvr` command is accompanied by several specialized variations for describing particular kinds of variables.

See Section 16.7 [Sample Function Definition], page 149, for a detailed example of a function definition, including the use of `@example` inside the definition.

16.2 Definition Command Continuation Lines

The heading line of a definition command can get very long. Therefore, Texinfo has a special syntax allowing them to be continued over multiple lines of the source file: a lone '@' at the end of each line to be continued. Here's an example:

```
@defun fn-name @
  arg1 arg2 arg3
This is the basic continued defun.
@end defun
```

produces:

fn-name *arg1 arg2 arg3*   [Function]
    This is the basic continued defun.

As you can see, the continued lines are combined, as if they had been typed on one source line.

Although this example only shows a one-line continuation, continuations may extend over any number of lines, in the same way; put an @ at the end of each line to be continued.

In general, any number of spaces or tabs before the @ continuation character are collapsed into a single space. There is one exception: the Texinfo processors will not fully collapse whitespace around a continuation inside braces. For example:

```
@deffn {Category @
  Name} ...
```

The output (not shown) has excess space between 'Category' and 'Name'. To avoid this, elide the unwanted whitespace in your input, or put the continuation @ outside braces.

@ does not function as a continuation character in *any* other context. Ordinarily, '@' followed by a whitespace character (space, tab, newline) produces a normal interword space (see Section 14.3.1 [Multiple Spaces], page 121).

16.3 Optional and Repeated Arguments

Some entities take optional or repeated arguments, conventionally specified by using square brackets and ellipses: an argument enclosed within square brackets is optional, and an argument followed by an ellipsis is optional and may be repeated more than once.

Thus, [*optional-arg*] means that *optional-arg* is optional and *repeated-args*'...' stands for zero or more arguments. Parentheses are used when several arguments are grouped into additional levels of list structure in Lisp.

Here is the `@defspec` line of an example of an imaginary (complicated) special form:

foobar (*var* [*from to* [*inc*]]) *body*...   [Special Form]

In this example, the arguments *from* and *to* are optional, but must both be present or both absent. If they are present, *inc* may optionally be specified as well. These arguments are grouped with the argument *var* into a list, to distinguish them from *body*, which includes all remaining elements of the form.

In a Texinfo source file, this `@defspec` line is written like this, including a continuation to avoid a long source line.

```
@defspec foobar (@var{var} [@var{from} @var{to} @
    [@var{inc}]]) @var{body}@dots{}
```

The function is listed in the Command and Variable Index under 'foobar'.

16.4 @deffnx, et al.: Two or More 'First' Lines

To create two or more 'first' or header lines for a definition, follow the first `@deffn` line by a line beginning with `@deffnx`. The `@deffnx` command works exactly like `@deffn` except that it does not generate extra vertical white space between it and the preceding line.

For example,

```
@deffn {Interactive Command} isearch-forward
@deffnx {Interactive Command} isearch-backward
These two search commands are similar except ...
@end deffn
```

produces

isearch-forward   [Interactive Command]
isearch-backward   [Interactive Command]
> These two search commands are similar except ...

Each definition command has an 'x' form: `@defunx`, `@defvrx`, `@deftypefunx`, etc.

The 'x' forms work similarly to `@itemx` (see Section 11.4.3 [@itemx], page 104).

16.5 The Definition Commands

Texinfo provides more than a dozen definition commands, all of which are described in this section.

The definition commands automatically enter the name of the entity in the appropriate index: for example, `@deffn`, `@defun`, and `@defmac` enter function names in the index of functions; `@defvr` and `@defvar` enter variable names in the index of variables.

Although the examples that follow mostly illustrate Lisp, the commands can be used for other programming languages.

16.5.1 Functions and Similar Entities

This section describes the commands for describing functions and similar entities:

`@deffn` *category name arguments*...

> The `@deffn` command is the general definition command for functions, interactive commands, and similar entities that may take arguments. You must choose a term to describe the category of entity being defined; for example, "Function" could be used if the entity is a function. The `@deffn` command is written at the beginning of a line and is followed on the same line by the category of entity being described, the name of this particular entity, and its arguments, if any. Terminate the definition with `@end deffn` on a line of its own.

> For example, here is a definition:

```
@deffn Command forward-char nchars
Move point forward @var{nchars} characters.
@end deffn
```

> This shows a rather terse definition for a "command" named `forward-char` with one argument, *nchars*.

> `@deffn` prints argument names such as *nchars* in slanted type in the printed output, because we think of these names as metasyntactic variables—they stand for the actual argument values. Within the text of the description, however, write an argument name explicitly with `@var` to refer to the value of the argument. In the example above, we used '`@var{nchars}`' in this way.

> In the extremely unusual case when an argument name contains '`--`', or another character sequence which is treated specially (see Section 1.9 [Conventions], page 9), use `@code` around the special characters. This avoids the conversion to typographic en-dashes and em-dashes.

> The template for `@deffn` is:

```
@deffn category name arguments...
body-of-definition
@end deffn
```

`@defun` *name arguments*...

> The `@defun` command is the definition command for functions. `@defun` is equivalent to '`@deffn Function ...`'. Terminate the definition with `@end defun` on a line of its own. Thus, the template is:

```
@defun function-name arguments...
body-of-definition
@end defun
```

`@defmac` *name arguments*...

> The `@defmac` command is the definition command for macros. `@defmac` is equivalent to '`@deffn Macro ...`' and works like `@defun`.

@defspec *name arguments...*

> The **@defspec** command is the definition command for special forms. (In Lisp, a special form is an entity much like a function; see Section "Special Forms" in *GNU Emacs Lisp Reference Manual*.) **@defspec** is equivalent to '**@deffn {Special Form} ...**' and works like **@defun**.

All these commands create entries in the index of functions.

16.5.2 Variables and Similar Entities

Here are the commands for defining variables and similar entities:

@defvr *category name*

> The **@defvr** command is a general definition command for something like a variable—an entity that records a value. You must choose a term to describe the category of entity being defined; for example, "Variable" could be used if the entity is a variable. Write the **@defvr** command at the beginning of a line and follow it on the same line by the category of the entity and the name of the entity.
>
> We recommend capitalizing the category name like a title. If the name of the category contains spaces, as in the name "User Option", enclose it in braces. Otherwise, the second word will be mistaken for the name of the entity. For example,
>
> ```
> @defvr {User Option} fill-column
> This buffer-local variable specifies
> the maximum width of filled lines.
> ...
> @end defvr
> ```
>
> Terminate the definition with **@end defvr** on a line of its own.
>
> The template is:
>
> ```
> @defvr category name
> body-of-definition
> @end defvr
> ```
>
> **@defvr** creates an entry in the index of variables for *name*.

@defvar *name*

> The **@defvar** command is the definition command for variables. **@defvar** is equivalent to '**@defvr Variable ...**'.
>
> For example:
>
> ```
> @defvar kill-ring
> ...
> @end defvar
> ```
>
> The template is:
>
> ```
> @defvar name
> body-of-definition
> @end defvar
> ```
>
> **@defvar** creates an entry in the index of variables for *name*.

`@defopt` *name*

> The `@defopt` command is the definition command for *user options*, i.e., variables intended for users to change according to taste; Emacs has many such (see Section "Variables" in *The GNU Emacs Manual*). `@defopt` is equivalent to '`@defvr {User Option} ...`' and works like `@defvar`. It creates an entry in the index of variables.

16.5.3 Functions in Typed Languages

The `@deftypefn` command and its variations are for describing functions in languages in which you must declare types of variables and functions, such as C and C++.

`@deftypefn` *category data-type name arguments...*

> The `@deftypefn` command is the general definition command for functions and similar entities that may take arguments and that are typed. The `@deftypefn` command is written at the beginning of a line and is followed on the same line by the category of entity being described, the type of the returned value, the name of this particular entity, and its arguments, if any.
>
> For example,
>
> ```
> @deftypefn {Library Function} int foobar @
>   (int @var{foo}, float @var{bar})
> ...
> @end deftypefn
> ```
>
> produces:
>
> int foobar (*int* foo, *float* bar)   [Library Function]
>   ...
>
> This means that `foobar` is a "library function" that returns an `int`, and its arguments are *foo* (an `int`) and *bar* (a `float`).
>
> Since in typed languages, the actual names of the arguments are typically scattered among data type names and keywords, Texinfo cannot find them without help. You can either (a) write everything as straight text, and it will be printed in slanted type; (b) use `@var` for the variable names, which will uppercase the variable names in Info and use the slanted typewriter font in printed output; (c) use `@var` for the variable names and `@code` for the type names and keywords, which will be dutifully obeyed.
>
> The template for `@deftypefn` is:
>
> ```
> @deftypefn category data-type name arguments ...
> body-of-description
> @end deftypefn
> ```
>
> Note that if the *category* or *data type* is more than one word then it must be enclosed in braces to make it a single argument.
>
> If you are describing a procedure in a language that has packages, such as Ada, you might consider using `@deftypefn` in a manner somewhat contrary to the convention described in the preceding paragraphs. For example:

```
@deftypefn stacks private push @
        (@var{s}:in out stack; @
        @var{n}:in integer)
    ...
@end deftypefn
```

(In these examples the **@deftypefn** arguments are shown using continuations (see Section 16.2 [Def Cmd Continuation Lines], page 140), but could be on a single line.)

In this instance, the procedure is classified as belonging to the package **stacks** rather than classified as a 'procedure' and its data type is described as **private**. (The name of the procedure is **push**, and its arguments are *s* and *n*.)

@deftypefn creates an entry in the index of functions for *name*.

@deftypefun *data-type name arguments...*

> The **@deftypefun** command is the specialized definition command for functions in typed languages. The command is equivalent to '**@deftypefn Function ...**'. The template is:

> ```
> @deftypefun type name arguments...
> body-of-description
> @end deftypefun
> ```

> **@deftypefun** creates an entry in the index of functions for *name*.

Ordinarily, the return type is printed on the same line as the function name and arguments, as shown above. In source code, GNU style is to put the return type on a line by itself. So Texinfo provides an option to do that: **@deftypefnnewline on**.

This affects typed functions only—not untyped functions, not typed variables, etc.. Specifically, it affects the commands in this section, and the analogous commands for object-oriented languages, namely **@deftypeop** and **@deftypemethod** (see Section 16.5.6.2 [Object-Oriented Methods], page 148).

Specifying **@deftypefnnewline off** reverts to the default.

16.5.4 Variables in Typed Languages

Variables in typed languages are handled in a manner similar to functions in typed languages. See Section 16.5.3 [Typed Functions], page 144. The general definition command **@deftypevr** corresponds to **@deftypefn** and the specialized definition command **@deftypevar** corresponds to **@deftypefun**.

@deftypevr *category data-type name*

> The **@deftypevr** command is the general definition command for something like a variable in a typed language—an entity that records a value. You must choose a term to describe the category of the entity being defined; for example, "Variable" could be used if the entity is a variable.

> The **@deftypevr** command is written at the beginning of a line and is followed on the same line by the category of the entity being described, the data type, and the name of this particular entity.

For example:

```
@deftypevr {Global Flag} int enable
...
@end deftypevr
```

produces the following:

`int enable`   [Global Flag]

    ...

The template is:

```
@deftypevr category data-type name
body-of-description
@end deftypevr
```

`@deftypevar data-type name`

       The `@deftypevar` command is the specialized definition command for variables in typed languages. `@deftypevar` is equivalent to '`@deftypevr Variable ...`'. The template is:

```
@deftypevar data-type name
body-of-description
@end deftypevar
```

These commands create entries in the index of variables.

16.5.5 Data Types

Here is the command for data types:

`@deftp category name attributes...`

       The `@deftp` command is the generic definition command for data types. The command is written at the beginning of a line and is followed on the same line by the category, by the name of the type (which is a word like `int` or `float`), and then by names of attributes of objects of that type. Thus, you could use this command for describing `int` or `float`, in which case you could use `data type` as the category. (A data type is a category of certain objects for purposes of deciding which operations can be performed on them.)

       In Lisp, for example, *pair* names a particular data type, and an object of that type has two slots called the CAR and the CDR. Here is how you would write the first line of a definition of `pair`.

```
@deftp {Data type} pair car cdr
...
@end deftp
```

The template is:

```
@deftp category name-of-type attributes...
body-of-definition
@end deftp
```

`@deftp` creates an entry in the index of data types.

16.5.6 Object-Oriented Programming

Here are the commands for formatting descriptions about abstract objects, such as are used in object-oriented programming. A class is a defined type of abstract object. An instance of a class is a particular object that has the type of the class. An instance variable is a variable that belongs to the class but for which each instance has its own value.

16.5.6.1 Object-Oriented Variables

These commands allow you to define different sorts of variables in object-oriented programming languages.

`@defcv` *category class name*

> The `@defcv` command is the general definition command for variables associated with classes in object-oriented programming. The `@defcv` command is followed by three arguments: the category of thing being defined, the class to which it belongs, and its name. For instance:
>
> ```
> @defcv {Class Option} Window border-pattern
> ...
> @end defcv
> ```
>
> produces:
>
> `border-pattern`   [Class Option of `Window`]
> ...
>
> `@defcv` creates an entry in the index of variables.

`@deftypecv` *category class data-type name*

> The `@deftypecv` command is the definition command for typed class variables in object-oriented programming. It is analogous to `@defcv` with the addition of the *data-type* parameter to specify the type of the instance variable. Ordinarily, the data type is a programming language construct that should be marked with `@code`. For instance:
>
> ```
> @deftypecv {Class Option} Window @code{int} border-pattern
> ...
> @end deftypecv
> ```
>
> produces:
>
> `int border-pattern`   [Class Option of `Window`]
> ...
>
> `@deftypecv` creates an entry in the index of variables.

`@defivar` *class name*

> The `@defivar` command is the definition command for instance variables in object-oriented programming. `@defivar` is equivalent to '`@defcv {Instance Variable} ...`'. For instance:
>
> ```
> @defivar Window border-pattern
> ...
> @end defivar
> ```
>
> produces:

border-pattern   [Instance Variable of `Window`]

   ...

`@defivar` creates an entry in the index of variables.

`@deftypeivar` *class data-type name*

The `@deftypeivar` command is the definition command for typed instance variables in object-oriented programming. It is analogous to `@defivar` with the addition of the *data-type* parameter to specify the type of the instance variable. Ordinarily, the data type is a programming language construct that should be marked with `@code`. For instance:

```
@deftypeivar Window @code{int} border-pattern
...
@end deftypeivar
```

produces:

int border-pattern   [Instance Variable of `Window`]

   ...

`@deftypeivar` creates an entry in the index of variables.

16.5.6.2 Object-Oriented Methods

These commands allow you to define different sorts of function-like entities resembling methods in object-oriented programming languages. These entities take arguments, as functions do, but are associated with particular classes of objects.

`@defop` *category class name arguments...*

The `@defop` command is the general definition command for these method-like entities.

For example, some systems have constructs called *wrappers* that are associated with classes as methods are, but that act more like macros than like functions. You could use `@defop Wrapper` to describe one of these.

Sometimes it is useful to distinguish methods and *operations*. You can think of an operation as the specification for a method. Thus, a window system might specify that all window classes have a method named `expose`; we would say that this window system defines an `expose` operation on windows in general. Typically, the operation has a name and also specifies the pattern of arguments; all methods that implement the operation must accept the same arguments, since applications that use the operation do so without knowing which method will implement it.

Often it makes more sense to document operations than methods. For example, window application developers need to know about the `expose` operation, but need not be concerned with whether a given class of windows has its own method to implement this operation. To describe this operation, you would write:

```
@defop Operation windows expose
```

The `@defop` command is written at the beginning of a line and is followed on the same line by the overall name of the category of operation, the name of the class of the operation, the name of the operation, and its arguments, if any.

The template is:

```
@defop category class name arguments...
body-of-definition
@end defop
```

`@defop` creates an entry, such as 'expose on windows', in the index of functions.

`@deftypeop` *category class data-type name arguments...*

The `@deftypeop` command is the definition command for typed operations in object-oriented programming. It is similar to `@defop` with the addition of the *data-type* parameter to specify the return type of the method. `@deftypeop` creates an entry in the index of functions.

`@defmethod` *class name arguments...*

The `@defmethod` command is the definition command for methods in object-oriented programming. A method is a kind of function that implements an operation for a particular class of objects and its subclasses.

`@defmethod` is equivalent to '`@defop Method ...`'. The command is written at the beginning of a line and is followed by the name of the class of the method, the name of the method, and its arguments, if any.

For example:

```
@defmethod bar-class bar-method argument
...
@end defmethod
```

illustrates the definition for a method called `bar-method` of the class `bar-class`. The method takes an argument.

`@defmethod` creates an entry in the index of functions.

`@deftypemethod` *class data-type name arguments...*

The `@deftypemethod` command is the definition command for methods in object-oriented typed languages, such as C++ and Java. It is similar to the `@defmethod` command with the addition of the *data-type* parameter to specify the return type of the method. `@deftypemethod` creates an entry in the index of functions.

The typed commands are affected by the `@deftypefnnewline` option (see Section 16.5.3 [Functions in Typed Languages], page 144).

16.6 Conventions for Writing Definitions

When you write a definition using `@deffn`, `@defun`, or one of the other definition commands, please take care to use arguments that indicate the meaning, as with the *count* argument to the `forward-word` function. Also, if the name of an argument contains the name of a type, such as *integer*, take care that the argument actually is of that type.

16.7 A Sample Function Definition

A function definition uses the `@defun` and `@end defun` commands. The name of the function follows immediately after the `@defun` command and it is followed, on the same line, by the parameter list.

Here is a definition from Section "Calling Functions" in *The GNU Emacs Lisp Reference Manual*.

> `apply` *function* **&rest** *arguments*   [Function]
>
> `apply` calls *function* with *arguments*, just like `funcall` but with one difference: the last of *arguments* is a list of arguments to give to *function*, rather than a single argument. We also say that this list is *appended* to the other arguments.
>
> `apply` returns the result of calling *function*. As with `funcall`, *function* must either be a Lisp function or a primitive function; special forms and macros do not make sense in `apply`.
>
> ```
> (setq f 'list)
>      ⇒ list
> (apply f 'x 'y 'z)
>   error   Wrong type argument: listp, z
> (apply '+ 1 2 '(3 4))
>      ⇒ 10
> (apply '+ '(1 2 3 4))
>      ⇒ 10
>
> (apply 'append '((a b c) nil (x y z) nil))
>      ⇒ (a b c x y z)
> ```
>
> An interesting example of using `apply` is found in the description of `mapcar`.

In the Texinfo source file, this example looks like this:

```
@defun apply function &rest arguments
@code{apply} calls @var{function} with
@var{arguments}, just like @code{funcall} but with one
difference: the last of @var{arguments} is a list of
arguments to give to @var{function}, rather than a single
argument.  We also say that this list is @dfn{appended}
to the other arguments.

@code{apply} returns the result of calling
@var{function}.  As with @code{funcall},
@var{function} must either be a Lisp function or a
primitive function; special forms and macros do not make
sense in @code{apply}.
```

```
@example
(setq f 'list)
    @result{} list
(apply f 'x 'y 'z)
@error{} Wrong type argument: listp, z
(apply '+ 1 2 '(3 4))
    @result{} 10
(apply '+ '(1 2 3 4))
    @result{} 10

(apply 'append '((a b c) nil (x y z) nil))
    @result{} (a b c x y z)
@end example

An interesting example of using @code{apply} is found
in the description of @code{mapcar}.
@end defun
```

In this manual, this function is listed in the Command and Variable Index under `apply`.

Ordinary variables and user options are described using a format like that for functions except that variables do not take arguments.

17 Internationalization

Texinfo has some support for writing in languages other than English, although this area still needs considerable work. (If you are yourself helping to translate the fixed strings written to documents, see Section 22.6 [Internationalization of Document Strings], page 210.)

For a list of the various accented and special characters Texinfo supports, see Section 14.4 [Inserting Accents], page 124.

17.1 @documentlanguage *ll*[*_cc*]: Set the Document Language

The @documentlanguage command declares the current document locale. Write it on a line by itself, near the beginning of the file, but after @setfilename (see Section 3.2.3 [@setfilename], page 31):

```
@documentlanguage ll[_cc]
```

Include a two-letter ISO 639-2 language code (*ll*) following the command name, optionally followed by an underscore and two-letter ISO 3166 two-letter country code (*cc*). If you have a multilingual document, the intent is to be able to use this command multiple times, to declare each language change. If the command is not used at all, the default is en_US for US English.

As with GNU Gettext (see *Gettext*), if the country code is omitted, the main dialect is assumed where possible. For example, de is equivalent to de_DE (German as spoken in Germany).

For Info and other online output, this command changes the translation of various *document strings* such as "see" in cross references (see Chapter 8 [Cross References], page 66), "Function' in defuns (see Chapter 16 [Definition Commands], page 139), and so on. Some strings, such as "Node:", "Next:", "Menu:", etc., are keywords in Info output, so are not translated there; they are translated in other output formats.

For TEX, this command causes a file txi-*locale*.tex to be read (if it exists). If @documentlanguage argument contains the optional '_cc' suffix, this is tried first. For example, with @documentlanguage de_DE, TEX first looks for txi-de_DE.tex, then txi-de.tex.

Such a txi-* file is intended to redefine the various English words used in TEX output, such as 'Chapter', 'See', and so on. We are aware that individual words like these cannot always be translated in isolation, and that a very different strategy would be required for ideographic (among other) scripts. Help in improving Texinfo's language support is welcome.

@documentlanguage also changes TEX's current hyphenation patterns, if the TEX program being run has the necessary support included. This will generally not be the case for tex itself, but will usually be the case for up-to-date distributions of the extended TEX programs etex (DVI output) and pdftex (PDF output). texi2dvi will use the extended TEXs if they are available (see Section 21.2 [Format with texi2dvi], page 177).

In September 2006, the W3C Internationalization Activity released a new recommendation for specifying languages: http://www.rfc-editor.org/rfc/bcp/bcp47.txt. When Gettext supports this new scheme, Texinfo will too.

Since the lists of language codes and country codes are updated relatively frequently, we don't attempt to list them here. The valid language codes are on the official home page for ISO 639, `http://www.loc.gov/standards/iso639-2/`. The country codes and the official web site for ISO 3166 can be found via `http://en.wikipedia.org/wiki/ISO_3166`.

17.2 @documentencoding *enc*: Set Input Encoding

The `@documentencoding` command declares the input document encoding, and can also affect the encoding of the output. Write it on a line by itself, with a valid encoding specification following, near the beginning of the file but after `@setfilename` (see Section 3.2.3 [`@setfilename`], page 31):

```
@documentencoding enc
```

Texinfo supports these encodings:

US-ASCII   This has no particular effect, but it's included for completeness.

UTF-8   The vast global character encoding, expressed in 8-bit bytes.

ISO-8859-1
ISO-8859-15
ISO-8859-2

These specify the standard encodings for Western European (the first two) and Eastern European languages (the third), respectively. ISO 8859-15 replaces some little-used characters from 8859-1 (e.g., precomposed fractions) with more commonly needed ones, such as the Euro symbol (€).

A full description of the encodings is beyond our scope here; one useful reference is `http://czyborra.com/charsets/iso8859.html`.

koi8-r   This is the commonly used encoding for the Russian language.

koi8-u   This is the commonly used encoding for the Ukrainian language.

Specifying an encoding *enc* has the following effects:

In Info output, a so-called 'Local Variables' section (see Section "File Variables" in *The GNU Emacs Manual*) is output including *enc*. This allows Info readers to set the encoding appropriately. It looks like this:

```
Local Variables:
coding: enc
End:
```

Also, in Info and plain text output, unless the option `--disable-encoding` is given to `makeinfo`, accent constructs and special characters, such as `@'e`, are output as the actual 8-bit or UTF-8 character in the given encoding where possible.

In HTML output, a '`<meta>`' tag is output, in the '`<head>`' section of the HTML, that specifies *enc*. Web servers and browsers cooperate to use this information so the correct encoding is used to display the page, if supported by the system. That looks like this:

```
<meta http-equiv="Content-Type" content="text/html;
    charset=enc">
```

In XML and Docbook output, UTF-8 is always used for the output, according to the conventions of those formats.

In TEX output, the characters which are supported in the standard Computer Modern fonts are output accordingly. For example, this means using constructed accents rather than precomposed glyphs. Using a missing character generates a warning message, as does specifying an unimplemented encoding.

Although modern TEX systems support nearly every script in use in the world, this wide-ranging support is not available in `texinfo.tex`, and it's not feasible to duplicate or incorporate all that effort. (Our plan to support other scripts is to create a LATEX back-end to `texi2any`, where the support is already present.)

For maximum portability of Texinfo documents across the many different user environments in the world, we recommend sticking to 7-bit ASCII in the input unless your particular manual needs a substantial amount of non-ASCII, e.g., it's written in German. You can use the `@U` command to insert an occasional needed character (see Section 14.10 [Inserting Unicode], page 133).

18 Conditionally Visible Text

The *conditional commands* allow you to use different text for different output formats, or for general conditions that you define. For example, you can use them to specify different text for the printed manual and the Info output.

The conditional commands comprise the following categories.

- Commands specific to an output format (Info, TEX, HTML, . . .).
- Commands specific to any output format *excluding* a given one (e.g., not Info, not TEX, . . .).
- 'Raw' formatter text for any output format, passed straight through with minimal (but not zero) interpretation of @-commands.
- Format-independent variable substitutions, and testing if a variable is set or clear.

18.1 Conditional Commands

Texinfo has an `@ifformat` environment for each output format, to allow conditional inclusion of text for a particular output format.

`@ifinfo` begins segments of text that should be ignored by TEX when it typesets the printed manual, and by `makeinfo` when not producing Info output. The segment of text appears only in the Info file and, for historical compatibility, the plain text output.

The environments for the other formats are analogous, but without the special historical case:

`@ifdocbook ... @end ifdocbook`
> Text to appear only in the Docbook output.

`@ifhtml ... @end ifhtml`
> Text to appear only in the HTML output.

`@ifplaintext ... @end ifplaintext`
> Text to appear only in the plain text output.

`@iftex ... @end iftex`
> Text to appear only in the printed manual.

`@ifxml ... @end ifxml`
> Text to appear only in the XML output.

The `@if...` and `@end if...` commands must appear on lines by themselves in your source file. The newlines following the commands are (more or less) treated as whitespace, so that the conditional text is flowed normally into a surrounding paragraph.

The `@if...` constructs are intended to conditionalize normal Texinfo source; see Section 18.3 [Raw Formatter Commands], page 157, for using underlying format commands directly.

Here is an example showing all these conditionals:

```
@iftex
This text will appear only in the printed manual.
@end iftex
```

```
@ifinfo
However, this text will appear only in Info and plain text.
@end ifinfo
@ifhtml
And this text will only appear in HTML.
@end ifhtml
@ifplaintext
Whereas this text will only appear in plain text.
@end ifplaintext
@ifxml
Notwithstanding that this will only appear in XML.
@end ifxml
@ifdocbook
Nevertheless, this will only appear in Docbook.
@end ifdocbook
```

The preceding example produces the following line:

This text will appear only in the printed manual.

Notice that you only see one of the input lines, depending on which version of the manual you are reading.

In complex documents, you may want Texinfo to issue an error message in some conditionals that should not ever be processed. The `@errormsg{text}` command will do this; it takes one argument, the text of the error message, which is expanded more or less as if it were Info text.

We mention `@errormsg{}` here even though it is not strictly related to conditionals, since in practice it is most likely to be useful in that context. Technically, it can be used anywhere. See Section 19.6 [External Macro Processors], page 172, for a caveat regarding the line numbers which `@errormsg` emits in TeX.

18.2 Conditional Not Commands

You can specify text to be included in any output format *other* than a given one with the `@ifnot...` environments:

```
@ifnotdocbook ... @end ifnotdocbook
@ifnothtml ... @end ifnothtml
@ifnotinfo ... @end ifnotinfo
@ifnotplaintext ... @end ifnotplaintext
@ifnottex ... @end ifnottex
@ifnotxml ... @end ifnotxml
```

The `@ifnot...` command and the `@end` command must appear on lines by themselves in your actual source file.

If the output file is being made in the given format, the region is *ignored*. Otherwise, it is included.

There is one exception (for historical compatibility): `@ifnotinfo` text is omitted for both Info and plain text output, not just Info. To specify text which appears only in Info and not in plain text, use `@ifnotplaintext`, like this:

```
@ifinfo
@ifnotplaintext
This will be in Info, but not plain text.
@end ifnotplaintext
@end ifinfo
```

The regions delimited by these commands are ordinary Texinfo source as with `@iftex`, not raw formatter source as with `@tex` (see Section 18.3 [Raw Formatter Commands], page 157).

18.3 Raw Formatter Commands

The `@if...` conditionals just described must be used only with normal Texinfo source. For instance, most features of plain TeX will not work within `@iftex`. The purpose of `@if...` is to provide conditional processing for Texinfo source, not provide access to underlying formatting features. For that, Texinfo provides so-called *raw formatter commands*. They should only be used when truly required (most documents do not need them).

The first raw formatter command is `@tex`. You can enter plain TeX completely, and use '\' in the TeX commands, by delineating a region with the `@tex` and `@end tex` commands. All plain TeX commands and category codes are restored within an `@tex` region. The sole exception is that the `@` character still introduces a command, so that `@end tex` can be recognized. Texinfo processors will not output material in such a region, unless TeX output is being produced.

In complex cases, you may wish to define new TeX macros within `@tex`. You must use `\gdef` to do this, not `\def`, because `@tex` regions are processed in a TeX group. If you need to make several definitions, you may wish to set `\globaldefs=1` (its value will be restored to zero as usual when the group ends at `@end tex`, so it won't cause problems with the rest of the document).

As an example, here is a displayed equation written in plain TeX:

```
@tex
$$ \chi^2 = \sum_{i=1}^N
           \left (y_i - (a + b x_i)
           \over \sigma_i\right)^2 $$
@end tex
```

The output of this example will appear only in a printed manual. If you are reading this in a format not generated by TeX, you will not see the equation that appears in the printed manual.

$$\chi^2 = \sum_{i=1}^N \left(\frac{y_i - (a + bx_i)}{\sigma_i} \right)^2$$

Analogously, you can use `@ifhtml ... @end ifhtml` to delimit Texinfo source to be included in HTML output only, and `@html ... @end html` for a region of raw HTML.

Likewise, you can use `@ifxml ... @end ifxml` to delimit Texinfo source to be included in XML output only, and `@xml ... @end xml` for a region of raw XML. Regions of raw text in other formats will also be present in the XML output, but with protection of XML characters and within corresponding elements. For example, the raw HTML text:

```
@html
<br />
@end html
```

will be included in the XML output as:

```
<html>
&lt;br /&gt;
</html>
```

Again likewise, you can use `@ifdocbook` ... `@end ifdocbook` to delimit Texinfo source to be included in Docbook output only, and `@docbook` ... `@end docbook` for a region of raw Docbook.

The behavior of newlines in raw regions is unspecified.

In all cases, in raw processing, `@` retains the same meaning as in the remainder of the document. Thus, the Texinfo processors must recognize and even execute, to some extent, the contents of the raw regions, regardless of the final output format. Therefore, specifying changes that globally affect the document inside a raw region leads to unpredictable and generally undesirable behavior. For example, using the `@kbdinputstyle` command inside a raw region is undefined.

The remedy is simple: don't do that. Use the raw formatter commands for their intended purpose, of providing material directly in the underlying format. When you simply want to give different Texinfo specifications for different output formats, use the `@if...` conditionals and stay in Texinfo syntax.

18.4 Inline Conditionals: `@inline`, `@inlineifelse`, `@inlineraw`

Texinfo provides a set of conditional commands with arguments given within braces:

`@inlinefmt{`*format, text*`}`

> Process the Texinfo *text* if *format* output is being generated.

`@inlinefmtifelse{`*format, then-text, else-text*`}`

> Process the Texinfo *then-text* if *format* output is being generated; otherwise, process *else-text*.

`@inlineraw{`*format, text*`}`

> Similar, but for raw *text* (see Section 18.3 [Raw Formatter Commands], page 157).

The supported *format* names are:

```
docbook  html  info  plaintext  tex  xml
```

For example,

```
@inlinefmt{html, @emph{HTML-only text}}
```

is nearly equivalent to

```
@ifhtml
@emph{HTML-only text}
@end ifhtml
```

except that no whitespace is added, as happens in the latter (environment) case.

In these commands, whitespace is ignored after the comma separating the arguments, as usual, but is *not* ignored at the end of *text*.

To insert a literal at sign, left brace, or right brace in one of the arguments, you must use the alphabetic commands `@atchar{}` (see Section 14.1.1 [Inserting an Atsign], page 119), and `@lbracechar{}` or `@rbracechar{}` (see Section 14.1.2 [Inserting Braces], page 119), or the parsing will become confused.

With `@inlinefmtifelse`, it is also necessary to use `@comma{}` to avoid mistaking a ',' in the text for the delimiter. With `@inlinefmt` and `@inlineraw`, `@comma{}` is not required (though it's fine to use it), since these commands always have exactly two arguments.

For TEX, the processed *text* cannot contain newline-delimited commands. Text to be ignored (i.e., for non-TEX) can, though.

Two other `@inline...` conditionals complement the `@ifset` and `@ifclear` commands; see the next section.

18.5 Flags: @set, @clear, conditionals, and @value

You can direct the Texinfo formatting commands to format or ignore parts of a Texinfo file with the `@set`, `@clear`, `@ifset`, and `@ifclear` commands.

Here are brief descriptions of these commands, see the following sections for more details:

`@set flag [value]`

> Set the variable *flag*, to the optional *value* if specified.

`@clear flag`

> Undefine the variable *flag*, whether or not it was previously defined.

`@ifset flag`

> If *flag* is set, text through the next `@end ifset` command is formatted. If *flag* is clear, text through the following `@end ifset` command is ignored.

`@inlineifset{flag, text}`

> Brace-delimited version of `@ifset`.

`@ifclear flag`

> If *flag* is set, text through the next `@end ifclear` command is ignored. If *flag* is clear, text through the following `@end ifclear` command is formatted.

`@inlineifclear{flag, text}`

> Brace-delimited version of `@ifclear`.

18.5.1 @set and @value

You use the `@set` command to specify a value for a flag, which is later expanded by the `@value` command.

A *flag* (aka *variable*) name is an identifier starting with an alphanumeric, '-', or '_'. Subsequent characters, if any, may not be whitespace, '@', braces, angle brackets, or any of '~`^+|'; other characters, such as '%', may work. However, it is best to use only letters and numerals in a flag name, not '-' or '_' or others—they will work in some contexts, but not all, due to limitations in TEX.

The value is the remainder of the input line, and can contain anything. However, unlike most other commands which take the rest of the line as a value, @set need not appear at the beginning of a line.

Write the @set command like this:

```
@set foo This is a string.
```

This sets the value of the flag foo to "This is a string.".

The Texinfo formatters then replace an @value{*flag*} command with the string to which *flag* is set. Thus, when foo is set as shown above, the Texinfo formatters convert this:

```
@value{foo}
```

to this:

```
This is a string.
```

You can write an @value command within a paragraph; but you must write an @set command on a line of its own.

If you write the @set command like this:

```
@set foo
```

without specifying a string, the value of foo is the empty string.

If you clear a previously set flag with @clear *flag*, a subsequent @value{*flag*} command will report an error.

For example, if you set foo as follows:

```
@set howmuch very, very, very
```

then the formatters transform

```
It is a @value{howmuch} wet day.
```

into

```
It is a very, very, very wet day.
```

If you write

```
@clear howmuch
```

then the formatters transform

```
It is a @value{howmuch} wet day.
```

into

```
It is a {No value for "howmuch"} wet day.
```

@value cannot be reliably used as the argument to an accent command (see Section 14.4 [Inserting Accents], page 124). For example, this fails:

```
@set myletter a
@'@value{myletter}
```

18.5.2 @ifset and @ifclear

When a *flag* is set, the Texinfo formatting commands format text between subsequent pairs of @ifset *flag* and @end ifset commands. When the *flag* is cleared, the Texinfo formatting commands do *not* format the text. @ifclear operates analogously.

Write the conditionally formatted text between @ifset *flag* and @end ifset commands, like this:

```
@ifset flag
conditional-text
@end ifset
```

For example, you can create one document that has two variants, such as a manual for a 'large' and 'small' model:

```
You can use this machine to dig up shrubs
without hurting them.

@set large

@ifset large
It can also dig up fully grown trees.
@end ifset

Remember to replant promptly ...
```

In the example, the formatting commands will format the text between `@ifset large` and `@end ifset` because the `large` flag is set.

When *flag* is cleared, the Texinfo formatting commands do *not* format the text between `@ifset flag` and `@end ifset`; that text is ignored and does not appear in either printed or Info output.

For example, if you clear the flag of the preceding example by writing an `@clear large` command after the `@set large` command (but before the conditional text), then the Texinfo formatting commands ignore the text between the `@ifset large` and `@end ifset` commands. In the formatted output, that text does not appear; in both printed and Info output, you see only the lines that say, "You can use this machine to dig up shrubs without hurting them. Remember to replant promptly ...".

If a flag is cleared with an `@clear flag` command, then the formatting commands format text between subsequent pairs of `@ifclear` and `@end ifclear` commands. But if the flag is set with `@set flag`, then the formatting commands do *not* format text between an `@ifclear` and an `@end ifclear` command; rather, they ignore that text. An `@ifclear` command looks like this:

```
@ifclear flag
```

18.5.3 `@inlineifset` and `@inlineifclear`

`@inlineifset` and `@inlineifclear` provide brace-delimited alternatives to the `@ifset` and `@ifclear` forms, similar to the other `@inline...` Commands (see Section 18.4 [Inline Conditionals], page 158). The same caveats about argument parsing given there apply here too.

`@inlineifset{var, text}`

> Process the Texinfo *text* if the flag *var* is defined.

`@inlineifclear{var, text}`

> Process the Texinfo *text* if the flag *var* is not defined.

Except for the syntax, their general behavior and purposes is the same as with `@ifset` and `@ifclear`, described in the previous section.

18.5.4 @value Example

You can use the @value command to minimize the number of places you need to change when you record an update to a manual. See Section C.2 [GNU Sample Texts], page 264, for the full text of an example of using this to work with Automake distributions.

This example is adapted from *The GNU Make Manual*.

1. Set the flags:

```
@set EDITION 0.35 Beta
@set VERSION 3.63 Beta
@set UPDATED 14 August 1992
@set UPDATE-MONTH August 1992
```

2. Write text for the @copying section (see Section 3.3.1 [@copying], page 33):

```
@copying
This is Edition @value{EDITION},
last updated @value{UPDATED},
of @cite{The GNU Make Manual},
for @code{make}, version @value{VERSION}.

Copyright ...

Permission is granted ...
@end copying
```

3. Write text for the title page, for people reading the printed manual:

```
@titlepage
@title GNU Make
@subtitle A Program for Directing Recompilation
@subtitle Edition @value{EDITION}, ...
@subtitle @value{UPDATE-MONTH}
@page
@insertcopying
...
@end titlepage
```

(On a printed cover, a date listing the month and the year looks less fussy than a date listing the day as well as the month and year.)

4. Write text for the Top node, for people reading the Info file:

```
@ifnottex
@node Top
@top Make

This is Edition @value{EDITION},
last updated @value{UPDATED},
of @cite{The GNU Make Manual},
for @code{make}, version @value{VERSION}.
@end ifnottex
```

After you format the manual, the `@value` constructs have been expanded, so the output contains text like this:

```
This is Edition 0.35 Beta, last updated 14 August 1992,
of `The GNU Make Manual', for `make', Version 3.63 Beta.
```

When you update the manual, you change only the values of the flags; you do not need to edit the three sections.

18.6 Testing for Texinfo Commands: `@ifcommanddefined`, `@ifcommandnotdefined`

Occasionally, you may want to arrange for your manual to test if a given Texinfo command is available and (presumably) do some sort of fallback formatting if not. There are conditionals `@ifcommanddefined` and `@ifcommandnotdefined` to do this. For example:

```
@ifcommanddefined node
Good, @samp{@@node} is defined.
@end ifcommanddefined
```

will output the expected 'Good, '@node' is defined.'.

This conditional will also consider true any new commands defined by the document via `@macro`, `@alias`, `@definfoenclose`, and `@def(code)index` (see Chapter 19 [Defining New Texinfo Commands], page 165). Caveat: the TeX implementation reports internal TeX commands, in addition to all the Texinfo commands, as being "defined"; the `makeinfo` implementation is reliable in this regard, however.

You can check the `NEWS` file in the Texinfo source distribution and linked from the Texinfo home page (`http://www.gnu.org/software/texinfo`) to see when a particular command was added.

These command-checking conditionals themselves were added in Texinfo 5.0, released in 2013—decades after Texinfo's inception. In order to test if they themselves are available, the predefined flag `txicommandconditionals` can be tested, like this:

```
@ifset txicommandconditionals
@ifcommandnotdefined foobarnode
(Good, '@foobarnode' is not defined.)
@end ifcommandnotdefined
@end ifset
```

Since flags (see the previous section) were added early in the existence of Texinfo, there is no problem with assuming they are available.

We recommend avoiding these tests whenever possible—which is usually the case. For many software packages, it is reasonable for all developers to have a given version of Texinfo (or newer) installed, and thus no reason to worry about older versions. (It is straightforward for anyone to download and install the Texinfo source; it does not have any problematic dependencies.)

The issue of Texinfo versions does not generally arise for end-users. With properly distributed packages, users need not process the Texinfo manual simply to build and install the package; they can use preformatted Info (or other) output files. This is desirable in general, to avoid unnecessary dependencies between packages (see Section "Releases" in *GNU Coding Standards*).

18.7 Conditional Nesting

Conditionals can be nested; however, the details are a little tricky. The difficulty comes with failing conditionals, such as `@ifhtml` when HTML is not being produced, where the included text is to be ignored. However, it is not to be *completely* ignored, since it is useful to have one `@ifset` inside another, for example—that is a way to include text only if two conditions are met. Here's an example:

```
@ifset somevar
@ifset anothervar
Both somevar and anothervar are set.
@end ifset
@ifclear anothervar
Somevar is set, anothervar is not.
@end ifclear
@end ifset
```

Technically, Texinfo requires that for a failing conditional, the ignored text must be properly nested with respect to that failing conditional. Unfortunately, it's not always feasible to check that *all* conditionals are properly nested, because then the processors could have to fully interpret the ignored text, which defeats the purpose of the command. Here's an example illustrating these rules:

```
@ifset a
@ifset b
@ifclear ok  - ok, ignored
@end junky   - ok, ignored
@end ifset
@c WRONG - missing @end ifset.
```

Finally, as mentioned above, all conditional commands must be on lines by themselves, with no text (even spaces) before or after. Otherwise, the processors cannot reliably determine which commands to consider for nesting purposes.

19 Defining New Texinfo Commands

Texinfo provides several ways to define new commands (in all cases, it's not recommended to try redefining existing commands):

- A Texinfo *macro* allows you to define a new Texinfo command as any sequence of text and/or existing commands (including other macros). The macro can have any number of *parameters*—text you supply each time you use the macro.

  Incidentally, these macros have nothing to do with the `@defmac` command, which is for documenting macros in the subject area of the manual (see Section 16.1 [Def Cmd Template], page 139).

- '`@alias`' is a convenient way to define a new name for an existing command.

- '`@definfoenclose`' allows you to define new commands with customized output for all non-TEX output formats.

Most generally of all (not just for defining new commands), it is possible to invoke any external macro processor and have Texinfo recognize so-called `#line` directives for error reporting.

If you want to do simple text substitution, `@set` and `@value` is the simplest approach (see Section 18.5 [@set @clear @value], page 159).

19.1 Defining Macros

You use the Texinfo `@macro` command to define a macro, like this:

```
@macro macroname{param1, param2, ...}
text ... \param1\ ...
@end macro
```

The *parameters param1, param2, ...* correspond to arguments supplied when the macro is subsequently used in the document (described in the next section).

For a macro to work consistently with TEX, *macroname* must consist entirely of letters: no digits, hyphens, underscores, or other special characters. So, we recommend using only letters. However, `makeinfo` will accept anything consisting of alphanumerics, and (except as the first character) '`-`'. The '`_`' character is excluded so that macros can be called inside `@math` without a following space (see Section 14.7 [Inserting Math], page 127).

If a macro needs no parameters, you can define it either with an empty list ('`@macro foo {}`') or with no braces at all ('`@macro foo`').

The definition or *body* of the macro can contain most Texinfo commands, including macro invocations. However, a macro definition that defines another macro does not work in TEX due to limitations in the design of `@macro`.

In the macro body, instances of a parameter name surrounded by backslashes, as in '`\param1\`' in the example above, are replaced by the corresponding argument from the macro invocation. You can use parameter names any number of times in the body, including zero.

To get a single '`\`' in the macro expansion, use '`\\`'. Any other use of '`\`' in the body yields a warning.

The newline characters after the `@macro` line and before the `@end macro` line are ignored, that is, not included in the macro body. All other whitespace is treated according to the usual Texinfo rules. However, there are still undesirable and unpredictable interactions between newlines, macros, and commands which are line-delimited, as warned about below (see Section 19.3 [Macro Details], page 168).

To allow a macro to be used recursively, that is, in an argument to a call to itself, you must define it with '`@rmacro`', like this:

```
@rmacro rmac {arg}
a\arg\b
@end rmacro
...
@rmac{1@rmac{text}2}
```

This produces the output 'a1atextb2b'. With '`@macro`' instead of '`@rmacro`', an error message is given.

You can undefine a macro *foo* with `@unmacro` *foo*. It is not an error to undefine a macro that is already undefined. For example:

```
@unmacro foo
```

19.2 Invoking Macros

After a macro is defined (see the previous section), you can *invoke* (use) it in your document like this:

```
@macroname {arg1, arg2, ...}
```

and the result will be more or less as if you typed the body of *macroname* at that spot. For example:

```
@macro foo {p, q}
Together: \p\ & \q\.
@end macro
@foo{a, b}
```

produces:

> Together: a & b.

Thus, the arguments and parameters are separated by commas and delimited by braces; any whitespace after (but not before) a comma is ignored. The braces are required in the invocation even when the macro takes no arguments, consistent with other Texinfo commands. For example:

```
@macro argless {}
No arguments here.
@end macro
@argless{}
```

produces:

> No arguments here.

Passing macro arguments containing commas requires special care, since commas also separate the arguments. To include a comma character in an argument, the most reliable method is to use the `@comma{}` command. For `makeinfo`, you can also prepend a backslash character, as in '\,', but this does not work with TeX.

It's not always necessary to worry about commas. To facilitate use of macros, `makeinfo` implements two rules for *automatic quoting* in some circumstances:

1. If a macro takes only one argument, all commas in its invocation are quoted by default. For example:

```
@macro TRYME{text}
@strong{TRYME: \text\}
@end macro


@TRYME{A nice feature, though it can be dangerous.}
```
will produce the following output

TRYME: A nice feature, though it can be dangerous.

And indeed, it can. Namely, `makeinfo` does not control the number of arguments passed to one-argument macros, so be careful when you invoke them.

2. If a macro invocation includes another command (including a recursive invocation of itself), any commas in the nested command invocation(s) are quoted by default. For example, in

```
@say{@strong{Yes, I do}, person one}
```
the comma after 'Yes' is implicitly quoted. Here's another example, with a recursive macro:

```
@rmacro cat{a,b}
\a\\b\
@end rmacro


@cat{@cat{foo, bar}, baz}
```
will produce the string 'foobarbaz'.

3. Otherwise, a comma should be explicitly quoted, as above, for it to be treated as a part of an argument.

In addition to the comma, characters that need to be quoted in macro arguments are curly braces and backslash. For example:

```
@macname {\\\{\}\,}
```
will pass the (almost certainly error-producing) argument '\{},' to *macname*.

Unfortunately, this has not been reliably implemented in TeX. When macros are used in the argument to other commands, for example, errors or incorrect output (the '\' "escape" being included literally) are likely to result.

If a macro is defined to take exactly one argument, it can (but need not) be invoked without any braces; then the entire rest of the line after the macro name is used as the argument. (Braces around the argument(s) are required in all other cases, i.e., if the macro takes either zero or more than one argument.) For example:

```
@macro bar {p}
Twice: \p\ & \p\.
@end macro
```

```
@bar aah
```

produces:

> Twice: aah & aah.

Likewise, if a macro is defined to take exactly one argument, and is invoked with braces, the braced text is passed as the argument, also regardless of commas. For example:

```
@macro bar {p}
Twice: \p\ & \p\.
@end macro
@bar{a,b}
```

produces:

> Twice: a,b & a,b.

If a macro is defined to take more than one argument, but is called with only one (in braces), the remaining arguments are set to the empty string, and no error is given. For example:

```
@macro addtwo {p, q}
Both: \p\\q\.
@end macro
@addtwo{a}
```

produces simply:

> Both: a.

19.3 Macro Details and Caveats

By design, macro expansion does not happen in the following contexts in `makeinfo`:

- `@macro` and `@unmacro` lines;
- `@if...` lines, including `@ifset` and similar;
- `@set`, `@clear`, `@value`;
- `@clickstyle` lines;
- `@end` lines.

Unfortunately, TEX may do some expansion in these situations, possibly yielding errors.

Also, quite a few macro-related constructs cause problems with TEX; some of the caveats are listed below. Thus, if you get macro-related errors when producing the printed version of a manual, you might try expanding the macros with `makeinfo` by invoking `texi2dvi` with the '-E' option (see Section 21.2 [Format with texi2dvi], page 177). Or, more reliably, eschew Texinfo macros altogether and use a language designed for macro processing, such as M4 (see Section 19.6 [External Macro Processors], page 172).

- As mentioned earlier, macro names must consist entirely of letters.
- It is not advisable to redefine any TEX primitive, plain, or Texinfo command name as a macro. Unfortunately this is a large and open-ended set of names, and the possible resulting errors are unpredictable.
- All macros are expanded inside at least one TEX group.
- Macro arguments cannot cross lines.

- Macros containing a command which must be on a line by itself, such as a conditional, cannot be invoked in the middle of a line. Similarly, macros containing line-oriented commands or text, such as @example environments, may behave unpredictably in TeX.

- White space is ignored at the beginnings of lines.

- Macros can't be reliably used in the argument to accent commands (see Section 14.4 [Inserting Accents], page 124).

- The backslash escape for commas in macro arguments does not work; @comma{} must be used.

- As a consequence, if a macro takes two or more arguments, and you want to pass an argument with the Texinfo command @, (to produce a cedilla, see Section 14.4 [Inserting Accents], page 124), you have to use @value or another work-around. Otherwise, TeX takes the comma as separating the arguments. Example:

```
@macro mactwo{argfirst, argsecond}
\argfirst\+\argsecond\.
@end macro
@set fc Fran@,cois
@mactwo{@value{fc}}
```

produces:

  François+.

The natural-seeming @mactwo{Fran@,cois} passes the two arguments 'Fran@' and 'cois' to the macro, and nothing good results. And, as just mentioned, although the comma can be escaped with a backslash for makeinfo ('@\,'), that doesn't work in TeX, so there is no other solution.

- It is usually best to avoid comments inside macro definitions, but see the next item.

- In general, the interaction of newlines in the macro definitions and invocations depends on the precise commands and context, notwithstanding the previous statements. You may be able to work around some problems with judicious use of @c to "comment out" a newline, but @c will cause problems in other cases. We are unable to make any general statements.

- In general, you can't arbitrarily substitute a macro (or @value) call for Texinfo command arguments, even when the text is the same. Texinfo is not M4 (or even plain TeX). It might work with some commands, it fails with others. Best not to do it at all. For instance, this fails:

```
@macro offmacro
off
@end macro
@headings @offmacro
```

This looks equivalent to @headings off, but for TeXnical reasons, it fails with a mysterious error message (namely, 'Paragraph ended before @headings was complete').

- Macros cannot define macros in the natural way. To do this, you must use conditionals and raw TeX. For example:

```
@ifnottex
@macro ctor {name, arg}
@macro \name\
```

```
something involving \arg\ somehow
@end macro
@end macro
@end ifnottex
@tex
\gdef\ctor#1{\ctorx#1,}
\gdef\ctorx#1,#2,{\def#1{something involving #2 somehow}}
@end tex
```

The `makeinfo` implementation also has the following limitations (by design):

- `@verbatim` and macros do not mix; for instance, you can't start a verbatim block inside a macro and end it outside (see Section 10.5 [`@verbatim`], page 92). Starting any environment inside a macro and ending it outside may or may not work, for that matter.

- Macros that completely define macros are ok, but it's not possible to have incompletely nested macro definitions. That is, `@macro` and `@end macro` (likewise for `@rmacro`) must be correctly paired. For example, you cannot start a macro definition within a macro, and then end that nested definition outside the macro.

In the `makeinfo` implementation before Texinfo 5.0, ends of lines from expansion of an `@macro` definition did not end an @-command line-delimited argument (`@chapter`, `@center`, etc.). This is no longer the case. For example:

```
@macro twolines{}
aaa
bbb
@end macro
@center @twolines{}
```

In the current `makeinfo`, this is equivalent to:

```
@center aaa
bbb
```

with just 'aaa' as the argument to `@center`. In the earlier implementation, it would have been parsed as this:

```
@center aaa bbb
```

19.4 '@alias *new=existing*'

The '`@alias`' command defines a new command to be just like an existing one. This is useful for defining additional markup names, thus preserving additional semantic information in the input even though the output result may be the same.

Write the '`@alias`' command on a line by itself, followed by the new command name, an equals sign, and the existing command name. Whitespace around the equals sign is optional and ignored if present. Thus:

```
@alias new = existing
```

For example, if your document contains citations for both books and some other media (movies, for example), you might like to define a macro `@moviecite{}` that does the same thing as an ordinary `@cite{}` but conveys the extra semantic information as well. You'd do this as follows:

```
@alias moviecite = cite
```

Macros do not always have the same effect as aliases, due to vagaries of argument parsing. Also, aliases are much simpler to define than macros. So the command is not redundant.

Unfortunately, it's not possible to alias Texinfo environments; for example, `@alias lang=example` is an error.

Aliases must not be recursive, directly or indirectly.

It is not advisable to redefine any TeX primitive, plain TeX, or Texinfo command name as an alias. Unfortunately this is a very large set of names, and the possible resulting errors from TeX are unpredictable.

`makeinfo` will accept the same identifiers for aliases as it does for macro names, that is, alphanumerics and (except as the first character) '`-`'.

19.5 `@definfoenclose`: Customized Highlighting

An `@definfoenclose` command may be used to define a highlighting command for all the non-TeX output formats. A command defined using `@definfoenclose` marks text by enclosing it in strings that precede and follow the text. You can use this to get closer control of your output.

Presumably, if you define a command with `@definfoenclose`, you will create a corresponding command for TeX, either in `texinfo.tex`, `texinfo.cnf`, or within an '`@iftex`' of '`@tex`' in your document.

Write an `@definfoenclose` command at the beginning of a line followed by three comma-separated arguments. The first argument to `@definfoenclose` is the @-command name (without the @); the second argument is the start delimiter string; and the third argument is the end delimiter string. The latter two arguments enclose the highlighted text in the output.

A delimiter string may contain spaces. Neither the start nor end delimiter is required. If you do not want a start delimiter but do want an end delimiter, you must follow the command name with two commas in a row; otherwise, the end delimiter string you intended will naturally be (mis)interpreted as the start delimiter string.

If you do an `@definfoenclose` on the name of a predefined command (such as `@emph`, `@strong`, `@t`, or `@i`), the enclosure definition will override the built-in definition. We don't recommend this.

An enclosure command defined this way takes one argument in braces, since it is intended for new markup commands (see Chapter 9 [Marking Text], page 78).

For example, you can write:

```
@definfoenclose phoo,//,\\
```

near the beginning of a Texinfo file to define `@phoo` as an Info formatting command that inserts '`//`' before and '`\\`' after the argument to `@phoo`. You can then write `@phoo{bar}` wherever you want '`//bar\\`' highlighted in Info.

For TeX formatting, you could write

```
@iftex
@global@let@phoo=@i
```

```
@end iftex
```

to define @phoo as a command that causes TeX to typeset the argument to @phoo in italics.

Each definition applies to its own formatter: one for TeX, the other for everything else. The raw TeX commands need to be in '@iftex'. @definfoenclose command need not be within '@ifinfo', unless you want to use different definitions for different output formats.

Here is another example: write

```
@definfoenclose headword, , :
```

near the beginning of the file, to define @headword as an Info formatting command that inserts nothing before and a colon after the argument to @headword.

'@definfoenclose' definitions must not be recursive, directly or indirectly.

19.6 External Macro Processors: Line Directives

Texinfo macros (and its other text substitution facilities) work fine in straightforward cases. If your document needs unusually complex processing, however, their fragility and limitations can be a problem. In this case, you may want to use a different macro processor altogether, such as M4 (see *M4*) or CPP (see *The C Preprocessor*).

With one exception, Texinfo does not need to know whether its input is "original" source or preprocessed from some other source file. Therefore, you can arrange your build system to invoke whatever programs you like to handle macro expansion or other preprocessing needs. Texinfo does not offer built-in support for any particular preprocessor, since no one program seemed likely to suffice for the requirements of all documents.

The one exception is line numbers in error messages. In that case, the line number should refer to the original source file, whatever it may be. There's a well-known mechanism for this: the so-called '#line' directive. Texinfo supports this.

19.6.1 '#line' Directive

An input line such as this:

```
#line 100 "foo.ptexi"
```

indicates that the next line was line 100 of the file foo.ptexi, and so that's what an error message should refer to. Both M4 (see Section "Preprocessor features" in *GNU M4*) and CPP (see Section "Line Control" in *The C Preprocessor*, and Section "Preprocessor Output" in *The C Preprocessor*) can generate such lines.

The makeinfo program recognizes these lines by default, except within @verbatim blocks (see Section 10.5 [@verbatim], page 92. Their recognition can be turned off completely with CPP_LINE_DIRECTIVES (see Section 22.5.4 [Other Customization Variables], page 204), though there is normally no reason to do so.

For those few programs (M4, CPP, Texinfo) which need to document '#line' directives and therefore have examples which would otherwise match the pattern, the command @hashchar{} can be used (see Section 14.1.5 [Inserting a Hashsign], page 120). The example line above looks like this in the source for this manual:

```
@hashchar{}line 100 "foo.ptexi"
```

The @hashchar command was added to Texinfo in 2013. If you don't want to rely on it, you can also use @set and @value to insert the literal '#':

```
@set hash #
@value{hash}line 1 "example.c"
```

Or, if suitable, an `@verbatim` environment can be used instead of `@example`. As mentioned above, `#line`-recognition is disabled inside verbatim blocks.

19.6.2 '#line' and TEX

As mentioned, `makeinfo` recognizes the '`#line`' directives described in the previous section. However, `texinfo.tex` does not and cannot. Therefore, such a line will be incorrectly typeset verbatim if TEX sees it. The solution is to use `makeinfo`'s macro expansion options before running TEX. There are three approaches:

- If you run `texi2dvi` or its variants (see Section 21.2 [Format with `texi2dvi`], page 177), you can pass `-E` and `texi2dvi` will run `makeinfo` first to expand macros and eliminate '`#line`'.

- If you run `makeinfo` or its variants (see Chapter 22 [Generic Translator `texi2any`], page 189), you can specify `--no-ifinfo --iftex -E somefile.out`, and then give `somefile.out` to `texi2dvi` in a separate command.

- Or you can run `makeinfo --dvi --Xopt -E`. (Or `--pdf` instead of `--dvi`.) `makeinfo` will then call `texi2dvi -E`.

One last caveat regarding use with TEX: since the `#line` directives are not recognized, the line numbers emitted by the `@errormsg{}` command (see Section 18.1 [Conditional Commands], page 155), or by TEX itself, are the (incorrect) line numbers from the derived file which TEX is reading, rather than the preprocessor-specified line numbers. This is another example of why we recommend running `makeinfo` for the best diagnostics (see Section 23.1.1 [`makeinfo` Advantages], page 213).

19.6.3 '#line' Syntax Details

Syntax details for the '`#line`' directive: the '`#`' character can be preceded or followed by whitespace, the word '`line`' is optional, and the file name can be followed by a whitespace-separated list of integers (these are so-called "flags" output by CPP in some cases). For those who like to know the gory details, the actual (Perl) regular expression which is matched is this:

```
/^\s*#\s*(line)? (\d+)(( "([^"]+)")(\s+\d+)*)?\s*$/
```

As far as we've been able to tell, the trailing integer flags only occur in conjunction with a filename, so that is reflected in the regular expression.

As an example, the following is a syntactically valid '`#line`' directive, meaning line 1 of /usr/include/stdio.h:

```
# 1 "/usr/include/stdio.h" 2 3 4
```

Unfortunately, the quoted filename ('`"..."`') has to be optional, because M4 (especially) can often generate '`#line`' directives within a single file. Since the '`line`' is also optional, the result is that lines might match which you wouldn't expect, e.g.,

```
# 1
```

The possible solutions are described above (see Section 19.6.1 [#line Directive], page 172).

20 Include Files

When a Texinfo processor sees an `@include` command in a Texinfo file, it processes the contents of the file named by the `@include` and incorporates them into the output files being created. Include files thus let you keep a single large document as a collection of conveniently small parts.

20.1 How to Use Include Files

To include another file within a Texinfo file, write the `@include` command at the beginning of a line and follow it on the same line by the name of a file to be included. For example:

```
@include buffers.texi
```

@-commands are expanded in file names. The one most likely to be useful is `@value` (see Section 18.5.1 [`@set @value`], page 159), and even then only in complicated situations.

An included file should simply be a segment of text that you expect to be included as is into the overall or *outer* Texinfo file; it should not contain the standard beginning and end parts of a Texinfo file. In particular, you should not start an included file with a line saying '`\input texinfo`'; if you do, that text is inserted into the output file literally. Likewise, you should not end an included file with an `@bye` command; nothing after `@bye` is formatted.

In the long-ago past, you were required to write an `@setfilename` line at the beginning of an included file, but no longer. Now, it does not matter whether you write such a line. If an `@setfilename` line exists in an included file, it is ignored.

20.2 `texinfo-multiple-files-update`

GNU Emacs Texinfo mode provides the `texinfo-multiple-files-update` command. This command creates or updates 'Next', 'Previous', and 'Up' pointers of included files as well as those in the outer or overall Texinfo file, and it creates or updates a main menu in the outer file. Depending on whether you call it with optional arguments, the command updates only the pointers in the first `@node` line of the included files or all of them:

`M-x texinfo-multiple-files-update`
> Called without any arguments:
>
> — Create or update the 'Next', 'Previous', and 'Up' pointers of the first `@node` line in each file included in an outer or overall Texinfo file.
>
> — Create or update the 'Top' level node pointers of the outer or overall file.
>
> — Create or update a main menu in the outer file.

`C-u M-x texinfo-multiple-files-update`
> Called with `C-u` as a prefix argument:
>
> — Create or update pointers in the first `@node` line in each included file.
>
> — Create or update the 'Top' level node pointers of the outer file.
>
> — Create and insert a master menu in the outer file. The master menu is made from all the menus in all the included files.

`C-u 8 M-x texinfo-multiple-files-update`
> Called with a numeric prefix argument, such as `C-u 8`:

- Create or update *all* the 'Next', 'Previous', and 'Up' pointers of all the included files.

- Create or update *all* the menus of all the included files.

- Create or update the 'Top' level node pointers of the outer or overall file.

- And then create a master menu in the outer file. This is similar to invoking `texinfo-master-menu` with an argument when you are working with just one file.

Note the use of the prefix argument in interactive use: with a regular prefix argument, just *C-u*, the `texinfo-multiple-files-update` command inserts a master menu; with a numeric prefix argument, such as *C-u 8*, the command updates *every* pointer and menu in *all* the files and then inserts a master menu.

20.3 Include Files Requirements

If you plan to use the `texinfo-multiple-files-update` command, the outer Texinfo file that lists included files within it should contain nothing but the beginning and end parts of a Texinfo file, and a number of `@include` commands listing the included files. It should not even include indices, which should be listed in an included file of their own.

Moreover, each of the included files must contain exactly one highest level node (conventionally, `@chapter` or equivalent), and this node must be the first node in the included file. Furthermore, each of these highest level nodes in each included file must be at the same hierarchical level in the file structure. Usually, each is an `@chapter`, an `@appendix`, or an `@unnumbered` node. Thus, normally, each included file contains one, and only one, chapter or equivalent-level node.

The outer file should contain only *one* node, the 'Top' node. It should *not* contain any nodes besides the single 'Top' node. The `texinfo-multiple-files-update` command will not process them.

20.4 Sample File with `@include`

Here is an example of an outer Texinfo file with `@include` files within it before running `texinfo-multiple-files-update`, which would insert a main or master menu:

```
\input texinfo @c -*-texinfo-*-
@setfilename include-example.info
@settitle Include Example

... See Appendix C [Sample Texinfo Files], page 263, for
examples of the rest of the frontmatter ...

@ifnottex
@node Top
@top Include Example
@end ifnottex
```

```
@include foo.texinfo
@include bar.texinfo
@include concept-index.texinfo
@bye
```

An included file, such as `foo.texinfo`, might look like this:

```
@node First
@chapter First Chapter

Contents of first chapter ...
```

The full contents of `concept-index.texinfo` might be as simple as this:

```
@node Concept Index
@unnumbered Concept Index

@printindex cp
```

The outer Texinfo source file for *The GNU Emacs Lisp Reference Manual* is named `elisp.texi`. This outer file contains a master menu with 417 entries and a list of 41 `@include` files.

20.5 Evolution of Include Files

When Info was first created, it was customary to create many small Info files on one subject. Each Info file was formatted from its own Texinfo source file. This custom meant that Emacs did not need to make a large buffer to hold the whole of a large Info file when someone wanted information; instead, Emacs allocated just enough memory for the small Info file that contained the particular information sought. This way, Emacs could avoid wasting memory.

References from one file to another were made by referring to the file name as well as the node name. (See Section 7.6 [Referring to Other Info Files], page 64. Also, see Section 8.4.5 [@xref with Four and Five Arguments], page 71.)

Include files were designed primarily as a way to create a single, large printed manual out of several smaller Info files. In a printed manual, all the references were within the same document, so TEX could automatically determine the references' page numbers. The Info formatting commands used include files only for creating joint indices; each of the individual Texinfo files had to be formatted for Info individually. (Each, therefore, required its own `@setfilename` line.)

However, because large Info files are now split automatically, it is no longer necessary to keep them small.

Nowadays, multiple Texinfo files are used mostly for large documents, such as *The GNU Emacs Lisp Reference Manual*, and for projects in which several different people write different sections of a document simultaneously.

In addition, the Info formatting commands have been extended to work with the `@include` command so as to create a single large Info file that is split into smaller files if necessary. This means that you can write menus and cross references without naming the different Texinfo files.

21 Formatting and Printing Hardcopy

Running the `texi2dvi` or `texi2pdf` command is the simplest way to create printable output. These commands are installed as part of the Texinfo package.

In more detail, three major shell commands are used to print formatted output from a Texinfo manual: one converts the Texinfo source into something printable, a second sorts indices, and a third actually prints the formatted document. When you use the shell commands, you can either work directly in the operating system shell or work within a shell inside GNU Emacs (or some other computing environment).

If you are using GNU Emacs, you can use commands provided by Texinfo mode instead of shell commands. In addition to the three commands to format a file, sort the indices, and print the result, Texinfo mode offers key bindings for commands to recenter the output buffer, show the print queue, and delete a job from the print queue.

Details are in the following sections.

21.1 Use TeX

The typesetting program called TeX is used to format a Texinfo document for printable output. TeX is a very powerful typesetting program and, when used correctly, does an exceptionally good job.

See Section 21.16 [Obtaining TeX], page 188, for information on how to obtain TeX. It is not included in the Texinfo package, being a vast suite of software in itself.

21.2 Format with `texi2dvi`

The `texi2dvi` program takes care of all the steps for producing a TeX DVI file from a Texinfo document. Similarly, `texi2pdf` produces a PDF file.

To run `texi2dvi` or `texi2pdf` on an input file `foo.texi`, do this (where 'prompt$ ' is your shell prompt):

```
prompt$ texi2dvi foo.texi
prompt$ texi2pdf foo.texi
```

As shown in this example, the input filenames to `texi2dvi` and `texi2pdf` must include any extension, such as '.texi'. (Under MS-DOS and perhaps in other circumstances, you may need to run 'sh texi2dvi foo.texi' instead of relying on the operating system to invoke the shell on the 'texi2dvi' script.)

One useful option to `texi2dvi` is '`--command=cmd`'. This inserts *cmd* on a line by itself after the `@setfilename` in a temporary copy of the input file before running TeX. With this, you can specify different printing formats, such as `@smallbook` (see Section 21.11 [@smallbook], page 186), `@afourpaper` (see Section 21.12 [A4 Paper], page 186), or `@pagesizes` (see Section 21.13 [@pagesizes], page 186), without actually changing the document source. (You can also do this on a site-wide basis with `texinfo.cnf`; see Section 21.9 [Preparing for TeX], page 184).

With the `--pdf` option, `texi2dvi` produces PDF output instead of DVI (see Section 21.15 [PDF Output], page 187), by running `pdftex` instead of `tex`. Alternatively, the command `texi2pdf` is an abbreviation for running '`texi2dvi --pdf`'. The command `pdftexi2dvi` is also provided as a convenience for AUC-TEX (see *AUC-TEX*, as it prefers to merely prepend 'pdf' to DVI producing tools to have PDF producing tools.

With the `--dvipdf` option, `texi2dvi` produces PDF output by running TEX and then a DVI-to-PDF program: if the `DVIPDF` environment variable is set, that value is used, else the first program extant among `dvipdfmx`, `dvipdfm`, `dvipdf`, `dvi2pdf`, `dvitopdf`. This method generally supports CJK typesetting better than `pdftex`.

With the `--ps` option, `texi2dvi` produces PostScript instead of DVI, by running `tex` and then `dvips` (see *Dvips*). (Or the value of the `DVIPS` environment variable, if set.)

`texi2dvi` can also be used to process LATEX files. Normally `texi2dvi` is able to guess the input file language by its contents and file name extension; however, if it guesses wrong you can explicitly specify the input language using `--language=`*lang* command line option, where *lang* is either 'latex' or 'texinfo'.

`texi2dvi` will use `etex` (or `pdfetex`) if they are available; this extended version of TEX is not required, and the DVI output is identical, but it runs faster in some cases, and provide additional tracing information when debugging `texinfo.tex`. (These days, `pdftex` and `pdfetex` are exactly the same, but we still run `pdfetex` to cater to ancient TEX installations.)

The option `-E` (equivalently, `-e` and `--expand`) does Texinfo macro expansion using `makeinfo` instead of the TEX implementation (see Section 19.3 [Macro Details], page 168). Each implementation has its own limitations and advantages. If this option is used, the string `@c _texi2dvi` must not appear at the beginning of a line in the source file.

For a list of all the options, run 'texi2dvi --help'.

21.3 Format with `tex`/`texindex`

You can do the basic formatting of a Texinfo file with the shell command `tex` followed by the name of the Texinfo file. For example:

```
tex foo.texi
```

TEX will produce a *DVI file* as well as several auxiliary files containing information for indices, cross references, etc. The DVI file (for *DeVice Independent* file) can be printed on virtually any device, perhaps after a further conversion (see the previous section).

The `tex` formatting command itself does not sort the indices; it writes an output file of unsorted index data. To generate a printed index after running the `tex` command, you first need a sorted index to work from. The `texindex` command sorts indices. (`texi2dvi`, described in the previous section, runs `tex` and `texindex` as necessary.)

`tex` outputs unsorted index files under names following a standard convention: the name of your main input file with any '.texi' or similar extension replaced by the two letter index name. For example, the raw index output files for the input file `foo.texi` would be, by default, `foo.cp`, `foo.vr`, `foo.fn`, `foo.tp`, `foo.pg` and `foo.ky`. Those are exactly the arguments to give to `texindex`.

Instead of specifying all the unsorted index file names explicitly, it's typical to use '??' as shell wildcards and give the command in this form:

```
texindex foo.??
```

This command will run `texindex` on all the unsorted index files, including any two letter indices that you have defined yourself using `@defindex` or `@defcodeindex`. You can safely run 'texindex foo.??' even if there are files with two letter extensions that are not index files, such as 'foo.el'. The texindex command reports but otherwise ignores such files.

For each file specified, texindex generates a sorted index file whose name is made by appending 's' to the input file name; for example, foo.cps is made from foo.cp. The @printindex command looks for a file with that name (see Section 4.1 [Printing Indices & Menus], page 45). TEX does not read the raw index output file, and texindex does not alter it.

After you have sorted the indices, you need to rerun tex on the Texinfo file. This regenerates the output file, this time with up-to-date index entries.

Finally, you may need to run tex one more time, to get the page numbers in the cross references correct.

To summarize, this is a five step process. (Alternatively, it's a one-step process: run texi2dvi; see the previous section.)

1. Run tex on your Texinfo file. This generates a DVI file (with undefined cross references and no indices), and the raw index files (with two letter extensions).

2. Run texindex on the raw index files. This creates the corresponding sorted index files (with three letter extensions).

3. Run tex again on your Texinfo file. This regenerates the DVI file, this time with indices and defined cross references, but with page numbers for the cross references from the previous run, generally incorrect.

4. Sort the indices again, with texindex.

5. Run tex one last time. This time the correct page numbers are written for the cross references.

21.3.1 Formatting Partial Documents

Sometimes you may wish to print a document while you know it is incomplete, or to print just one chapter of a document. In such a case, the usual auxiliary files that TEX creates and warnings TEX gives about undefined cross references are just nuisances. You can avoid them with the @novalidate command, which you must give *before* the @setfilename command (see Section 3.2.3 [@setfilename], page 31).

Thus, the beginning of your file would look approximately like this:

```
\input texinfo
@novalidate
@setfilename myfile.info
...
```

@novalidate also turns off validation in makeinfo, just like its --no-validate option (see Section 22.4 [Pointer Validation], page 196).

Furthermore, you need not run texindex each time after you run tex. The tex formatting command simply uses whatever sorted index files happen to exist from a previous use of texindex. If those are out of date, that is usually ok while you are creating or debugging a document.

21.3.2 Details of `texindex`

In Texinfo version 6, released in 2015, the `texindex` program was completely reimplemented. The principal functional difference is that index entries beginning with a left brace or right brace ('{' resp. '}') can work properly. For example, these simple index entries are processed correctly, including the "index initial" shown in the index:

```
@cindex @{
@cindex @}
...
@printindex cp
```

However, to enable this behavior, it's necessary (for the time being) to give a special option to TeX early in a source document:

```
@tex
\global\usebracesinindexestrue
@end tex
```

This is because the previous `texindex` implementation aborted with an incorrect error message ('No page number in \entry...') on such index entries when handled in the normal way. Therefore TeX wrote out an incorrect "sort string" using the '|' character; this did not affect the text of the entry, but the index initial was the incorrect '|', and sorting was not perfect.

Because of that fatal error, and because relatively few documents have index entries beginning with braces, we want to provide some transition time for installations to have the new `texindex`. At some point in the future, we'll make `\usebracesinindexes` true by default (the above TeX code will continue to work fine).

Although not a matter of functionality, readers may be interested to know that the new `texindex` is a literate program (http://en.wikipedia.org/wiki/Literate_programming) using Texinfo for documentation and (portable) `awk` for code. A single source file, `texindex/ti.twjr` in this case, produces the runnable program, a printable document, and an online document.

The system is called `texiwebjr` and was created by Arnold Robbins, who also wrote the new `texindex`. Not coincidentally, he is also the long-time maintainer of Gawk, see *The GNU Awk User's Guide*). The file `texindex/Makefile.am` shows example usage of the system.

21.4 Print with `lpr` from Shell

The way to print a DVI file depends on your system installation. Two common ones are 'dvips foo.dvi -o' to make a PostScript file first and then print that, and 'lpr -d foo.dvi' to print a DVI file directly.

For example, the following commands will (probably) suffice to sort the indices, format, and print this manual using the `texi2dvi` shell script (see Section 21.2 [Format with texi2dvi], page 177).

```
texi2dvi texinfo.texi
dvips texinfo.dvi -o
lpr texinfo.ps
```

Depending on the `lpr` setup on your machine, you might able to combine the last two steps into `lpr -d texinfo.dvi`.

You can also generate a PDF file by running `texi2pdf` instead of `texi2dvi`; a PDF is often directly printable. Or you can generate a PCL file by using `dvilj` instead of `dvips`, if you have a printer that prefers that format.

`lpr` is a standard program on Unix systems, but it is usually absent on MS-DOS/MS-Windows. If so, just create a PostScript or PDF or PCL file, whatever is most convenient, and print that in the usual way for your machine (e.g., by sending to the appropriate port, usually 'PRN').

21.5 Printing From an Emacs Shell

You can give formatting and printing commands from a shell within GNU Emacs, just like any other shell command. To create a shell within Emacs, type *M-x shell* (see Section "Shell" in *The GNU Emacs Manual*). In this shell, you can format and print the document. See Chapter 21 [Format and Print Hardcopy], page 177, for details.

You can switch to and from the shell buffer while `tex` is running and do other editing. If you are formatting a long document on a slow machine, this can be very convenient.

For example, you can use `texi2dvi` from an Emacs shell. Here is one way to use `texi2pdf` to format and print *Using and Porting GNU CC* from a shell within Emacs:

```
texi2pdf gcc.texi
lpr gcc.pdf
```

See the next section for more information about formatting and printing in Texinfo mode.

21.6 Formatting and Printing in Texinfo Mode

Texinfo mode provides several predefined key commands for TeX formatting and printing. These include commands for sorting indices, looking at the printer queue, killing the formatting job, and recentering the display of the buffer in which the operations occur.

C-c C-t C-b
M-x texinfo-tex-buffer
        Run `texi2dvi` on the current buffer.

C-c C-t C-r
M-x texinfo-tex-region
        Run TeX on the current region.

C-c C-t C-i
M-x texinfo-texindex
        Sort the indices of a Texinfo file formatted with `texinfo-tex-region`.

C-c C-t C-p
M-x texinfo-tex-print
        Print a DVI file that was made with `texinfo-tex-region` or `texinfo-tex-buffer`.

`C-c C-t C-q`
`M-x tex-show-print-queue`
>Show the print queue.

`C-c C-t C-d`
`M-x texinfo-delete-from-print-queue`
>Delete a job from the print queue; you will be prompted for the job number shown by a preceding `C-c C-t C-q` command (`texinfo-show-tex-print-queue`).

`C-c C-t C-k`
`M-x tex-kill-job`
>Kill the currently running TeX job started by either `texinfo-tex-region` or `texinfo-tex-buffer`, or any other process running in the Texinfo shell buffer.

`C-c C-t C-x`
`M-x texinfo-quit-job`
>Quit a TeX formatting job that has stopped because of an error by sending an x to it. When you do this, TeX preserves a record of what it did in a `.log` file.

`C-c C-t C-l`
`M-x tex-recenter-output-buffer`
>Redisplay the shell buffer in which the TeX printing and formatting commands are run to show its most recent output.

Thus, the usual sequence of commands for formatting a buffer is as follows (with comments to the right):

C-c C-t C-b	Run `texi2dvi` on the buffer.
C-c C-t C-p	Print the DVI file.
C-c C-t C-q	Display the printer queue.

The Texinfo mode TeX formatting commands start a subshell in Emacs called the `*tex-shell*`. The `texinfo-tex-command`, `texinfo-texindex-command`, and `tex-dvi-print-command` commands are all run in this shell.

You can watch the commands operate in the '`*tex-shell*`' buffer, and you can switch to and from and use the '`*tex-shell*`' buffer as you would any other shell buffer.

The formatting and print commands depend on the values of several variables. The default values are:

Variable	Default value
`texinfo-texi2dvi-command`	`"texi2dvi"`
`texinfo-tex-command`	`"tex"`
`texinfo-texindex-command`	`"texindex"`
`texinfo-delete-from-print-queue-command`	`"lprm"`
`texinfo-tex-trailer`	`"@bye"`
`tex-start-of-header`	`"%**start"`
`tex-end-of-header`	`"%**end"`
`tex-dvi-print-command`	`"lpr -d"`
`tex-show-queue-command`	`"lpq"`

You can change the values of these variables with the *M-x set-variable* command (see Section "Examining and Setting Variables" in *The GNU Emacs Manual*), or with your `.emacs` initialization file (see Section "Init File" in *The GNU Emacs Manual*).

Beginning with version 20, GNU Emacs offers a user-friendly interface, called *Customize*, for changing values of user-definable variables. See Section "Easy Customization Interface" in *The GNU Emacs Manual*, for more details about this. The Texinfo variables can be found in the 'Development/Docs/Texinfo' group, once you invoke the *M-x customize* command.

21.7 Using the Local Variables List

Yet another way to apply the TeX formatting command to a Texinfo file is to put that command in a *local variables list* at the end of the Texinfo file. You can then specify the `tex` or `texi2dvi` commands as a `compile-command` and have Emacs run it by typing *M-x compile*. This creates a special shell called the `*compilation*` buffer in which Emacs runs the compile command. For example, at the end of the `gdb.texi` file, after the `@bye`, you could put the following:

```
Local Variables:
compile-command: "texi2dvi gdb.texi"
End:
```

This technique is most often used by programmers who also compile programs this way; see Section "Compilation" in *The GNU Emacs Manual*.

21.8 TeX Formatting Requirements Summary

Every Texinfo file that is to be input to TeX must begin with a `\input` command, and must contain an `@setfilename` command:

```
\input texinfo
@setfilename arg-not-used-by-TeX
```

The first command instructs TeX to load the macros it needs to process a Texinfo file and the second command opens auxiliary files.

Every Texinfo file must end with a line that terminates TeX's processing and forces out unfinished pages:

```
@bye
```

Strictly speaking, these lines are all a Texinfo file needs to be processed successfully by TeX.

Usually, however, the beginning includes an `@settitle` command to define the title of the printed manual, a title page, a copyright page, permissions, and a table of contents. Besides `@bye`, the end of a file usually includes indices. (Not to mention that most manuals contain a body of text as well.)

For more information, see:

- Section 3.2.4 [`@settitle`], page 32.
- Section 3.7.2 [`@setchapternewpage`], page 41.
- Appendix D [Headings], page 269.

21.9 Preparing for TeX

TeX needs to know where to find the `texinfo.tex` file that the '\input texinfo' command on the first line reads. The `texinfo.tex` file tells TeX how to handle @-commands; it is included in all standard GNU distributions. The latest version released for general use is available from the usual GNU servers and mirrors:

```
http://ftp.gnu.org/gnu/texinfo/texinfo.tex
http://ftpmirror.gnu.org/texinfo/texinfo.tex
```

The latest development version is available from the Texinfo source repository:

```
http://svn.savannah.gnu.org/viewvc/trunk/doc/texinfo.tex?root=texinfo&view=log
```

`texinfo.tex` is essentially a standalone file, and compatibility is of utmost concern; so, if you need or want to try a newer version than came with your system, it nearly always suffices to download it and put it anywhere that TeX will find it (first). You can replace any existing `texinfo.tex` with a newer version (of course saving the original in case of disaster).

Also, you should install `epsf.tex`, if it is not already installed from another distribution. More details are at the end of the description of the `@image` command (see Section 12.2 [Images], page 109).

To use quotation marks other than those used in English, you'll need to have the European Computer Modern fonts (e.g., `ecrm1000`) and (for PDF output) CM-Super fonts (see Section 14.5 [Inserting Quotation Marks], page 125).

To use the `@euro` command, you'll need the '`feym*`' fonts (e.g., `feymr10`). See Section 14.8.6 [@euro], page 129.

All of the above files (and a whole lot more) should be installed by default in a reasonable TeX installation.

Optionally, you may create a file `texinfo.cnf` for site configuration. This file is read by TeX when the `@setfilename` command is executed (see Section 3.2.3 [@setfilename], page 31). You can put any commands you like there, according to local site-wide conventions. They will be read by TeX when processing any Texinfo document. For example, if `texinfo.cnf` contains the line '`@afourpaper`' (see Section 21.12 [A4 Paper], page 186), then all Texinfo documents will be processed with that page size in effect. If you have nothing to put in `texinfo.cnf`, you do not need to create it.

If neither of the above locations for these system files suffice, you can specify the directories explicitly. For `texinfo.tex`, you can do this by writing the complete path for the file after the `\input` command. Another way, that works for both `texinfo.tex` and `texinfo.cnf` (and any other file TeX might read), is to set the `TEXINPUTS` environment variable in your `.profile` or `.cshrc` file.

Whether you use `.profile` or `.cshrc` depends on whether you use a Bourne shell-compatible (`sh`, `bash`, `ksh`, ...) or C shell-compatible (`csh`, `tcsh`) command interpreter, respeictvely.

In a `.profile` file, you could use the following `sh` command sequence:

```
TEXINPUTS=.:/home/me/mylib:
export TEXINPUTS
```

While in a `.cshrc` file, you could use the following `csh` command sequence:

```
setenv TEXINPUTS .:/home/me/mylib:
```

On MS-DOS/MS-Windows, you'd do this (note the use of the ';' character as directory separator, instead of ':'):

```
set TEXINPUTS=.;d:/home/me/mylib;c:
```

It is customary for DOS/Windows users to put such commands in the `autoexec.bat` file, or in the Windows registry.

These settings would cause TeX to look for `\input` file first in the current directory, indicated by the '.', then in a hypothetical user 'me''s `mylib` directory, and finally in the system directories. (A leading, trailing, or doubled ':' indicates searching the system directories at that point.)

21.10 Overfull "hboxes"

TeX is sometimes unable to typeset a line within the normal margins. This most often occurs when TeX comes upon what it interprets as a long word that it cannot hyphenate, such as an electronic mail network address or a very long identifier. When this happens, TeX prints an error message like this:

```
Overfull @hbox (20.76302pt too wide)
```

(In TeX, lines are in "horizontal boxes", hence the term, "hbox". '@hbox' is a TeX primitive not used in the Texinfo language.)

TeX also provides the line number in the Texinfo source file and the text of the offending line, which is marked at all the places that TeX considered hyphenation. See Section E.3 [Debugging with TeX], page 275, for more information about typesetting errors.

If the Texinfo file has an overfull hbox, you can rewrite the sentence so the overfull hbox does not occur, or you can decide to leave it. A small excursion into the right margin often does not matter and may not even be noticeable.

If you have many overfull boxes and/or an antipathy to rewriting, you can coerce TeX into greatly increasing the allowable interword spacing, thus (if you're lucky) avoiding many of the bad line breaks, like this:

```
@tex
\global\emergencystretch = .9\hsize
@end tex
```

(You should adjust the fraction as needed.) This huge value for `\emergencystretch` cannot be the default, since then the typeset output would generally be of noticeably lower quality; its default value is '.15\hsize'. `\hsize` is the TeX dimension containing the current line width.

For any overfull boxes you do have, TeX will print a large, ugly, black rectangle beside the line that contains the overfull hbox unless told otherwise. This is so you will notice the location of the problem if you are correcting a draft.

To prevent such a monstrosity from marring your final printout, write the following in the beginning of the Texinfo file on a line of its own, before the `@titlepage` command:

```
@finalout
```

21.11 @smallbook: Printing "Small" Books

By default, TeX typesets pages for printing in an 8.5 by 11 inch format. However, you can direct TeX to typeset a document in a 7 by 9.25 inch format that is suitable for bound books by inserting the following command on a line by itself at the beginning of the Texinfo file, before the title page:

    @smallbook

(Since many books are about 7 by 9.25 inches, this command might better have been called the @regularbooksize command, but it came to be called the @smallbook command by comparison to the 8.5 by 11 inch format.)

If you write the @smallbook command between the start-of-header and end-of-header lines, the Texinfo mode TeX region formatting command, texinfo-tex-region, will format the region in "small" book size (see Section 3.2.2 [Start of Header], page 31).

See Section 10.8 [@small...], page 94, for information about commands that make it easier to produce examples for a smaller manual.

See Section 21.2 [Format with texi2dvi], page 177, and Section 21.9 [Preparing for TeX], page 184, for other ways to format with @smallbook that do not require changing the source file.

21.12 Printing on A4 Paper

You can tell TeX to format a document for printing on European size A4 paper (or A5) with the @afourpaper (or @afivepaper) command. Write the command on a line by itself near the beginning of the Texinfo file, before the title page. For example, this is how you would write the header for this manual:

    \input texinfo   @c -*-texinfo-*-
    @c %**start of header
    @setfilename texinfo
    @settitle Texinfo
    @afourpaper
    @c %**end of header

See Section 21.2 [Format with texi2dvi], page 177, and Section 21.9 [Preparing for TeX], page 184, for other ways to format for different paper sizes that do not require changing the source file.

You may or may not prefer the formatting that results from the command @afourlatex. There's also @afourwide for A4 paper in wide format.

21.13 @pagesizes [*width*][, *height*]: Custom Page Sizes

You can explicitly specify the height and (optionally) width of the main text area on the page with the @pagesizes command. Write this on a line by itself near the beginning of the Texinfo file, before the title page. The height comes first, then the width if desired, separated by a comma. Examples:

    @pagesizes 200mm,150mm

and

```
@pagesizes 11.5in
```

This would be reasonable for printing on B5-size paper. To emphasize, this command specifies the size of the *text area*, not the size of the paper (which is 250 mm by 177 mm for B5, 14 in by 8.5 in for legal).

To make more elaborate changes, such as changing any of the page margins, you must define a new command in `texinfo.tex` or `texinfo.cnf`.

See Section 21.2 [Format with `texi2dvi`], page 177, and Section 21.9 [Preparing for TeX], page 184, for other ways to specify `@pagesizes` that do not require changing the source file.

21.14 Cropmarks and Magnification

You can (attempt to) direct TeX to print cropmarks at the corners of pages with the `@cropmarks` command. Write the `@cropmarks` command on a line by itself near the beginning of the Texinfo file, before the title page, like this:

```
@cropmarks
```

This command is mainly for printers that typeset several pages on one sheet of film; but you can attempt to use it to mark the corners of a book set to 7 by 9.25 inches with the `@smallbook` command. (Printers will not produce cropmarks for regular sized output that is printed on regular sized paper.) Since different printing machines work in different ways, you should explore the use of this command with a spirit of adventure. You may have to redefine the command in `texinfo.tex`.

The `@cropmarks` command is recognized and ignored in non-TeX output formats.

You can attempt to direct TeX to typeset pages larger or smaller than usual with the `\mag` TeX command. Everything that is typeset is scaled proportionally larger or smaller. (`\mag` stands for "magnification".) This is *not* a Texinfo @-command, but is a raw TeX command that is prefixed with a backslash. You have to write this command between `@tex` and `@end tex` (see Section 18.3 [Raw Formatter Commands], page 157).

Follow the `\mag` command with an '=' and then a number that is 1000 times the magnification you desire. For example, to print pages at 1.2 normal size, write the following near the beginning of the Texinfo file, before the title page:

```
@tex
\global\mag=1200
@end tex
```

With some printing technologies, you can print normal-sized copies that look better than usual by giving a larger-than-normal master to your print shop. They do the reduction, thus effectively increasing the resolution.

Depending on your system, DVI files prepared with a nonstandard-`\mag` may not print or may print only with certain magnifications. Be prepared to experiment.

21.15 PDF Output

The simplest way to generate PDF output from Texinfo source is to run the convenience script `texi2pdf` (or `pdftexi2dvi`); this executes the `texi2dvi` script with the `--pdf` option (see Section 21.2 [Format with `texi2dvi`], page 177). If for some reason you want to process the document by hand, you can run the `pdftex` program instead of plain `tex`. That is, run '`pdftex foo.texi`' instead of '`tex foo.texi`'.

PDF stands for 'Portable Document Format'. It was invented by Adobe Systems some years ago for document interchange, based on their PostScript language. Related links:

- GNU GV, a Ghostscript-based PDF reader (`http://www.gnu.org/software/gv/`). (It can also preview PostScript documents.)

- `xpdf`, a freely available standalone PDF reader (`http://www.foolabs.com/xpdf/`) for the X window system.

- PDF at Wikipedia (`https://en.wikipedia.org/wiki/Portable_Document_Format`).

At present, Texinfo does not provide '`@ifpdf`' or '`@pdf`' commands as for the other output formats, since PDF documents contain many internal low-level offsets and cross-references that would be hard or impossible to specify at the Texinfo source level.

PDF files require dedicated software to be displayed, unlike the plain ASCII formats (Info, HTML) that Texinfo supports. They also tend to be much larger than the DVI files output by TeX by default. Nevertheless, a PDF file does define an actual typeset document in a self-contained file, notably including all the fonts that are used, so it has its place.

21.16 Obtaining TeX

TeX is a document formatter that is used by the FSF for its documentation. It is the easiest way to get printed output (e.g., PDF and PostScript) for Texinfo manuals. TeX is freely redistributable, and you can get it over the Internet or on physical media. See `http://tug.org/texlive`.

22 texi2any: The Generic Translator for Texinfo

texi2any is the generic translator for Texinfo that can produce different output formats and is highly customizable. It supports these formats:

Info (by default, or with --info),
HTML (with --html),
plain text (with --plaintext),
Docbook (with --docbook),
Texinfo XML (with --xml).

makeinfo is an alias for texi2any. By default, both texi2any and makeinfo generate Info output; indeed, there are no differences in behavior based on the name.

Beside these default formats, command line options to texi2any can change many aspects of the output. Beyond that, initialization files provide even more control over the final output—nearly anything not specified in the Texinfo input file. Initialization files are written in Perl, like the main program, and anything which can be specified on the command line can also be specified within a initialization file.

The rest of this chapter goes into the details.

22.1 texi2any: A Texinfo Reference Implementation

Above, we called texi2any "the" translator for Texinfo instead of just "a" translator, even though (of course) it's technically and legally possible for other implementations to be written. The reason is that alternative implementations are very likely to have subtle, or not-so-subtle, differences in behavior, and thus Texinfo documents would become dependent on the processor. Therefore, it is important to have a reference implementation that defines parts of the language not fully specified by the manual (often intentionally so). It is equally important to have consistent command-line options and other behavior for all processors.

For this reason, the once-independent texi2html Perl Texinfo processor was made compatible with the C implementation of makeinfo, to avoid continuing with two different implementations (see Section 1.14 [History], page 14). The current implementation, texi2any, serves as the reference implementation. It inherited the design of customization and other features from texi2html (for more on texi2html compatibility, see Section 22.8 [texi2html], page 211). However, texi2any is a full reimplementation: it constructs a tree-based representation of the input document for all back-ends to work from.

Extensive tests of the language were developed at the same time as texi2any; we plead with anyone thinking of writing a program to parse Texinfo input to at least make use of these tests.

The texi2html wrapper script (see Section 22.8 [texi2html], page 211) provides a very simple example of calling texi2any from a shell script; it's in util/texi2html in the Texinfo sources. More consequentially, texi-elements-by-size is an example Perl script using the Texinfo::Parser module interface; it's also in the util source directory. (Its functionality may also be useful to authors; see [texi-elements-by-size], page 261.)

With the release of texi2any as the reference implementation, development of both the C implementation of makeinfo and texi2html has been halted. Going forward, we ask authors of Texinfo documents to use only texi2any.

22.2 Invoking `texi2any/makeinfo` from a Shell

To process a Texinfo file, invoke `texi2any` or `makeinfo` (the two names are synonyms for the same program; we'll use the names interchangeably) followed by the name of the Texinfo file. Also select the format you want to output with the appropriate command line option (default is Info). Thus, to create the Info file for Bison, type the following to the shell:

```
texi2any --info bison.texinfo
```

You can specify more than one input file name; each is processed in turn. If an input file name is '-', standard input is read.

The `texi2any` program accept many options. Perhaps the most basic are those that change the output format. By default, `texi2any` outputs Info.

Each command line option is either a long name preceded by '--' or a single letter preceded by '-'. You can use abbreviations for the long option names as long as they are unique.

For example, you could use the following shell command to create an Info file for `bison.texinfo` in which lines are filled to only 68 columns:

```
texi2any --fill-column=68 bison.texinfo
```

You can write two or more options in sequence, like this:

```
texi2any --no-split --fill-column=70 ...
```

(This would keep the Info file together as one possibly very long file and would also set the fill column to 70.)

The options are (approximately in alphabetical order):

`--commands-in-node-names`

> This option now does nothing, but remains for compatibility. (It used to ensure that @-commands in node names were expanded throughout the document, especially `@value`. This is now done by default.)

`--conf-dir=path`

> Prepend *path* to the directory search list for finding customization files that may be loaded with `--init-file` (see below). The *path* value can be a single directory, or a list of several directories separated by the usual path separator character (':' on Unix-like systems, ';' on Windows).

`--css-include=file`

> When producing HTML, literally include the contents of *file*, which should contain W3C cascading style sheets specifications, in the '`<style>`' block of the HTML output. If *file* is '-', read standard input. See Section 24.3 [HTML CSS], page 225.

`--css-ref=url`

> When producing HTML, add a '`<link>`' tag to the output which references a cascading style sheet at *url*. This allows using standalone style sheets.

`-D var`
`-D 'var value'`

> Cause the Texinfo variable *var* to be defined. This is equivalent to `@set var` in the Texinfo file (see Section 18.5 [@set @clear @value], page 159).

The argument to the option is always one word to the shell; if it contains internal whitespace, the first word is taken as the variable name and the remainder as the value. For example, `-D 'myvar someval'` is equivalent to `@set myvar someval`.

`--disable-encoding`
`--enable-encoding`

> By default, or with `--enable-encoding`, output accented and special characters in Info and plain text output based on '`@documentencoding`'. With `--disable-encoding`, 7-bit ASCII transliterations are output. See Section 17.2 [`@documentencoding`], page 153, and Section 14.4 [Inserting Accents], page 124.

`--docbook`

> Generate Docbook output (rather than Info).

`--document-language=`*lang*

> Use *lang* to translate Texinfo keywords which end up in the output document. The default is the locale specified by the `@documentlanguage` command if there is one, otherwise English (see Section 17.1 [`@documentlanguage`], page 152).

`--dvi`   Generate a TeX DVI file using `texi2dvi`, rather than Info (see Section 22.3 [`texi2any` Printed Output], page 196).

`--dvipdf`   Generate a PDF file using `texi2dvi --dvipdf`, rather than Info (see Section 22.3 [`texi2any` Printed Output], page 196).

`--error-limit=`*limit*
`-e` *limit* Report *LIMIT* errors before aborting (on the assumption that continuing would be useless); default 100.

`--fill-column=`*width*
`-f` *width* Specify the maximum number of columns in a line; this is the right-hand edge of a line. Paragraphs that are filled will be filled to this width. (Filling is the process of breaking up and connecting lines so that lines are the same length as or shorter than the number specified as the fill column. Lines are broken between words.) The default value is 72.

`--footnote-style=`*style*
`-s` *style* Set the footnote style to *style*: either 'end' for the end node style (the default) or 'separate' for the separate node style. The value set by this option overrides the value set in a Texinfo file by an `@footnotestyle` command (see Section 12.3.2 [Footnote Styles], page 112).

> When the footnote style is 'separate', `makeinfo` makes a new node containing the footnotes found in the current node. When the footnote style is 'end', `makeinfo` places the footnote references at the end of the current node.

> In HTML, when the footnote style is 'end', or if the output is not split, footnotes are put at the end of the output. If set to 'separate', and the output is split, they are placed in a separate file.

`--force`
`-F`   Ordinarily, if the input file has errors, the output files are not created. With this option, they are preserved.

`--help`
`-h`   Print a message with available options and basic usage, then exit successfully.

`--html`   Generate HTML output (rather than Info). By default, the HTML output is split into one output file per Texinfo source node, and the split output is written into a subdirectory based on the name of the top-level Info file. See Chapter 24 [Generating HTML], page 223.

`-I path`   Append *path* to the directory search list for finding files that are included using the `@include` command. By default, `texi2any` searches only the current directory. If *path* is not given, the current directory is appended. The *path* value can be a single directory or a list of several directories separated by the usual path separator character (':' on Unix-like systems, ';' on Windows).

`--ifdocbook`
`--ifhtml`
`--ifinfo`
`--ifplaintext`
`--iftex`
`--ifxml`   For the given format, process '`@if`*format*' and '`@`*format*' commands, and do not process '`@ifnot`*format*', regardless of the format being output. For instance, if `--iftex` is given, then '`@iftex`' and '`@tex`' blocks will be read, and '`@ifnottex`' blocks will be ignored.

`--info`   Generate Info output. By default, if the output file contains more than about 300,000 bytes, it is split into shorter subfiles of about that size. The name of the output file and any subfiles is determined by `@setfilename` (see Section 3.2.3 [`@setfilename`], page 31). See Section 23.1.5 [Tag and Split Files], page 215.

`--init-file=`*file*
             Load *file* as code to modify the behavior and output of the generated manual. It is customary to use the `.pm` or the `.init` extensions for these customization files, but that is not enforced; the *file* name can be anything. The `--conf-dir` option (see above) can be used to add to the list of directories in which these customization files are searched for.

`--internal-links=`*file*
             In HTML mode, output a tab-separated file containing three columns: the internal link to an indexed item or item in the table of contents, the name of the index (or table of contents) in which it occurs, and the term which was indexed or entered. The items are in the natural sorting order for the given element. This dump can be useful for post-processors.

`--macro-expand=`*file*
`-E file`   Output the Texinfo source, with all Texinfo macros expanded, to *file*. Normally, the result of macro expansion is used internally by `makeinfo` and then discarded.

`--no-headers`
             Do not include menus or node separator lines in the output.

             When generating Info, this is the same as using `--plaintext`, resulting in a simple plain text file. Furthermore, `@setfilename` is ignored, and output is to standard output unless overridden with `-o`. (This behavior is for backward compatibility.)

When generating HTML, and output is split, also output navigation links only at the beginning of each file. If output is not split, do not include navigation links at the top of each node at all. See Chapter 24 [Generating HTML], page 223.

`--no-ifdocbook`
`--no-ifhtml`
`--no-ifinfo`
`--no-ifplaintext`
`--no-iftex`
`--no-ifxml`

For the given format, do not process '`@ifformat`' and '`@format`' commands, and do process '`@ifnotformat`', regardless of the format being output. For instance, if `--no-ifhtml` is given, then '`@ifhtml`' and '`@html`' blocks will not be read, and '`@ifnothtml`' blocks will be.

`--no-node-files`
`--node-files`

When generating HTML, create redirection files for anchors and any nodes not already output with the file name corresponding to the node name (see Section 24.4.2 [HTML Xref Node Name Expansion], page 227). This makes it possible for section- and chapter-level cross-manual references to succeed (see Section 24.4.6 [HTML Xref Configuration], page 231).

If the output is split, this is enabled by default. If the output is not split, `--node-files` enables the creation of the redirection files, in addition to the monolithic main output file. `--no-node-files` suppresses the creation of redirection files in any case. This option has no effect with any output format other than HTML. See Chapter 24 [Generating HTML], page 223.

`--no-number-footnotes`

Suppress automatic footnote numbering. By default, footnotes are numbered sequentially within a node, i.e., the current footnote number is reset to 1 at the start of each node.

`--no-number-sections`
`--number-sections`

With `--number_sections` (the default), output chapter, section, and appendix numbers as in printed manuals. This works only with hierarchically-structured manuals. You should specify `--no-number-sections` if your manual is not normally structured.

`--no-pointer-validate`
`--no-validate`

Suppress the pointer-validation phase of `makeinfo`—a dangerous thing to do. This can also be done with the `@novalidate` command (see Section 21.1 [Use TeX], page 177). Normally, consistency checks are made to ensure that cross references can be resolved, etc. See Section 22.4 [Pointer Validation], page 196.

`--no-warn`

> Suppress warning messages (but not error messages).

`--output=file`

`-o file`   Specify that the output should be directed to *file*. This overrides any file name specified in an `@setfilename` command found in the Texinfo source. If neither `@setfilename` nor this option are specified, the input file name is used to determine the output name. See Section 3.2.3 [`@setfilename`], page 31.

> If *file* is '-', output goes to standard output and '`--no-split`' is implied.

> If *file* is a directory or ends with a '/' the usual rules are used to determine the output file name (namely, use `@setfilename` or the input file name) but the files are written to the *file* directory. For example, '`makeinfo -o bar/ foo.texi`', with or without `--no-split`, will write `bar/foo.info`, and possibly other files, under `bar/`.

> When generating HTML and output is split, *file* is used as the name for the directory into which all files are written. For example, '`makeinfo -o bar --html foo.texi`' will write `bar/index.html`, among other files.

`--output-indent=val`

> This option now does nothing, but remains for compatibility. (It used to alter indentation in XML/Docbook output.)

`-P path`   Prepend *path* to the directory search list for `@include`. If *path* is not given, the current directory is prepended. See '`-I`' above.

`--paragraph-indent=indent`

`-p indent`   Set the paragraph indentation style to *indent*. The value set by this option overrides the value set in a Texinfo file by an `@paragraphindent` command (see Section 3.7.4 [`@paragraphindent`], page 43). The value of *indent* is interpreted as follows:

> `'asis'`   Preserve any existing indentation (or lack thereof) at the beginnings of paragraphs.

> `'0' or 'none'`
> > Delete any existing indentation.

> *num*   Indent each paragraph by *num* spaces.

> The default is to indent by two spaces, except for paragraphs following a section heading, which are not indented.

`--pdf`   Generate a PDF file using `texi2dvi --pdf`, rather than Info (see Section 22.3 [`texi2any` Printed Output], page 196).

`--plaintext`

> Output a plain text file (rather than Info): do not include menus or node separator lines in the output. This results in a straightforward plain text file that you can (for example) send in email without complications, or include in a distribution (for example, an `INSTALL` file).

> With this option, `@setfilename` is ignored and the output goes to standard output by default; this can be overridden with `-o`.

`--ps`   Generate a PostScript file using `texi2dvi --ps`, rather than Info (see Section 22.3 [texi2any Printed Output], page 196).

`--set-customization-variable var=value`
`-c var=value`

Set the customization variable *var* to *value*. The = is optional, but both *var* and *value* must be quoted to the shell as necessary so the result is a single word. Many aspects of `texi2any` behavior and output may be controlled by customization variables, beyond what can be set in the document by @-commands and with other command line switches. See Section 22.5 [Customization Variables], page 197.

`--split=how`
`--no-split`

When generating Info, by default large output files are split into smaller subfiles, of approximately 300k bytes. When generating HTML, by default each output file contains one node (see Chapter 24 [Generating HTML], page 223). `--no-split` suppresses this splitting of the output.

Alternatively, `--split=how` may be used to specify at which level the HTML output should be split. The possible values for *how* are:

'chapter'   The output is split at @chapter and other sectioning @-commands at this level (@appendix, etc.).

'section'   The output is split at @section and similar.

'node'   The output is split at every node. This is the default.

Plain text output can be split similarly to HTML. This may be useful for extracting sections from a Texinfo document and making them available as separate files.

`--split-size=num`

Keep Info files to at most *num* characters if possible; default is 300,000. (However, a single node will never be split across Info files.)

`--transliterate-file-names`

Enable transliteration of 8-bit characters in node names for the purpose of file name creation. See Section 24.4.4 [HTML Xref 8-bit Character Expansion], page 230.

`-U var`   Cause *var* to be undefined. This is equivalent to @clear *var* in the Texinfo file (see Section 18.5 [@set @clear @value], page 159).

`--verbose`

Cause `makeinfo` to display messages saying what it is doing. Normally, `makeinfo` only outputs messages if there are errors or warnings.

`--version`
`-V`   Print the version number, then exit successfully.

`--Xopt str`

Pass *str* (a single shell word) to `texi2dvi`; may be repeated (see Section 22.3 [texi2any Printed Output], page 196).

`--xml`   Generate Texinfo XML output (rather than Info).

   `makeinfo` also reads the environment variable `TEXINFO_OUTPUT_FORMAT` to determine the output format, if not overridden by a command line option. The value should be one of:

    docbook dvi dvipdf html info pdf plaintext ps xml

   If not set or otherwise specified, Info output is the default.

   The customization variable of the same name is also read; if set, that overrides an environment variable setting, but not a command-line option. See Section 22.5.2 [Customization Variables and Options], page 198.

22.3 `texi2any` Printed Output

To justify the name Texinfo-to-*any*, `texi2any` has basic support for creating printed output in the various formats: TEX DVI, PDF, and PostScript. This is done via the simple method of executing the `texi2dvi` program when those output formats are requested, after checking the validity of the input to give users the benefit of `texi2any`'s error checking. If you don't want such error checking, perhaps because your manual plays advanced TEX tricks together with `texinfo.tex`, just invoke `texi2dvi` directly.

   The output format options for this are `--dvi`, `--dvipdf`, `--pdf`, and `--ps`. See Section 21.2 [Format with `texi2dvi`], page 177, for more details on these options and general `texi2dvi` operation. In addition, the `--verbose`, `--silent`, and `--quiet` options are passed on if specified; the `-I` and `-o` options are likewise passed on with their arguments, and `--debug` without its argument.

   The only option remaining that is related to the `texi2dvi` invocation is `--Xopt`. Here, just the argument is passed on and multiple `--Xopt` options accumulate. This provides a way to construct an arbitrary command line for `texi2dvi`. For example, running

    texi2any --Xopt -t --Xopt @a4paper --pdf foo.texi

is equivalent to running

    texi2dvi -t @a4paper --pdf foo.texi

except for the validity check.

   Although one might wish that other options to `texi2any` would take effect, they don't. For example, running '`texi2any --no-number-sections --dvi foo.texi`' still results in a DVI file with numbered sections. (Perhaps this could be improved in the future, if requests are received.)

   The actual name of the command that is invoked is specified by the `TEXI2DVI` customization variable (see Section 22.5.4 [Other Customization Variables], page 204). As you might guess, the default is '`texi2dvi`'.

   `texi2any` itself does not generate any normal output when it invokes `texi2dvi`, only diagnostic messages.

22.4 Pointer Validation

If you do not suppress pointer validation with the '`--no-validate`' option or the `@novalidate` command in the source file (see Section 21.1 [Use TEX], page 177), `makeinfo` will check the validity of the Texinfo file.

Most validation checks are different depending on whether node pointers are explicitly or implicitly determined. With explicit node pointers, here is the list of what is checked:

1. If a 'Next', 'Previous', or 'Up' node reference is a reference to a node in the current file and is not an external reference such as to (`dir`), then the referenced node must exist.

2. Every node except the 'Top' node must have an 'Up' pointer.

3. The node referenced by an 'Up' pointer must itself reference the current node through a menu item, unless the node referenced by 'Up' has the form '(*file*)'.

With implicit node pointers, the above error cannot occur, as such. (Which is a major reason why we recommend using this feature of `makeinfo`, and not specifying any node pointers yourself.)

Instead, `makeinfo` checks that the tree constructed from the document's menus matches the tree constructed from the sectioning commands. For example, if a chapter-level menu mentions nodes *n1* and *n2*, in that order, nodes *n1* and *n2* must be associated with `@section` commands in the chapter.

Finally, with both explicit and implicit node pointers, `makeinfo` checks that every node except the 'Top' node is referenced in a menu.

22.5 Customization Variables

Warning: These customization variable names and meanings may change in any Texinfo release. We always try to avoid incompatible changes, but we cannot absolutely promise, since needs change over time.

Many aspects of the behavior and output of `texi2any` may be modified by modifying so-called *customization variables*. These fall into a few general categories:

- Those associated with @-commands; for example, `@documentlanguage`.

- Those associated with command-line options; for example, the customization variable `SPLIT` is associated with the `--split` command-line option, and `TEXINFO_OUTPUT_FORMAT` allows specifying the output format.

- Those associated with customizing the HTML output.

- Other ad hoc variables.

Customization variables may set on the command line using `--set-customization-variable '`*var value*`'` (quoting the variable/value pair to the shell) or `--set-customization-variable `*var*`=`*value* (using =). A special *value* is 'undef', which sets the variable to this special "undefined" Perl value.

The sections below give the details for each of these.

22.5.1 Customization Variables for @-Commands

Each of the following @-commands has an associated customization variable with the same name (minus the leading `@`):

```
@allowcodebreaks @clickstyle @codequotebacktick
@codequoteundirected @contents @deftypefnnewline
@documentdescription @documentencoding @documentlanguage
@evenfooting     @evenfootingmarks
@evenheading     @evenheadingmarks
@everyfooting    @everyfootingmarks
```

```
@everyheading  @everyheadingmarks
@exampleindent @firstparagraphindent
@fonttextsize  @footnotestyle @frenchspacing @headings
@kbdinputstyle @novalidate
@oddfooting    @oddfootingmarks
@oddheading    @oddheadingmarks
@pagesizes     @paragraphindent
@setchapternewpage @setcontentsaftertitlepage
@setfilename
@setshortcontentsaftertitlepage @shortcontents
@urefbreakstyle @xrefautomaticsectiontitle
```

Setting such a customization variable to a value 'foo' is similar to executing `@cmd foo`. It is not exactly the same, though, since any side effects of parsing the Texinfo source are not redone. Also, some variables do not take Texinfo code when generating particular formats, but an argument that is already formatted. This is the case, for example, for HTML for `documentdescription`.

22.5.2 Customization Variables and Options

The following table gives the customization variables associated with some command line options. See Section 22.2 [Invoking texi2any], page 190, for the meaning of the options.

Option	Variable
--enable-encoding	ENABLE_ENCODING
--document-language	documentlanguage
--error-limit	ERROR_LIMIT
--fill-column	FILLCOLUMN
--footnote-style	footnotestyle
--force	FORCE
--internal-links	INTERNAL_LINKS
--macro-expand	MACRO_EXPAND
--headers	HEADERS, SHOW_MENU
--no-warn	NO_WARN
--no-validate	novalidate
--number-footnotes	NUMBER_FOOTNOTES
--number-sections	NUMBER_SECTIONS
--node-files	NODE_FILES
--output	OUT, OUTFILE, SUBDIR
--paragraph-indent	paragraphindent
--silent	SILENT
--split	SPLIT
--split-size	SPLIT_SIZE
--transliterate-file-names	TRANSLITERATE_FILE_NAMES
--verbose	VERBOSE

Setting such a customization variable to a value 'foo' is essentially the same as specifying the --*opt*=foo if the option takes an argument, or --*opt* if not.

In addition, the customization variable `TEXINFO_OUTPUT_FORMAT` allows specifying what `makeinfo` outputs, either one of the usual output formats that can be specified with options, or various other forms:

'docbook'
'dvi'
'dvipdf'
'html'
'info'
'pdf'
'plaintext'
'ps'
'xml'   These correspond to the command-line options (and `TEXINFO_OUTPUT_FORMAT`
               environment variable values) of the same name. See Section 22.2 [Invoking
               texi2any], page 190.

'debugcount'
               Instead of generating a regular output format, output the count of bytes and
               lines obtained when converting to Info, and other information.

'debugtree'
               Instead of generating a regular output format, output a text representation of
               the tree obtained by parsing the input texinfo document.

'parse'   Do only Texinfo source parsing; there is no output.

'plaintexinfo'
               Output the Texinfo source with all the macros, `@include` and `@value{}` ex-
               panded. This is similar to setting `--macro-expand`, but instead of being output
               in addition to the normal conversion, output of Texinfo is the main output.

'rawtext'   Output raw text, with minimal formatting. For example, footnotes are ignored
               and there is no paragraph filling. This is used by the parser for file names and
               copyright text in HTML comments, for example.

'structure'
               Do only Texinfo source parsing and determination of the document structure;
               there is no output.

'texinfosxml'
               Output the document in TexinfoSXML representation, a syntax for writing
               XML data using Lisp S-expressions.

'textcontent'
               Output the text content only, stripped of commands; this is useful for spell
               checking or word counting, for example. The trivial `detexinfo` script setting
               this is in the `util` directory of the Texinfo source as an example. It's one line:
                    exec texi2any -c TEXINPUT_OUTPUT_FORMAT=textcontent "$@"

22.5.3 HTML Customization Variables

This table gives the customization variables which apply to HTML output only. A few other
customization variable apply to both HTML and other output formats; those are given in
the next section.

AVOID_MENU_REDUNDANCY
               For HTML. If set, and the menu entry and menu description are the same,
               then do not print the menu description; default false.

`AFTER_BODY_OPEN`

>   For HTML. If set, the corresponding text will appear at the beginning of each HTML file; default unset.

`AFTER_ABOUT`

>   For HTML, when an About-element is output. If set, the corresponding text will appear at the end of the About element; default unset.

`AFTER_OVERVIEW`
`AFTER_TOC_LINES`

>   For HTML. If set, the corresponding text is output after the short table of contents for `AFTER_OVERVIEW` and after the table of contents for `AFTER_TOC_LINES`; otherwise, a default string is used. At the time of writing, a `</div>` element is closed.

>   In general, you should set `BEFORE_OVERVIEW` if `AFTER_OVERVIEW` is set, and you should set `BEFORE_TOC_LINES` if `AFTER_TOC_LINES` is set.

`BASEFILENAME_LENGTH`

>   For HTML. The maximum length of the base filenames; default 245. Changing this would make cross-manual references to such long node names invalid (see Section 24.4.1 [HTML Xref Link Basics], page 226).

`BEFORE_OVERVIEW`
`BEFORE_TOC_LINES`

>   For HTML. If set, the corresponding text is output before the short table of contents for `BEFORE_OVERVIEW` and before the table of contents for `BEFORE_TOC_LINES`, otherwise a default string is used. At the time of writing, a `<div ...>` element is opened.

>   In general you should set `AFTER_OVERVIEW` if `BEFORE_OVERVIEW` is set, and you should set `AFTER_TOC_LINES` if `BEFORE_TOC_LINES` is set.

`BIG_RULE`   For HTML. Rule used after and before the top element and before special elements, but not for footers and headers; default `<hr>`.

`BODYTEXT`   For HTML, the text appearing in `<body>`. By default, sets the HTML `lang` attribute to the document language (see Section 17.1 [@documentlanguage], page 152).

`CASE_INSENSITIVE_FILENAMES`

>   For HTML. Construct output file names as if the filesystem were case insensitive (see Section 24.2 [HTML Splitting], page 224); default false.

`CHAPTER_HEADER_LEVEL`

>   For HTML. Header formatting level used for chapter level sectioning commands; default '2'.

`CHECK_HTMLXREF`

>   For HTML. Check that manuals which are the target of external cross references (see Section 8.4.5 [Four and Five Arguments], page 71) are present in `htmlxref.cnf` (see Section 24.4.6 [HTML Xref Configuration], page 231); default false.

COMPLEX_FORMAT_IN_TABLE
> For HTML. If set, use tables for indentation of complex formats; default false.

CSS_LINES
> For HTML. CSS output, automatically determined by default (see Section 24.3 [HTML CSS], page 225).

DATE_IN_HEADER
> For HTML. Put the document generation date in the header; off by default.

DEF_TABLE
> For HTML. If set, a `<table>` construction for `@deffn` and similar @-commands is used (looking more like the TeX output), instead of definition lists; default false.

DEFAULT_RULE
> For HTML. Rule used between element, except before and after the top element, and before special elements, and for footers and headers; default `<hr>`.

DO_ABOUT   For HTML. If set to 0 never do an About special element; if set to 1 always do an About special element; default 0.

EXTERNAL_DIR
> For HTML. Base directory for external manuals; default none. It is better to use the general external cross reference mechanism (see Section 24.4.6 [HTML Xref Configuration], page 231) than this variable.

EXTRA_HEAD
> For HTML. Additional text appearing within `<head>`; default unset.

FOOTNOTE_END_HEADER_LEVEL
> For HTML. Header formatting level used for the footnotes header with the 'end' footnotestyle; default '4'. See Section 12.3.2 [Footnote Styles], page 112.

FOOTNOTE_SEPARATE_HEADER_LEVEL
> For HTML. Header formatting level used for the footnotes header with the 'separate' footnotestyle; default '4'. See Section 12.3.2 [Footnote Styles], page 112.

FRAMES   For HTML. If set, a file describing the frame layout is generated, together with a file with the short table of contents; default false.

FRAMESET_DOCTYPE
> For HTML. Same as DOCTYPE, but for the file containing the frame description.

HEADER_IN_TABLE
> For HTML. Use tables for header formatting rather than a simple `<div>` element; default false.

ICONS   For HTML. Use icons for the navigation panel; default false.

IMAGE_LINK_PREFIX
> For HTML. If set, the associated value is prepended to the image file links; default unset.

`INLINE_CONTENTS`

> For HTML. If set, output the contents where the `@contents` and similar @-commands are located; default true. This is ignored if `@set*contentsaftertitlepage` is set (see Section 3.5 [Contents], page 38).

`INLINE_CSS_STYLE`

> For HTML. Put CSS directly in HTML elements rather than at the beginning of the output; default false.

`KEEP_TOP_EXTERNAL_REF`

> For HTML. If set, do not ignore 'Top' as the first argument for an external ref to a manual, as is done by default. See Section 8.5 [Top Node Naming], page 72.

`L2H`

> For HTML. If set, `latex2html` is used to convert `@math` and `@tex` sections; default false. Best used with `--iftex`.

`L2H_CLEAN`

> (Relevant only if `L2H` is set.) If set, the intermediate files generated in relation with `latex2html` are removed; default true.

`L2H_FILE`

> (Relevant only if `L2H` is set.) If set, the given file is used as `latex2html`'s init file; default unset.

`L2H_HTML_VERSION`

> (Relevant only if `L2H` is set.) The HTML version used in the `latex2html` call; default unset.

`L2H_L2H`

> (Relevant only if `L2H` is set.) The program invoked as `latex2html`; default is `latex2html`.

`L2H_SKIP`

> (Relevant only if `L2H` is set.) If set to a true value, the actual call to `latex2html` is skipped; previously generated content is reused instead. If set to 0, the cache is not used at all. If set to 'undef', the cache is used for as many TeX fragments as possible and for any remaining the command is run. The default is 'undef'.

`L2H_TMP`

> (Relevant only if `L2H` is set.) Set the directory used for temporary files. None of the file name components in this directory name may start with '.'; otherwise, `latex2html` will fail (because of `dvips`). The default is the empty string, which means the current directory.

`MAX_HEADER_LEVEL`

> For HTML. Maximum header formatting level used (higher header formatting level numbers correspond to lower sectioning levels); default '4'.

`MENU_SYMBOL`

> For HTML. Symbol used in front of menu entries when node names are used for menu entries formatting; default '`&bull;`'.

`MONOLITHIC`

> For HTML. Output only one file including the table of contents. Set by default, but only relevant when the output is not split.

`NO_CSS`

> For HTML. Do not use CSS; default false. See Section 24.3 [HTML CSS], page 225.

NODE_FILE_EXTENSION
> For HTML. Extension for node files if NODE_FILENAMES is set; default 'html'.

PRE_ABOUT
> For HTML, when an About element is output. If set to a text string, this text will appear at the beginning of the About element. If set to a reference on a subroutine, the result of the subroutine call will appear at the beginning of the About element. If not set (the default), default text is used.

PRE_BODY_CLOSE
> For HTML. If set, the given text will appear at the footer of each HTML file; default unset.

PROGRAM_NAME_IN_FOOTER
> For HTML. If set, output the program name and miscellaneous related information in the page footers; default false.

SHORTEXTN
> For HTML. If set, use '.htm' as extension; default false.

SHOW_TITLE
> For HTML. If set, output the title at the beginning of the document; default true.

SIMPLE_MENU
> For HTML. If set, use a simple preformatted style for the menu, instead of breaking down the different parts of the menu; default false. See Section 7.3 [Menu Parts], page 63.

TOC_LINKS
> For HTML. If set, links from headings to toc entries are created; default false.

TOP_FILE This file name may be used for the top-level file. The extension is set appropriately, if necessary. This is used to override the default, and is, in general, only taken into account when output is split, and for HTML.

TOP_NODE_FILE
> For HTML. File name used for the Top node, if NODE_FILENAMES is set; default is index.

TOP_NODE_FILE_TARGET
> For HTML. File name used for the Top node in cross references; default is index.

TOP_NODE_UP_URL
> For HTML. A url used for (dir) references; the default is undef, meaning that the normal rules apply, typically leading to a link to 'dir.html' from an implicit or explicit reference to '(dir)' (see Section 24.4 [HTML Xref], page 226). For more about the Top node pointers, see Section 6.1.4 [First Node], page 57. For overriding the Up pointer in other formats, see TOP_NODE_UP in Section 22.5.4 [Other Customization Variables], page 204.

USE_ACCESSKEY
> For HTML. Use accesskey in cross references; default true.

USE_ISO   For HTML. Use entities for doubled single-quote characters (see Section 14.5 [Inserting Quotation Marks], page 125), and '---' and '--' (see Section 1.9 [Conventions], page 9); default true.

USE_LINKS
            For HTML. Generate `<link>` elements in the HTML `<head>` output; default true.

USE_REL_REV
            For HTML. Use `rel` in cross references; default true.

VERTICAL_HEAD_NAVIGATION
            For HTML. If set, a vertical navigation panel is used; default false.

WORDS_IN_PAGE
            For HTML, with output split at nodes. Specifies the approximate minimum page length at which a navigation panel is placed at the bottom of a page. To avoid ever having the navigation buttons at the bottom of a page, set this to a sufficiently large number. The default is 300.

XREF_USE_FLOAT_LABEL
            For HTML. If set, for the float name in cross references, use the float label instead of the type followed by the float number (see Section 12.1.1 [`@float`], page 107). The default is off.

XREF_USE_NODE_NAME_ARG
            For HTML. Only relevant for cross reference commands with no cross reference name (second argument). If set to 1, use the node name (first) argument in cross reference @-commands for the text displayed as the hyperlink. If set to 0, use the node name if `USE_NODES` is set, otherwise the section name. If set to 'undef', use the first argument in preformatted environments, otherwise use the node name or section name depending on `USE_NODES`. The default is 'undef'.

22.5.4 Other Customization Variables

This table gives the remaining customization variables, which apply to multiple formats, or affect global behavior, or otherwise don't fit into the categories of the previous sections.

CLOSE_QUOTE_SYMBOL
            When a closing quote is needed, use this character; default `&rsquo;` in HTML, `&#8217;` in Docbook. The default for Info is the same as `OPEN_QUOTE_SYMBOL` (see below).

CPP_LINE_DIRECTIVES
            Recognize `#line` directives in a "preprocessing" pass (see Section 19.6 [External Macro Processors], page 172); on by default.

DEBUG   If set, debugging output is generated; default is off (zero).

DOCTYPE   For Docbook, HTML, XML. Specifies the `SystemLiteral`, the entity's system identifier. This is a URI which may be used to retrieve the entity, and identifies the canonical DTD for the document. The default value is different for each of HTML, Docbook and Texinfo XML.

`DUMP_TEXI`

> For debugging. If set, no conversion is done, only parsing and macro expansion. If the option `--macro-expand` is set, the Texinfo source is also expanded to the corresponding file. Default false.

`DUMP_TREE`

> For debugging. If set, the tree constructed upon parsing a Texinfo document is output to standard error; default false.

`ENABLE_ENCODING_USE_ENTITY`

> For HTML, XML. If `--enable-encoding` is set, and there is an entity corresponding with the letter or the symbol being output, prefer the entity. Set by default for HTML, but not XML.

`EXTERNAL_CROSSREF_SPLIT`

> For cross references to other manuals, this determines if the other manual is considered to be split or monolithic. By default, it is set based on the value of `SPLIT`. See Section 24.4 [HTML Xref], page 226, and see Section 24.4.6 [HTML Xref Configuration], page 231.

`EXTENSION`

> The extension added to the output file name. The default is different for each output format.

`FIX_TEXINFO`

> For "plain Texinfo" (see the `PLAINTEXINFO` item). If set to false, the resulting Texinfo does not have all errors corrected, such as missing '`@end`'; default true. This variable is only relevant when expanding Texinfo; other converters always try to output something sane even if the input is erroneous.

`IGNORE_BEFORE_SETFILENAME`

> If set, begin outputting at `@setfilename`, if `@setfilename` is present; default true.

`IGNORE_SPACE_AFTER_BRACED_COMMAND_NAME`

> If set, spaces are ignored after an @-command that takes braces. Default true, matching the TeX behavior.

`INDEX_ENTRY_COLON`

> Symbol used between the index entry and the associated node or section; default ':'.

`INDEX_SPECIAL_CHARS_WARNING`

> If set, warn about ':' in index entry, as it leads to invalid entries in index menus in output Info files. For Info and plaintext only.

`INFO_SPECIAL_CHARS_WARNING`

> If set, warn about problematic constructs for Info output (such as the string '::') in node names, menu items, and cross references; default true. Do not warn about index entries, since parsing problems there don't prevent navigation; readers can still relatively easily find their way to the node in question.

`INLINE_INSERTCOPYING`

    If set, `@insertcopying` is replaced by the `@copying` content (see Section 3.3.1 [`@copying`], page 33) as if `@insertcopying` were a user-defined macro; default false.

`INPUT_ENCODING_NAME`

    Normalized encoding name suitable for output. Should be a usable charset name in HTML, typically one of the preferred IANA encoding names. You should not need to use this variable, since it is set by `@documentencoding` (see Section 17.2 [`@documentencoding`], page 153).

`INPUT_PERL_ENCODING`

    Perl encoding used to process the Texinfo source. You should not need to use that variable, since it is set by `@documentencoding` (see Section 17.2 [`@documentencoding`], page 153).

`MACRO_BODY_IGNORES_LEADING_SPACE`

    Ignore white space at the beginning of user defined macro body line, mimicking a TeX limitation (see Section 19.3 [Macro Details], page 168). Default off.

`MAX_MACRO_CALL_NESTING`

    The maximal number of recursive calls of @-commands defined through `@rmacro`; default 100000. The purpose of this variable is to avoid infinite recursions.

`MENU_ENTRY_COLON`

    Symbol used between the menu entry and the description; default ':'.

`NO_USE_SETFILENAME`

    If set, do not use `@setfilename` to set the document name; instead, base the output document name only on the input file name. The default is false.

`NODE_FILENAMES`

    If set, node names are used to construct file names. By default, it is set if the output is split by node, or if `NODE_FILES` is set and the output is split in any way.

`NODE_NAME_IN_INDEX`

    If set, use node names in index entries, otherwise prefer section names; default true.

`NODE_NAME_IN_MENU`

    If set, use node names in menu entries, otherwise prefer section names; default true.

`OPEN_QUOTE_SYMBOL`

    When an opening quote is needed, e.g., for '`@samp`' output, use the specified character; default `&lsquo;` for HTML, `&#8216;` for Docbook. For Info, the default depends on the enabled document encoding (see Section 17.2 [`@documentencoding`], page 153); if no document encoding is set, or the encoding is US-ASCII, etc., '`'`' is used. This character usually appears as an undirected single quote on modern systems. If the document encoding is Unicode, the Info output uses a Unicode left quote.

`OUTPUT_ENCODING_NAME`

> Normalized encoding name used for output files. Should be a usable charset
> name in HTML, typically one of the preferred IANA encoding names. By
> default, if an input encoding is set (typically through `@documentencoding` or
> `INPUT_ENCODING_NAME`), this information is used to set the output encoding
> name. If no input encoding is specified, the default output encoding name
> may be set by the output format. In particular, the XML-based formats use
> `utf-8` for `OUTPUT_ENCODING_NAME` if the encoding is not otherwise specified.
> See Section 17.2 [`@documentencoding`], page 153.

`OVERVIEW_LINK_TO_TOC`

> If set, the cross references in the Overview link to the corresponding Table of
> Contents entries; default true.

`PACKAGE`
`PACKAGE_VERSION`
`PACKAGE_AND_VERSION`
`PACKAGE_URL`
`PACKAGE_NAME`

> The implementation's short package name, package version, package name and
> version concatenated, package url, and full package name, respectively. By de-
> fault, these variables are all set through Autoconf, Automake, and `configure`.

`PREFIX`   The output file prefix, which is prepended to some output file names. By
default it is set by `@setfilename` or from the input file (see Section 3.2.3
[`@setfilename`], page 31). How this value is used depends on the value of
other customization variables or command line options, such as whether the
output is split and `NODE_FILENAMES`. The default is unset.

`PROGRAM`   Name of the program used. By default, it is set to the name of the program
launched, with a trailing '`.pl`' removed.

`RENAMED_NODES_FILE`

> If set, use the value for the renamed nodes description file. If not set, the
> file is *doc_basename-noderename.cnf*. See Section 24.4.7 [HTML Xref Link
> Preservation], page 232.

`RENAMED_NODES_REDIRECTIONS`

> If set, create redirection files for renamed nodes. Set by default when generating
> HTML.

`SHOW_MENU`

> If set, Texinfo menus are output. By default, it is set unless generating Docbook
> or if `--no-headers` is specified.

`SORT_ELEMENT_COUNT`

> If set, the name of a file to which a list of elements (nodes or sections, de-
> pending on the output format) is dumped, sorted by the number of lines they
> contain after removal of @-commands; default unset. This is used by the pro-
> gram `texi-elements-by-size` in the `util/` directory of the Texinfo source
> distribution (see [texi-elements-by-size], page 261).

`SORT_ELEMENT_COUNT_WORDS`

> When dumping the elements-by-size file (see preceding item), use word counts instead of line counts; default false.

`TEST`   If set to true, some variables which are normally dynamically generated anew for each run (date, program name, version) are set to fixed and given values. This is useful to compare the output to a reference file, as is done for the tests. The default is false.

`TEXI2DVI` Name of the command used to produce PostScript, PDF, and DVI; default `texi2dvi`. See Section 22.3 [`texi2any` Printed Output], page 196.

`TEXI2HTML`

> Generate HTML and try to be as compatible as possible with `texi2html`; default false.

`TEXINFO_COLUMN_FOR_DESCRIPTION`

> Used with the `indent_menu_descriptions` tree transformation, described below; default 32 (matching `texinfo-column-for-description` in Emacs)).

`TEXINFO_DTD_VERSION`

> For XML. Version of the DTD used in the XML output preamble. The default is set based on a variable in `configure.ac`.

`TEXTCONTENT_COMMENT`

> For stripped text content output (i.e., when `TEXINFO_OUTPUT_FORMAT` is set to `textcontent`). If set, also output comments. Default false.

`TOP_NODE_UP`

> Up node for the Top node; default '`(dir)`'. For overriding the url in HTML output, see `TOP_NODE_UP_URL` in Section 22.5.3 [HTML Customization Variables], page 199.

`TREE_TRANSFORMATIONS`

> The associated value is a comma separated list of transformations that can be applied to the Texinfo tree prior to outputting the result. If more than one is specified, the ordering is irrelevant; each is always applied at the necessary point during processing.
>
> The only one executed by default is '`move_index_entries_after_items`' for HTML and Docbook output. Here's an example of updating the master menu in a document:
>
> ```
> makeinfo \
>   -c TREE_TRANSFORMATIONS=regenerate_master_menu \
>   -c PLAINTEXINFO=1 \
>   mydoc.texi \
>   -o /tmp/out
> ```
>
> (Caveat: Since `PLAINTEXINFO` output does expand Texinfo macros and conditionals, it's necessary to remove any such differences before installing the updates in the original document. This will be remedied in a future release.)

The following transformations are currently supported (many are used in the `pod2texi` utility distributed with Texinfo; see Section 22.7 [Invoking `pod2texi`], page 211):

'`complete_tree_nodes_menus`'

> Add menu entries or whole menus for nodes associated with sections of any level, based on the sectioning tree.

'`fill_gaps_in_sectioning`'

> Adds empty `@unnumbered...` sections in a tree to fill gaps in sectioning. For example, an `@unnumberedsec` will be inserted if an `@chapter` is followed by an `@subsection`.

'`indent_menu_descriptions`'

> Reformat menus so that descriptions start at column `TEXINFO_COLUMN_DESCRIPTION`.

'`insert_nodes_for_sectioning_commands`'

> Insert nodes for sectioning commands lacking a corresponding node.

'`move_index_entries_after_items`'

> In `@enumerate` and `@itemize`, move index entries appearing just before an `@item` to just after the `@item`. Comment lines between index entries are moved too. As mentioned, this is always done for HTML and Docbook output.

'`regenerate_master_menu`'

> Update the Top node master menu, either replacing the (first) `@detailmenu` in the Top node menu, or creating it at the end of the Top node menu.

'`simple_menu`'

> Mostly the same as `SIMPLE_MENU`: use a simple preformatted style for the menu. It differs from setting `SIMPLE_MENU` in that `SIMPLE_MENU` only has an effect in HTML output.

`USE_NODES`

Preferentially use nodes to decide where elements are separated. If set to false, preferentially use sectioning to decide where elements are separated. The default is true.

`USE_NODE_TARGET`

If set, use the node associated with a section for the section target in cross references; default true.

`USE_NUMERIC_ENTITY`

For HTML and XML. If set, use numeric entities instead of ASCII characters when there is no named entity. By default, set to true for HTML.

`USE_UP_NODE_FOR_ELEMENT_UP`

Fill in up sectioning direction with node direction when there is no sectioning up direction. In practice this can only happen when there is no `@top` section. Not set by default.

USE_SETFILENAME_EXTENSION

Default is on for Info, off for other output. If set, use exactly what @setfilename gives for the output file name, including the extension. You should not need to explicitly set this variable.

USE_TITLEPAGE_FOR_TITLE

Use the full @titlepage as the title, not a simple title string; default false.

USE_UNIDECODE

If set to false, do not use the Text::Unidecode Perl module to transliterate more characters; default true.

22.6 Internationalization of Document Strings

texi2any writes fixed strings into the output document at various places: cross references, page footers, the help page, alternate text for images, and so on. The string chosen depends on the value of the documentlanguage at the time of the string being output (see Section 17.1 [@documentlanguage], page 152, for the Texinfo command interface).

The Gettext framework is used for those strings (see *Gettext*). The libintl-perl package is used as the gettext implementation; more specifically, the pure Perl implementation is used, so Texinfo can support consistent behavior across all platforms and installations, which would not otherwise be possible. libintl-perl is included in the Texinfo distribution and always installed, to ensure that it is available if needed. It is also possible to use the system gettext (the choice can be made at build-time).

The Gettext domain 'texinfo_document' is used for the strings. Translated strings are written as Texinfo, and may include @-commands. In translated strings, the varying parts of the string are not usually denoted by %s and the like, but by '{arg_name}'. (This convention is common for gettext in Perl and is fully supported in GNU Gettext; see Section "Perl Format Strings" in *GNU Gettext*.) For example, in the following, '{section}' will be replaced by the section name:

```
see {section}
```

These Perl-style brace format strings are used for two reasons: first, changing the order of printf arguments is only available since Perl 5.8.0; second, and more importantly, the order of arguments is unpredictable, since @-command expansion may lead to different orders depending on the output format.

The expansion of a translation string is done like this:

1. First, the string is translated. The locale is *@documentlanguage.@documentencoding*.

   If the *@documentlanguage* has the form '11_CC', that is tried first, and then just '11'. If that does not exist, and the encoding is not us-ascii, then us-ascii is tried.

   The idea is that if there is a us-ascii encoding, it means that all the characters in the charset may be expressed as @-commands. For example, there is a fr.us-ascii locale that can accommodate any encoding, since all the Latin 1 characters have associated @-commands. On the other hand, Japanese has only a translation ja.utf-8, since there are no @-commands for Japanese characters.

2. Next, the string is expanded as Texinfo, and converted. The arguments are substituted; for example, '{arg_name}' is replaced by the corresponding actual argument.

In the following example, '{date}', '{program_homepage}' and '{program}' are the arguments of the string. Since they are used in `@uref`, their order is not predictable. '{date}', '{program_homepage}' and '{program}' are substituted after the expansion:

```
Generated on @emph{{date}} using
@uref{{program_homepage}, @emph{{program}}}.
```

This approach is admittedly a bit complicated. Its usefulness is that it supports having translations available in different encodings for encodings which can be covered by @-commands, and also specifying how the formatting for some commands is done, independently of the output format—yet still be language-dependent. For example, the '`@pxref`' translation string can be like this:

```
see {node_file_href} section `{section}\' in @cite{{book}}
```

which allows for specifying a string independently of the output format, while nevertheless with rich formatting it may be translated appropriately in many languages.

22.7 Invoking `pod2texi`: Convert POD to Texinfo

The `pod2texi` program translates Perl pod documentation file(s) to Texinfo. There are two basic modes of operation: generating a standalone manual from each input pod, or (if `--base-level=1` or higher is given) generating Texinfo subfiles suitable for use with `@include`.

Although ordinarily this documentation in the Texinfo manual would be the best place to look, in this case we have documented all the options and examples in the `pod2texi` program itself, since it may be useful outside of the rest of Texinfo. Thus, please see the output of `pod2texi --help`, the version on the web at `http://www.gnu.org/software/texinfo/manual/pod2texi.html`, etc.

For an example of using `pod2texi` to make Texinfo out of the Perl documentation itself, see `contrib/perldoc-all` (`http://svn.savannah.gnu.org/viewvc/trunk/contrib/perldoc-all/?root=texinfo`) in the Texinfo source distribution (the output is available at `http://www.gnu.org/software/perl/manual`).

22.8 `texi2html`: Ancestor of `texi2any`

Conceptually, the `texi2html` program is the parent of today's `texi2any` program. `texi2html` was developed independently, originally by Lionel Cons in 1998; at the time, `makeinfo` could not generate HTML. Many other people contributed to `texi2html` over the years.

The present `texi2any` uses little of the actual code of `texi2html`, and has quite a different basic approach to the implementation (namely, parsing the Texinfo document into a tree), but still, there is a family resemblance.

By design, `texi2any` supports nearly all the features of `texi2html` in some way. However, we did not attempt to maintain strict compatibility, so no `texi2html` executable is installed by the Texinfo package. An approximation can be run with an invocation like this (available as `util/texi2html` in the Texinfo source):

```
texi2any --set-customization-variable TEXI2HTML=1 ...
```

but, to emphasize, this is *not* a drop-in replacement for the previous `texi2html`. Here are the biggest differences:

- Most blatantly, the command line options of texi2html are now customization variables, for the most part. A table of approximate equivalents is given below.

- The program-level customization API is very different in texi2any.

- Indices cannot be split.

- Translated strings cannot be customized; we hope to introduce this feature in texi2any in the future.

Aside from the last, we do not intend to reimplement these differences. Therefore, the route forward for authors is alter manuals and build processes as necessary to use the new features and methods of texi2any. The texi2html maintainers (one of whom is the principal author of texi2any) do not intend to make further releases.

Here is the table showing texi2html options and corresponding texi2any customization variables.

```
--toc-links              TOC_LINKS
--short-ext              SHORTEXTN
--prefix                 PREFIX
--short-ref              SHORT_REF
--idx-sum                IDX_SUMMARY
--def-table              DEF_TABLE
--ignore-preamble-text   IGNORE_PREAMBLE_TEXT
--html-xref-prefix       EXTERNAL_DIR
--l2h                    L2H
--l2h-l2h                L2H_L2H
--l2h-skip               L2H_SKIP
--l2h-tmp                L2H_TMP
--l2h-file               L2H_FILE
--l2h-clean              L2H_CLEAN
--use-nodes              USE_NODES
--monolithic             MONOLITHIC
--top-file               TOP_FILE
--toc-file               TOC_FILE
--frames                 FRAMES
--menu                   SHOW_MENU
--debug                  DEBUG
--doctype                DOCTYPE
--frameset-doctype       FRAMESET_DOCTYPE
--test                   TEST
```

Finally, any texi2html users seeking more detailed information can check the draft file doc/texi2oldapi.texi in the Texinfo source repository. It consists mainly of very rough notes, but may still be useful to some.

23 Creating and Installing Info Files

This chapter describes how to create and install Info files. See Section 1.6 [Info Files], page 7, for general information about the file format itself.

23.1 Creating an Info File

`makeinfo` is a program that converts a Texinfo file into an Info file, HTML file, or plain text. `texinfo-format-region` and `texinfo-format-buffer` are GNU Emacs functions that convert Texinfo to Info.

For information on installing the Info file in the Info system, see Section 23.2 [Installing an Info File], page 216.

23.1.1 `makeinfo` Advantages

The `makeinfo` utility creates an Info file from a Texinfo source providing better error messages than either of the Emacs formatting commands. We recommend it. The `makeinfo` program is independent of Emacs. You can run `makeinfo` in any of three ways: from an operating system shell, from a shell inside Emacs, or by typing the `C-c C-m C-r` or the `C-c C-m C-b` command in Texinfo mode in Emacs.

The `texinfo-format-region` and the `texinfo-format-buffer` commands may be useful if you cannot run `makeinfo`.

23.1.2 Running `makeinfo` Within Emacs

You can run `makeinfo` in GNU Emacs Texinfo mode by using either the `makeinfo-region` or the `makeinfo-buffer` commands. In Texinfo mode, the commands are bound to `C-c C-m C-r` and `C-c C-m C-b` by default.

`C-c C-m C-r`
`M-x makeinfo-region`
> Format the current region for Info.

`C-c C-m C-b`
`M-x makeinfo-buffer`
> Format the current buffer for Info.

When you invoke `makeinfo-region` the output goes to a temporary buffer. When you invoke `makeinfo-buffer` output goes to the file set with `@setfilename` (see Section 3.2.3 [@setfilename], page 31).

The Emacs `makeinfo-region` and `makeinfo-buffer` commands run the `makeinfo` program in a temporary shell buffer. If `makeinfo` finds any errors, Emacs displays the error messages in the temporary buffer.

You can parse the error messages by typing `C-x `` (next-error). This causes Emacs to go to and position the cursor on the line in the Texinfo source that `makeinfo` thinks caused the error. See Section "Running **make** or Compilers Generally" in *The GNU Emacs Manual*, for more information about using the **next-error** command.

In addition, you can kill the shell in which the `makeinfo` command is running or make the shell buffer display its most recent output.

C-c C-m C-k
M-x makeinfo-kill-job
>   Kill the current running `makeinfo` job (from `makeinfo-region` or `makeinfo-buffer`).

C-c C-m C-l
M-x makeinfo-recenter-output-buffer
>   Redisplay the `makeinfo` shell buffer to display its most recent output.

(Note that the parallel commands for killing and recentering a TEX job are *C-c C-t C-k* and *C-c C-t C-l*. See Section 21.6 [Texinfo Mode Printing], page 181.)

You can specify options for `makeinfo` by setting the `makeinfo-options` variable with either the *M-x customize* or the *M-x set-variable* command, or by setting the variable in your `.emacs` initialization file.

For example, you could write the following in your `.emacs` file:

```
(setq makeinfo-options
       "--paragraph-indent=0 --no-split
       --fill-column=70 --verbose")
```

For more information, see [makeinfo Options], page 190, as well as "Easy Customization Interface," "Examining and Setting Variables," and "Init File" in *The GNU Emacs Manual.*

23.1.3 The `texinfo-format...` Commands

In GNU Emacs in Texinfo mode, you can format part or all of a Texinfo file with the `texinfo-format-region` command. This formats the current region and displays the formatted text in a temporary buffer called '`*Info Region*`'.

Similarly, you can format a buffer with the `texinfo-format-buffer` command. This command creates a new buffer and generates the Info file in it. Typing *C-x C-s* will save the Info file under the name specified by the `@setfilename` line which must be near the beginning of the Texinfo file.

C-c C-e C-r
`texinfo-format-region`
>   Format the current region for Info.

C-c C-e C-b
`texinfo-format-buffer`
>   Format the current buffer for Info.

The `texinfo-format-region` and `texinfo-format-buffer` commands provide you with some error checking, and other functions can provide you with further help in finding formatting errors. These procedures are described in an appendix; see Appendix E [Catching Mistakes], page 274. However, the `makeinfo` program provides better error checking (see Section 23.1.2 [makeinfo in Emacs], page 213).

23.1.4 Batch Formatting

You can format Texinfo files for Info using `batch-texinfo-format` and Emacs batch mode. You can run Emacs in batch mode from any shell, including a shell inside of Emacs. (See Section "Initial Options" in *The GNU Emacs Manual.*)

Here is a shell command to format all the files that end in `.texinfo` in the current directory:

```
emacs -batch -funcall batch-texinfo-format *.texinfo
```

Emacs processes all the files listed on the command line, even if an error occurs while attempting to format some of them.

Run `batch-texinfo-format` only with Emacs in batch mode as shown; it is not interactive. It kills the batch mode Emacs on completion.

`batch-texinfo-format` is convenient if you lack `makeinfo` and want to format several Texinfo files at once. When you use Batch mode, you create a new Emacs process. This frees your current Emacs, so you can continue working in it. (When you run `texinfo-format-region` or `texinfo-format-buffer`, you cannot use that Emacs for anything else until the command finishes.)

23.1.5 Tag Files and Split Files

If a Texinfo file has more than 30,000 bytes, `texinfo-format-buffer` automatically creates a tag table for its Info file; `makeinfo` always creates a tag table. With a *tag table*, Info can jump to new nodes more quickly than it can otherwise.

In addition, if the Texinfo file contains more than about 300,000 bytes, `texinfo-format-buffer` and `makeinfo` split the large Info file into shorter *indirect* subfiles of about 300,000 bytes each. Big files are split into smaller files so that Emacs does not need to make a large buffer to hold the whole of a large Info file; instead, Emacs allocates just enough memory for the small, split-off file that is needed at the time. This way, Emacs avoids wasting memory when you run Info. (Before splitting was implemented, Info files were always kept short and *include files* were designed as a way to create a single, large printed manual out of the smaller Info files. See Chapter 20 [Include Files], page 174, for more information. Include files are still used for very large documents, such as *The Emacs Lisp Reference Manual*, in which each chapter is a separate file.)

When a file is split, Info itself makes use of a shortened version of the original file that contains just the tag table and references to the files that were split off. The split-off files are called *indirect* files.

The split-off files have names that are created by appending '-1', '-2', '-3' and so on to the file name specified by the `@setfilename` command. The shortened version of the original file continues to have the name specified by `@setfilename`.

At one stage in writing this document, for example, the Info file was saved as the file `test-texinfo` and that file looked like this:

```
Info file: test-texinfo,    -*-Text-*-
produced by texinfo-format-buffer
from file: new-texinfo-manual.texinfo


^
_
Indirect:
test-texinfo-1: 102
test-texinfo-2: 50422
```

```
test-texinfo-3: 101300
^_^L
Tag table:
(Indirect)
Node: overview^?104
Node: info file^?1271
Node: printed manual^?4853
Node: conventions^?6855
   ...
```

(But `test-texinfo` had far more nodes than are shown here.) Each of the split-off, indirect files, `test-texinfo-1`, `test-texinfo-2`, and `test-texinfo-3`, is listed in this file after the line that says 'Indirect:'. The tag table is listed after the line that says 'Tag table:'.

In the list of indirect files, the number following the file name records the cumulative number of bytes in the preceding indirect files, not counting the file list itself, the tag table, or any permissions text in the first file. In the tag table, the number following the node name records the location of the beginning of the node, in bytes from the beginning of the (unsplit) output.

If you are using `texinfo-format-buffer` to create Info files, you may want to run the `Info-validate` command. (The `makeinfo` command does such a good job on its own, you do not need `Info-validate`.) However, you cannot run the *M-x Info-validate* node-checking command on indirect files. For information on how to prevent files from being split and how to validate the structure of the nodes, see Section E.6.1 [Using `Info-validate`], page 279.

23.2 Installing an Info File

Info files are usually kept in the `info` directory. You can read Info files using the standalone Info program or the Info reader built into Emacs. (See *Info*, for an introduction to Info.)

23.2.1 The Directory File `dir`

For Info to work, the `info` directory must contain a file that serves as a top level directory for the Info system. By convention, this file is called `dir`. (You can find the location of this file within Emacs by typing *C-h i* to enter Info and then typing *C-x C-f* to see the pathname to the `info` directory.)

The `dir` file is itself an Info file. It contains the top level menu for all the Info files in the system. The menu looks like this:

```
* Menu:
* Info:     (info).     Documentation browsing system.
* Emacs:    (emacs).    The extensible, self-documenting
                        text editor.
* Texinfo: (texinfo).   With one source file, make
                        either a printed manual using
                        @TeX{} or an Info file.
   ...
```

Each of these menu entries points to the 'Top' node of the Info file that is named in parentheses. (The menu entry does not need to specify the 'Top' node, since Info goes to the 'Top' node if no node name is mentioned. See Section 7.6 [Nodes in Other Info Files], page 64.)

Thus, the 'Info' entry points to the 'Top' node of the info file and the 'Emacs' entry points to the 'Top' node of the emacs file.

In each of the Info files, the 'Up' pointer of the 'Top' node refers back to the dir file. For example, the line for the 'Top' node of the Emacs manual looks like this in Info:

```
File: emacs  Node: Top, Up: (DIR), Next: Distrib
```

In this case, the dir file name is written in uppercase letters—it can be written in either upper- or lowercase. This is not true in general, it is a special case for dir.

23.2.2 Listing a New Info File

To add a new Info file to your system, you must write a menu entry to add to the menu in the dir file in the info directory. For example, if you were adding documentation for GDB, you would write the following new entry:

```
* GDB: (gdb).          The source-level C debugger.
```

The first part of the menu entry is the menu entry name, followed by a colon. The second part is the name of the Info file, in parentheses, followed by a period. The third part is the description.

The name of an Info file often has a .info extension. Thus, the Info file for GDB might be called either gdb or gdb.info. The Info reader programs automatically try the file name both with and without .info[1]; so it is better to avoid clutter and not to write '.info' explicitly in the menu entry. For example, the GDB menu entry should use just 'gdb' for the file name, not 'gdb.info'.

23.2.3 Info Files in Other Directories

If an Info file is not in the info directory, there are three ways to specify its location:

1. Write the pathname in the dir file as the second part of the menu.

2. Specify the Info directory name in the INFOPATH environment variable in your .profile or .cshrc initialization file. (Only you and others who set this environment variable will be able to find Info files whose location is specified this way.)

3. If you are using Emacs, list the name of the file in a second dir file, in its directory; and then add the name of that directory to the Info-directory-list variable in your personal or site initialization file.

   This variable tells Emacs where to look for dir files (the files must be named dir). Emacs merges the files named dir from each of the listed directories. (In Emacs version 18, you can set the Info-directory variable to the name of only one directory.)

For example, to reach a test file in the /home/bob/info directory, you could add an entry like this to the menu in the standard dir file:

```
* Test: (/home/bob/info/info-test).  Bob's own test file.
```

In this case, the absolute file name of the info-test file is written as the second part of the menu entry.

---

[1] On MS-DOS/MS-Windows systems, Info will try the .inf extension as well.

If you don't want to edit the system `dir` file, you can tell Info where to look by setting the `INFOPATH` environment variable in your shell startup file. This works with both the Emacs and standalone Info readers.

Specifically, if you use a Bourne-compatible shell such as `sh` or `bash` for your shell command interpreter, you set the `INFOPATH` environment variable in the `.profile` initialization file; but if you use `csh` or `tcsh`, you set the variable in the `.cshrc` initialization file. On MS-DOS/MS-Windows systems, you must set `INFOPATH` in your `autoexec.bat` file or in the registry. Each type of shell uses a different syntax.

- In a `.cshrc` file, you could set the `INFOPATH` variable as follows:

      setenv INFOPATH .:~/info:/usr/local/emacs/info

- In a `.profile` file, you would achieve the same effect by writing:

      INFOPATH=.:$HOME/info:/usr/local/emacs/info
      export INFOPATH

- In a `autoexec.bat` file, you write this command (note the use of ';' as the directory separator, and a different syntax for using values of other environment variables):

      set INFOPATH=.;%HOME%/info;c:/usr/local/emacs/info

The '.' indicates the current directory as usual. Emacs uses the `INFOPATH` environment variable to initialize the value of Emacs's own `Info-directory-list` variable. The standalone Info reader merges any files named `dir` in any directory listed in the `INFOPATH` variable into a single menu presented to you in the node called '(dir)Top'.

However you set `INFOPATH`, if its last character is a colon (on MS-DOS/MS-Windows systems, use a semicolon instead), this is replaced by the default (compiled-in) path. This gives you a way to augment the default path with new directories without having to list all the standard places. For example (using `sh` syntax):

      INFOPATH=/home/bob/info:
      export INFOPATH

will search `/home/bob/info` first, then the standard directories. Leading or doubled colons are not treated specially.

When you create your own `dir` file for use with `Info-directory-list` or `INFOPATH`, it's easiest to start by copying an existing `dir` file and replace all the text after the '* Menu:' with your desired entries. That way, the punctuation and special *CTRL-_* characters that Info needs will be present.

As one final alternative, which works only with Emacs Info, you can change the `Info-directory-list` variable. For example:

```
(add-hook 'Info-mode-hook '(lambda ()
    (add-to-list 'Info-directory-list
(expand-file-name "~/info"))))
```

23.2.4 Installing Info Directory Files

When you install an Info file onto your system, you can use the program `install-info` to update the Info directory file `dir`. Normally the makefile for the package runs `install-info`, just after copying the Info file into its proper installed location.

In order for the Info file to work with `install-info`, you include the commands `@dircategory` and `@direntry`...`@end direntry` in the Texinfo source file. Use `@direntry` to specify the menu entries to add to the Info directory file, and use `@dircategory` to specify which part of the Info directory to put it in. Here is how these commands are used in this manual:

```
@dircategory Texinfo documentation system
@direntry
* Texinfo: (texinfo).           The GNU documentation format.
* install-info: (texinfo)Invoking install-info. ...
...
@end direntry
```

Here's what this produces in the Info file:

```
INFO-DIR-SECTION Texinfo documentation system
START-INFO-DIR-ENTRY
* Texinfo: (texinfo).           The GNU documentation format.
* install-info: (texinfo)Invoking install-info. ...
...
END-INFO-DIR-ENTRY
```

The `install-info` program sees these lines in the Info file, and that is how it knows what to do.

Always use the `@direntry` and `@dircategory` commands near the beginning of the Texinfo input, before the first `@node` command. If you use them later on in the input, `install-info` will not notice them.

`install-info` will automatically reformat the description of the menu entries it is adding. As a matter of convention, the description of the main entry (above, 'The GNU documentation format') should start at column 32, starting at zero (as in `what-cursor-position` in Emacs). This will make it align with most others. Description for individual utilities best start in column 48, where possible. For more information about formatting see the '`--calign`', '`--align`', and '`--max-width`' options in Section 23.2.5 [Invoking install-info], page 220.

If you use `@dircategory` more than once in the Texinfo source, each usage specifies the 'current' category; any subsequent `@direntry` commands will add to that category.

When choosing a category name for the `@dircategory` command, we recommend consulting the Free Software Directory (`http://www.gnu.org/directory`). If your program is not listed there, or listed incorrectly or incompletely, please report the situation to the directory maintainers (`http://directory.fsf.org`) so that the category names can be kept in sync.

Here are a few examples (see the `util/dir-example` file in the Texinfo distribution for large sample `dir` file):

Emacs
Localization
Printing
Software development
Software libraries
Text creation and manipulation

Each 'Invoking' node for every program installed should have a corresponding `@direntry`. This lets users easily find the documentation for the different programs they can run, as with the traditional `man` system.

23.2.5 Invoking `install-info`

`install-info` inserts menu entries from an Info file into the top-level `dir` file in the Info system (see the previous sections for an explanation of how the `dir` file works). `install-info` also removes menu entries from the `dir` file. It's most often run as part of software installation, or when constructing a `dir` file for all manuals on a system. Synopsis:

    install-info [option...] [info-file [dir-file]]

If *info-file* or *dir-file* are not specified, the options (described below) that define them must be. There are no compile-time defaults, and standard input is never used. `install-info` can read only one Info file and write only one `dir` file per invocation.

If *dir-file* (however specified) does not exist, `install-info` creates it if possible (with no entries).

If any input file is compressed with `gzip` (see *Gzip*), `install-info` automatically uncompresses it for reading. And if *dir-file* is compressed, `install-info` also automatically leaves it compressed after writing any changes. If *dir-file* itself does not exist, `install-info` tries to open *dir-file*`.gz`, *dir-file*`.xz`, *dir-file*`.bz2`, *dir-file*`.lz`, and *dir-file*`.lzma`, in that order.

Options:

`--add-once`
> Specifies that the entry or entries will only be put into a single section.

`--align=`*column*
> Specifies the column that the second and subsequent lines of menu entry's description will be formatted to begin at. The default for this option is '35'. It is used in conjunction with the '`--max-width`' option. *column* starts counting at 1.

`--append-new-sections`
> Instead of alphabetizing new sections, place them at the end of the DIR file.

`--calign=`*column*
> Specifies the column that the first line of menu entry's description will be formatted to begin at. The default for this option is '33'. It is used in conjunction with the '`--max-width`' option. When the name of the menu entry exceeds this column, entry's description will start on the following line. *column* starts counting at 1.

`--debug`   Report what is being done.

`--delete` Delete the entries in *info-file* from *dir-file*. The file name in the entry in *dir-file* must be *info-file* (except for an optional '`.info`' in either one). Don't insert any new entries. Any empty sections that result from the removal are also removed.

`--description=`*text*
> Specify the explanatory portion of the menu entry. If you don't specify a description (either via '`--entry`', '`--item`' or this option), the description is taken from the Info file itself.

`--dir-file=`*name*
> Specify file name of the Info directory file. This is equivalent to using the *dir-file* argument.

`--dry-run`

> Same as '`--test`'.

`--entry=text`

> Insert *text* as an Info directory entry; *text* should have the form of an Info menu item line plus zero or more extra lines starting with whitespace. If you specify more than one entry, they are all added. If you don't specify any entries, they are determined from information in the Info file itself.

`--help`   Display a usage message with basic usage and all available options, then exit successfully.

`--info-file=file`

> Specify Info file to install in the directory. This is equivalent to using the *info-file* argument.

`--info-dir=dir`

> Specify the directory where the directory file `dir` resides. Equivalent to '`--dir-file=dir/dir`'.

`--infodir=dir`

> Same as '`--info-dir`'.

`--item=text`

> Same as '`--entry=text`'. An Info directory entry is actually a menu item.

`--keep-old`

> Do not replace pre-existing menu entries. When '`--remove`' is specified, this option means that empty sections are not removed.

`--max-width=column`

> Specifies the column that the menu entry's description will be word-wrapped at. *column* starts counting at 1.

`--maxwidth=column`

> Same as '`--max-width`'.

`--menuentry=text`

> Same as '`--name`'.

`--name=text`

> Specify the name portion of the menu entry. If the *text* does not start with an asterisk '`*`', it is presumed to be the text after the '`*`' and before the parentheses that specify the Info file. Otherwise *text* is taken verbatim, and is taken as defining the text up to and including the first period (a space is appended if necessary). If you don't specify the name (either via '`--entry`', '`--item`' or this option), it is taken from the Info file itself. If the Info does not contain the name, the basename of the Info file is used.

`--no-indent`

> Suppress formatting of new entries into the `dir` file.

`--quiet`
`--silent`   Suppress warnings, etc., for silent operation.

`--remove`   Same as '`--delete`'.

`--remove-exactly`

> Also like '`--delete`', but only entries if the Info file name matches exactly; `.info` and/or `.gz` suffixes are *not* ignored.

`--section=sec`

> Put this file's entries in section *sec* of the directory. If you specify more than one section, all the entries are added in each of the sections. If you don't specify any sections, they are determined from information in the Info file itself. If the Info file doesn't specify a section, the menu entries are put into the Miscellaneous section.

`--section regex sec`

> Same as '`--regex=regex --section=sec --add-once`'.
>
> `install-info` tries to detect when this alternate syntax is used, but does not always guess correctly. Here is the heuristic that `install-info` uses:
>
> 1. If the second argument to `--section` starts with a hyphen, the original syntax is presumed.
> 2. If the second argument to `--section` is a file that can be opened, the original syntax is presumed.
> 3. Otherwise the alternate syntax is used.
>
> When the heuristic fails because your section title starts with a hyphen, or it happens to be a filename that can be opened, the syntax should be changed to '`--regex=regex --section=sec --add-once`'.

`--regex=regex`

> Put this file's entries into any section that matches *regex*. If more than one section matches, all of the entries are added in each of the sections. Specify *regex* using basic regular expression syntax, more or less as used with **grep**, for example.

`--test`   Suppress updating of the directory file.

`--version`

> Display version information and exit successfully.

24 Generating HTML

`makeinfo` generates Info output by default, but given the `--html` option, it will generate HTML, for web browsers and other programs. This chapter gives some details on such HTML output.

`makeinfo` has many user-definable customization variables with which you can influence the HTML output. See Section 22.5 [Customization Variables], page 197.

`makeinfo` can also produce output in XML and Docbook formats, but we do not as yet describe these in detail. See Section 1.3 [Output Formats], page 4, for a brief overview of all the output formats.

24.1 HTML Translation

First, the HTML generated by `makeinfo` is standard HTML 4. It also tries to be compatible with earlier standards (e.g., HTML 2.0, RFC-1866). Thus, please report output from an error-free run of `makeinfo` which has practical browser portability problems as a bug (see Section 1.1 [Reporting Bugs], page 3).

Some known exceptions to HTML 3.2 (using '`--init-file=html32.pm`' produces strict HTML 3.2 output; see Section 22.2 [Invoking `texi2any`], page 190):

1. HTML 3.2 tables are generated for the `@multitable` command (see Section 11.5 [Multi-column Tables], page 104), but they should degrade reasonably in browsers without table support.

2. The HTML 4 '`lang`' attribute on the '`<html>`' attribute is used.

3. Entities that are not in the HTML 3.2 standard are also used.

4. CSS is used (see Section 24.3 [HTML CSS], page 225).

5. A few HTML 4 elements are used: `thead`, `abbr`, `acronym`.

To achieve maximum portability and accessibility among browsers (both graphical and text-based), systems, and users, the HTML output is intentionally quite plain and generic. It has always been our goal for users to be able to customize the output to their wishes via CSS (see Section 24.3 [HTML CSS], page 225) or other means (see Section 22.5 [Customization Variables], page 197. If you cannot accomplish a reasonable customization, feel free to report that.

However, we do not wish to depart from our basic goal of widest readability for the core output. For example, using fancy CSS may make it possible for the HTML output to more closely resemble the TeX output in some details, but this result is not even close to being worth the ensuing difficulties.

It is also intentionally not our goal, and not even possible, to pass through every conceivable validation test without any diagnostics. Different validation tests have different goals, often about pedantic enforcement of some standard or another. Our overriding goal is to help users, not blindly comply with standards.

To repeat what was said at the top: please report output from an error-free run of `makeinfo` which has *practical* browser portability problems as a bug (see Section 1.1 [Reporting Bugs], page 3).

A few other general points about the HTML output follow.

Navigation bar: By default, a navigation bar is inserted at the start of each node, analogous to Info output. If the '`--no-headers`' option is used, the navigation bar is only inserted at the beginning of split files. Header `<link>` elements in split output can support Info-like navigation with browsers like Lynx and Emacs W3 which implement this HTML 1.0 feature.

Footnotes: for HTML, when the footnote style is '`end`', or if the output is not split, footnotes are put at the end of the output. If the footnoet style is set to '`separate`', and the output is split, they are placed in a separate file. See Section 12.3.2 [Footnote Styles], page 112.

Raw HTML: `makeinfo` will include segments of Texinfo source between `@ifhtml` and `@end ifhtml` in the HTML output (but not any of the other conditionals, by default). Source between `@html` and `@end html` is passed without change to the output (i.e., suppressing the normal escaping of input '`<`', '`>`' and '`&`' characters which have special significance in HTML). See Section 18.1 [Conditional Commands], page 155.

24.2 HTML Splitting

When splitting output at nodes (which is the default), `makeinfo` writes HTML output into (basically) one output file per Texinfo source `@node`.

Each output file name is the node name with spaces replaced by '`-`'s and special characters changed to '`_`' followed by their code point in hex (see Section 24.4 [HTML Xref], page 226). This is to make it portable and easy to use as a filename. In the unusual case of two different nodes having the same name after this treatment, they are written consecutively to the same file, with HTML anchors so each can be referred to independently.

If `makeinfo` is run on a system which does not distinguish case in file names, nodes which are the same except for case (e.g., '`index`' and '`Index`') will also be folded into the same output file with anchors. You can also pretend to be on a case insensitive filesystem by setting the customization variable `CASE_INSENSITIVE_FILENAMES`.

It is also possible to split at chapters or sections with `--split` (see Section 22.2 [Invoking `texi2any`], page 190). In that case, the file names are constructed after the name of the node associated with the relevant sectioning command. Also, unless `--no-node-files` is specified, a redirection file is output for every node in order to more reliably support cross references to that manual (see Section 24.4 [HTML Xref], page 226).

When splitting, the HTML output files are written into a subdirectory, with the name chosen as follows:

1. `makeinfo` first tries the subdirectory with the base name from `@setfilename` (that is, any extension is removed). For example, HTML output for `@setfilename gcc.info` would be written into a subdirectory named '`gcc/`'.

2. If that directory cannot be created for any reason, then `makeinfo` tries appending '`.html`' to the directory name. For example, output for `@setfilename texinfo` would be written to '`texinfo.html/`'.

3. If the '`name.html`' directory can't be created either, `makeinfo` gives up.

In any case, the top-level output file within the directory is always named '`index.html`'.

Monolithic output (`--no-split`) is named according to `@setfilename` (with any
'.info' extension is replaced with '.html'), `--output` (the argument is used literally), or
based on the input file name as a last resort (see Section 3.2.3 [`@setfilename`], page 31).

24.3 HTML CSS

Cascading Style Sheets (CSS for short) is an Internet standard for influencing the display
of HTML documents: see `http://www.w3.org/Style/CSS/`.

By default, `makeinfo` includes a few simple CSS commands to better implement the
appearance of some Texinfo environments. Here are two of them, as an example:

```
pre.display { font-family:inherit }
pre.smalldisplay { font-family:inherit; font-size:smaller }
```

A full explanation of CSS is (far) beyond this manual; please see the reference above. In
brief, however, the above tells the web browser to use a 'smaller' font size for `@smalldisplay`
text, and to use the same font as the main document for both `@smalldisplay` and `@display`.
By default, the HTML '`<pre>`' command uses a monospaced font.

You can influence the CSS in the HTML output with two `makeinfo` options: `--css-include=file` and `--css-ref=url`.

The option `--css-ref=url` adds to each output HTML file a '`<link>`' tag referencing a CSS at the given *url*. This allows using external style sheets. You may find the
file `texi2html/examples/texinfo-bright-colors.css` useful for visualizing the CSS elements in Texinfo output.

The option `--css-include=file` includes the contents *file* in the HTML output, as
you might expect. However, the details are somewhat tricky, as described in the following,
to provide maximum flexibility.

The CSS file may begin with so-called '`@import`' directives, which link to external CSS
specifications for browsers to use when interpreting the document. Again, a full description
is beyond our scope here, but we'll describe how they work syntactically, so we can explain
how `makeinfo` handles them.

There can be more than one '`@import`', but they have to come first in the file, with
only whitespace and comments interspersed, no normal definitions. (Technical exception: an
'`@charset`' directive may precede the '`@import`''s. This does not alter `makeinfo`'s behavior,
it just copies the '`@charset`' if present.) Comments in CSS files are delimited by '`/* ...
*/`', as in C. An '`@import`' directive must be in one of these two forms:

```
@import url(http://example.org/foo.css);
@import "http://example.net/bar.css";
```

As far as `makeinfo` is concerned, the crucial characters are the '`@`' at the beginning and
the semicolon terminating the directive. When reading the CSS file, it simply copies any
such '`@`'-directive into the output, as follows:

- If *file* contains only normal CSS declarations, it is included after `makeinfo`'s default
  CSS, thus overriding it.
- If *file* begins with '`@import`' specifications (see below), then the '`import`''s are included
  first (they have to come first, according to the standard), and then `makeinfo`'s default
  CSS is included. If you need to override `makeinfo`'s defaults from an '`@import`', you
  can do so with the '`! important`' CSS construct, as in:

```
pre.smallexample { font-size: inherit ! important }
```

- If *file* contains both '`@import`' and inline CSS specifications, the '`@import`''s are included first, then `makeinfo`'s defaults, and lastly the inline CSS from *file*.

- Any @-directive other than '`@import`' and '`@charset`' is treated as a CSS declaration, meaning `makeinfo` includes its default CSS and then the rest of the file.

If the CSS file is malformed or erroneous, `makeinfo`'s output is unspecified. `makeinfo` does not try to interpret the meaning of the CSS file in any way; it just looks for the special '`@`' and '`;`' characters and blindly copies the text into the output. Comments in the CSS file may or may not be included in the output.

In addition to the possibilities offered by CSS, `makeinfo` has many user-definable customization variables with which you can influence the HTML output. See Section 22.5 [Customization Variables], page 197.

24.4 HTML Cross References

Cross references between Texinfo manuals in HTML format become, in the end, a standard HTML `<a>` link, but the details are unfortunately complex. This section describes the algorithm used in detail, so that Texinfo can cooperate with other programs, such as `texi2html`, by writing mutually compatible HTML files.

This algorithm may or may not be used for links *within* HTML output for a Texinfo file. Since no issues of compatibility arise in such cases, we do not need to specify this.

We try to support references to such "external" manuals in both monolithic and split forms. A *monolithic* (mono) manual is entirely contained in one file, and a *split* manual has a file for each node. (See Section 24.2 [HTML Splitting], page 224.)

The algorithm was primarily devised by Patrice Dumas in 2003–04.

24.4.1 HTML Cross Reference Link Basics

For our purposes, an HTML link consists of four components: a host name, a directory part, a file part, and a target part. We always assume the `http` protocol. For example:

```
http://host/dir/file.html#target
```

The information to construct a link comes from the node name and manual name in the cross reference command in the Texinfo source (see Chapter 8 [Cross References], page 66), and from *external information* (see Section 24.4.6 [HTML Xref Configuration], page 231).

We now consider each part in turn.

The *host* is hardwired to be the local host. This could either be the literal string '`localhost`', or, according to the rules for HTML links, the '`http://localhost/`' could be omitted entirely.

The *dir* and *file* parts are more complicated, and depend on the relative split/mono nature of both the manual being processed and the manual that the cross reference refers to. The underlying idea is that there is one directory for Texinfo manuals in HTML, and a given *manual* is either available as a monolithic file `manual.html`, or a split subdirectory `manual/*.html`. Here are the cases:

- If the present manual is split, and the referent manual is also split, the directory is '`../referent/`' and the file is the expanded node name (described later).

- If the present manual is split, and the referent manual is mono, the directory is '../' and the file is *referent*.html.

- If the present manual is mono, and the referent manual is split, the directory is *referent*/ and the file is the expanded node name.

- If the present manual is mono, and the referent manual is also mono, the directory is ./ (or just the empty string), and the file is *referent*.html.

Another rule, that only holds for filenames, is that base filenames are truncated to 245 characters, to allow for an extension to be appended and still comply with the 255-character limit which is common to many filesystems. Although technically this can be changed with the `BASEFILENAME_LENGTH` customization variable (see Section 22.5.4 [Other Customization Variables], page 204), doing so would make cross-manual references to such nodes invalid.

Any directory part in the filename argument of the source cross reference command is ignored. Thus, `@xref{,,,../foo}` and `@xref{,,,foo}` both use 'foo' as the manual name. This is because any such attempted hardwiring of the directory is very unlikely to be useful for both Info and HTML output.

Finally, the *target* part is always the expanded node name.

Whether the present manual is split or mono is determined by user option; `makeinfo` defaults to split, with the `--no-split` option overriding this.

Whether the referent manual is split or mono, however, is another bit of the external information (see Section 24.4.6 [HTML Xref Configuration], page 231). By default, `makeinfo` uses the same form of the referent manual as the present manual.

Thus, there can be a mismatch between the format of the referent manual that the generating software assumes, and the format it's actually present in. See Section 24.4.5 [HTML Xref Mismatch], page 230.

24.4.2 HTML Cross Reference Node Name Expansion

As mentioned in the previous section, the key part of the HTML cross reference algorithm is the conversion of node names in the Texinfo source into strings suitable for XHTML identifiers and filenames. The restrictions are similar for each: plain ASCII letters, numbers, and the '-' and '_' characters are all that can be used. (Although HTML anchors can contain most characters, XHTML is more restrictive.)

Cross references in Texinfo can refer either to nodes or anchors (see Section 6.3 [@anchor], page 59). However, anchors are treated identically to nodes in this context, so we'll continue to say "node" names for simplicity.

A special exception: the Top node (see Section 3.6 [The Top Node], page 39) is always mapped to the file index.html, to match web server software. However, the HTML *target* is 'Top'. Thus (in the split case):

```
@xref{Top,,, emacs, The GNU Emacs Manual}.
⇒ <a href="emacs/index.html#Top">
```

1. The standard ASCII letters (a-z and A-Z) are not modified. All other characters may be changed as specified below.

2. The standard ASCII numbers (0-9) are not modified except when a number is the first character of the node name. In that case, see below.

3. Multiple consecutive space, tab and newline characters are transformed into just one space. (It's not possible to have newlines in node names with the current implementation, but we specify it anyway, just in case.)

4. Leading and trailing spaces are removed.

5. After the above has been applied, each remaining space character is converted into a '-' character.

6. Other ASCII 7-bit characters are transformed into '_00xx', where xx is the ASCII character code in (lowercase) hexadecimal. This includes '_', which is mapped to '_005f'.

7. If the node name does not begin with a letter, the literal string 'g_t' is prefixed to the result. (Due to the rules above, that string can never occur otherwise; it is an arbitrary choice, standing for "GNU Texinfo".) This is necessary because XHTML requires that identifiers begin with a letter.

For example:

```
@node A  node --- with _'%
⇒ A-node-_002d_002d_002d-with-_005f_0027_0025
```

Example translations of common characters:

- '_' ⇒ '_005f'
- '-' ⇒ '_002d'
- 'A node' ⇒ 'A-node'

On case-folding computer systems, nodes differing only by case will be mapped to the same file. In particular, as mentioned above, Top always maps to the file `index.html`. Thus, on a case-folding system, Top and a node named 'Index' will both be written to `index.html`. Fortunately, the targets serve to distinguish these cases, since HTML target names are always case-sensitive, independent of operating system.

24.4.3 HTML Cross Reference Command Expansion

Node names may contain @-commands (see Section 6.1.3 [Node Line Requirements], page 56). This section describes how they are handled.

First, comments are removed.

Next, any @value commands (see Section 18.5.1 [@set @value], page 159) and macro invocations (see Section 19.2 [Invoking Macros], page 166) are fully expanded.

Then, for the following commands, the command name and braces are removed, and the text of the argument is recursively transformed:

```
@asis @b @cite @code @command @dfn @dmn @dotless
@emph @env @file @i @indicateurl @kbd @key
@samp @sansserif @sc @slanted @strong @sub @sup
@t @U @var @verb @w
```

For @sc, any letters are capitalized.

In addition, the following commands are replaced by constant text, as shown below. If any of these commands have non-empty arguments, as in @TeX{bad}, it is an error, and the result is unspecified. In this table, '(space)' means a space character and '(nothing)' means the empty string. The notation 'U+*hhhh*' means Unicode code point *hhhh* (in hex, as usual).

There are further transformations of many of these expansions to yield the final file or other target name, such as space characters to '-', etc., according to the other rules.

`@(newline)`	(space)
`@(space)`	(space)
`@(tab)`	(space)
`@!`	'!'
`@*`	(space)
`@-`	(nothing)
`@.`	'.'
`@:`	(nothing)
`@?`	'?'
`@@`	'@'
`@{`	'{'
`@}`	'}'
`@LaTeX`	'LaTeX'
`@TeX`	'TeX'
`@arrow`	U+2192
`@bullet`	U+2022
`@comma`	','
`@copyright`	U+00A9
`@dots`	U+2026
`@enddots`	'...'
`@equiv`	U+2261
`@error`	'error-->'
`@euro`	U+20AC
`@exclamdown`	U+00A1
`@expansion`	U+21A6
`@geq`	U+2265
`@leq`	U+2264
`@minus`	U+2212
`@ordf`	U+00AA
`@ordm`	U+00BA
`@point`	U+2605
`@pounds`	U+00A3
`@print`	U+22A3
`@questiondown`	U+00BF
`@registeredsymbol`	U+00AE
`@result`	U+21D2
`@textdegree`	U+00B0
`@tie`	(space)

Quotation mark @-commands (`@quotedblright{}` and the like), are likewise replaced by their Unicode values. Normal quotation *characters* (e.g., ASCII ' and ') are not altered. See Section 14.5 [Inserting Quotation Marks], page 125.

Any @acronym, @abbr, @email, and @image commands are replaced by their first argument. (For these commands, all subsequent arguments are optional, and ignored here.) See Section 9.1.14 [@acronym], page 85, and Section 9.1.16 [@email], page 86, and Section 12.2 [Images], page 109.

Accents are handled according to the next section.

Any other command is an error, and the result is unspecified.

24.4.4 HTML Cross Reference 8-bit Character Expansion

Usually, characters other than plain 7-bit ASCII are transformed into the corresponding Unicode code point(s) in Normalization Form C, which uses precomposed characters where available. (This is the normalization form recommended by the W3C and other bodies.) This holds when that code point is 0xffff or less, as it almost always is.

These will then be further transformed by the rules above into the string '_hhhh', where hhhh is the code point in hex.

For example, combining this rule and the previous section:

```
@node @b{A} @TeX{} @u{B} @point{}@enddots{}
⇒ A-TeX-B_0306-_2605_002e_002e_002e
```

Notice: 1) @enddots expands to three periods which in turn expands to three '_002e''s; 2) @u{B} is a 'B' with a breve accent, which does not exist as a pre-accented Unicode character, therefore expands to 'B_0306' (B with combining breve).

When the Unicode code point is above 0xffff, the transformation is '__xxxxxx', that is, two leading underscores followed by six hex digits. Since Unicode has declared that their highest code point is 0x10ffff, this is sufficient. (We felt it was better to define this extra escape than to always use six hex digits, since the first two would nearly always be zeros.)

This method works fine if the node name consists mostly of ASCII characters and contains only few 8-bit ones. But if the document is written in a language whose script is not based on the Latin alphabet (for example, Ukrainian), it will create file names consisting almost entirely of '_xxxx' notations, which is inconvenient and all but unreadable. To handle such cases, makeinfo offers the --transliterate-file-names command line option. This option enables transliteration of node names into ASCII characters for the purposes of file name creation and referencing. The transliteration is based on phonetic principles, which makes the generated file names more easily understanable.

For the definition of Unicode Normalization Form C, see Unicode report UAX#15, http://www.unicode.org/reports/tr15/. Many related documents and implementations are available elsewhere on the web.

24.4.5 HTML Cross Reference Mismatch

As mentioned earlier (see Section 24.4.1 [HTML Xref Link Basics], page 226), the generating software may need to guess whether a given manual being cross referenced is available in split or monolithic form—and, inevitably, it might guess wrong. However, when the *referent* manual is generated, it is possible to handle at least some mismatches.

In the case where we assume the referent is split, but it is actually available in mono, the only recourse would be to generate a manual/ subdirectory full of HTML files which redirect back to the monolithic manual.html. Since this is essentially the same as a split manual in the first place, it's not very appealing.

On the other hand, in the case where we assume the referent is mono, but it is actually available in split, it is possible to use JavaScript to redirect from the putatively monolithic `manual.html` to the different `manual/node.html` files. Here's an example:

```
function redirect() {
  switch (location.hash) {
    case "#Node1":
      location.replace("manual/Node1.html#Node1"); break;
    case "#Node2" :
      location.replace("manual/Node2.html#Node2"); break;
    ...
    default:;
  }
}
```

Then, in the `<body>` tag of `manual.html`:

```
<body onLoad="redirect();">
```

Once again, this is something the software which generated the *referent* manual has to do in advance, it's not something the software generating the cross reference in the present manual can control.

24.4.6 HTML Cross Reference Configuration: `htmlxref.cnf`

`makeinfo` reads a file named `htmlxref.cnf` to gather information for cross references to other manuals in HTML output. It is looked for in the following directories:

`./`   (the current directory)

`./.texinfo/`
          (under the current directory)

`~/.texinfo/`
          (where ~ is the current user's home directory)

sysconfdir`/texinfo/`
          (where *sysconfdir* is the system configuration directory specified at compile-time, e.g., `/usr/local/etc`)

datadir`/texinfo/`
          (likewise specified at compile time, e.g., `/usr/local/share`)

All files found are used, with earlier entries overriding later ones. The Texinfo distribution includes a default file which handles many GNU manuals; it is installed in the last of the above directories, i.e., *datadir*`/texinfo/htmlxref.cnf`.

The file is line-oriented. Lines consisting only of whitespace are ignored. Comments are indicated with a '#' at the beginning of a line, optionally preceded by whitespace. Since '#' can occur in urls (like almost any character), it does not otherwise start a comment.

Each non-blank non-comment line must be either a *variable assignment* or *manual information*.

A variable assignment line looks like this:

```
varname = varvalue
```

Whitespace around the '=' is optional and ignored. The *varname* should consist of letters; case is significant. The *varvalue* is an arbitrary string, continuing to the end of the line. Variables are then referenced with '`${varname}`'; variable references can occur in the *varvalue*.

A manual information line looks like this:

```
manual keyword urlprefix
```

with *manual* the short identifier for a manual, *keyword* being one of: `mono`, `node`, `section`, `chapter`, and *urlprefix* described below. Variable references can occur only in the *urlprefix*. For example (used in the canonical `htmlxref.cnf`):

```
G = http://www.gnu.org
GS = ${G}/software
hello mono    ${GS}/hello/manual/hello.html
hello chapter ${GS}/hello/manual/html_chapter/
hello section ${GS}/hello/manual/html_section/
hello node    ${GS}/hello/manual/html_node/
```

If the keyword is `mono`, *urlprefix* gives the host, directory, and file name for *manual* as one monolithic file.

If the keyword is `node`, `section`, or `chapter`, *urlprefix* gives the host and directory for *manual* split into nodes, sections, or chapters, respectively.

When available, `makeinfo` will use the "corresponding" value for cross references between manuals. That is, when generating monolithic output (`--no-split`), the `mono` url will be used, when generating output that is split by node, the `node` url will be used, etc. However, if a manual is not available in that form, anything that is available can be used. Here is the search order for each style:

```
node    ⇒ node,    section, chapter, mono
section ⇒ section, chapter, node,    mono
chapter ⇒ chapter, section, node,    mono
mono    ⇒ mono,    chapter, section, node
```

These section- and chapter-level cross-manual references can succeed only when the target manual was created using `--node-files`; this is the default for split output.

If you have additions or corrections to the `htmlxref.cnf` distributed with Texinfo, please email `bug-texinfo@gnu.org` as usual. You can get the latest version from `http://ftpmirror.gnu.org/texinfo/htmlxref.cnf`.

24.4.7 HTML Cross Reference Link Preservation: *manual*-`noderename.cnf`

Occasionally changes in a program require removing (or renaming) nodes in the manual in order to have the best documentation. Given the nature of the web, however, links may exist anywhere to such a removed node (renaming appears the same as removal for this purpose), and it's not ideal for those links to simply break.

Therefore, Texinfo provides a way for manual authors to specify old node names and the new nodes to which the old names should be redirected, via the file *manual*-`noderename.cnf`, where *manual* is the base name of the manual. For example, the manual `texinfo.texi` would be supplemented by a file `texinfo-noderename.cnf`.

(This name can be overridden by setting the `RENAMED_NODES_FILE` customization variable; see Section 22.5 [Customization Variables], page 197).

The file is read in pairs of lines, as follows:

```
old-node-name
@@{} new-node-name
```

The usual conversion from Texinfo node names to HTML names is applied; see this entire section for details (see Section 24.4 [HTML Xref], page 226). The unusual '`@@{}`' separator is used because it is not a valid Texinfo construct, so can't appear in the node names.

The effect is that `makeinfo` generates a redirect from *old-node-name* to *new-node-name* when producing HTML output. Thus, external links to the old node are preserved.

Lines consisting only of whitespace are ignored. Comments are indicated with an '`@c`' at the beginning of a line, optionally preceded by whitespace.

Another approach to preserving links to deleted or renamed nodes is to use anchors (see Section 6.3 [`@anchor`], page 59). There is no effective difference between the two approaches.

Appendix A @-Command List

Here is an alphabetical list of the @-commands in Texinfo. Square brackets, [ ], indicate optional arguments; an ellipsis, '...', indicates repeated text.

　　　More specifics on the general syntax of different @-commands are given in the section below.

@whitespace
　　　　　　　An @ followed by a space, tab, or newline produces a normal, stretchable, interword space. See Section 14.3.1 [Multiple Spaces], page 121.

@!　　　　Produce an exclamation point that ends a sentence (usually after an end-of-sentence capital letter). See Section 14.3.3 [Ending a Sentence], page 123.

@"
@'　　　　Generate an umlaut or acute accent, respectively, over the next character, as in ö and ó. See Section 14.4 [Inserting Accents], page 124.

@*　　　　Force a line break. See Section 15.2 [Line Breaks], page 135.

@,{c}　　Generate a cedilla accent under c, as in ç. See Section 14.4 [Inserting Accents], page 124.

@-　　　　Insert a discretionary hyphenation point. See Section 15.3 [@- @hyphenation], page 136.

@.　　　　Produce a period that ends a sentence (usually after an end-of-sentence capital letter). See Section 14.3.3 [Ending a Sentence], page 123.

@/　　　　Produces no output, but allows a line break. See Section 15.2 [Line Breaks], page 135.

@:　　　　Tell TeX to refrain from inserting extra whitespace after an immediately preceding period, question mark, exclamation mark, or colon, as TeX normally would. See Section 14.3.2 [Not Ending a Sentence], page 122.

@=　　　　Generate a macron (bar) accent over the next character, as in ō. See Section 14.4 [Inserting Accents], page 124.

@?　　　　Produce a question mark that ends a sentence (usually after an end-of-sentence capital letter). See Section 14.3.3 [Ending a Sentence], page 123.

@@
@atchar{}
　　　　　　　Insert an at sign, '@'. See Section 14.1.1 [Inserting an Atsign], page 119.

@
@backslashchar{}
　　　　　　　Insert a backslash, '\'; @backslashchar{} works anywhere, while @\ works only inside @math. See Section 14.1.4 [Inserting a Backslash], page 120, and Section 14.7 [Inserting Math], page 127.

@^
@`　　　　Generate a circumflex (hat) or grave accent, respectively, over the next character, as in ô and è. See Section 14.4 [Inserting Accents], page 124.

`@{`

`@lbracechar{}`
> Insert a left brace, '{'. See Section 14.1.2 [Inserting Braces], page 119.

`@}`

`@rbracechar{}`
> Insert a right brace, '}'. See Section 14.1.2 [Inserting Braces], page 119.

`@~`   Generate a tilde accent over the next character, as in Ñ. See Section 14.4 [Inserting Accents], page 124.

`@AA{}`

`@aa{}`   Generate the uppercase and lowercase Scandinavian A-ring letters, respectively: Å, å. See Section 14.4 [Inserting Accents], page 124.

`@abbr{abbreviation}`
> Indicate a general abbreviation, such as 'Comput.'. See Section 9.1.13 [`@abbr`], page 85.

`@acronym{acronym}`
> Indicate an acronym in all capital letters, such as 'NASA'. See Section 9.1.14 [`@acronym`], page 85.

`@AE{}`

`@ae{}`   Generate the uppercase and lowercase AE ligatures, respectively: Æ, æ. See Section 14.4 [Inserting Accents], page 124.

`@afivepaper`
> Change page dimensions for the A5 paper size. See Section 21.12 [A4 Paper], page 186.

`@afourlatex`
`@afourpaper`
`@afourwide`
> Change page dimensions for the A4 paper size. See Section 21.12 [A4 Paper], page 186.

`@alias new=existing`
> Make the command '`@new`' a synonym for the existing command '`@existing`'. See Section 19.4 [`@alias`], page 170.

`@allowcodebreaks true-false`
> Control breaking at '-' and '_' in TeX. See Section 15.4 [`@allowcodebreaks`], page 136.

`@anchor{name}`
> Define *name* as the current location for use as a cross reference target. See Section 6.3 [`@anchor`], page 59.

`@appendix title`
> Begin an appendix. The title appears in the table of contents. In Info, the title is underlined with asterisks. See Section 5.4 [`@unnumbered @appendix`], page 49.

`@appendixsec` *title*
`@appendixsection` *title*

> Begin an appendix section within an appendix. The section title appears in the table of contents. In Info, the title is underlined with equal signs. `@appendixsection` is a longer spelling of the `@appendixsec` command. See Section 5.7 [`@unnumberedsec @appendixsec @heading`], page 50.

`@appendixsubsec` *title*

> Begin an appendix subsection. The title appears in the table of contents. In Info, the title is underlined with hyphens. See Section 5.9 [`@unnumberedsubsec @appendixsubsec @subheading`], page 50.

`@appendixsubsubsec` *title*

> Begin an appendix subsubsection. The title appears in the table of contents. In Info, the title is underlined with periods. See Section 5.10 [`@subsubsection`], page 51.

`@arrow{}` Generate a right arrow glyph: '→'. Used by default for `@click`. See Section 14.9.8 [Click Sequences], page 133.

`@asis`   Used following `@table`, `@ftable`, and `@vtable` to print the table's first column without highlighting ("as is"). See [`@asis`], page 103.

`@author` *author*

> Typeset *author* flushleft and underline it. See Section 3.4.3 [`@title @subtitle @author`], page 36.

`@b{text}` Set *text* in a **bold** font. No effect in Info. See Section 9.2.3 [Fonts], page 87.

`@bullet{}`

> Generate a large round dot, ● ('*' in Info). Often used with `@table`. See Section 14.8.5 [`@bullet`], page 129.

`@bye`   Stop formatting a file. The formatters do not see anything in the input file following `@bye`. See Chapter 4 [Ending a File], page 45.

`@c` *comment*

> Begin a comment in Texinfo. The rest of the line does not appear in any output. A synonym for `@comment`. *DEL* also starts a comment. See Section 1.10 [Comments], page 10.

`@caption` Define the full caption for an `@float`. See Section 12.1.2 [`@caption @shortcaption`], page 108.

`@cartouche`

> Highlight an example or quotation by drawing a box with rounded corners around it. Pair with `@end cartouche`. No effect in Info. See Section 10.16 [`@cartouche`], page 98.

`@center` *line-of-text*

> Center the line of text following the command. See Section 3.4.2 [`@titlefont @center @sp`], page 35.

@centerchap *line-of-text*

>   Like **@chapter**, but centers the chapter title. See Section 5.3 [**@chapter**], page 48.

@chapheading *title*

>   Print an unnumbered chapter-like heading, but omit from the table of contents. In Info, the title is underlined with asterisks. See Section 5.5 [**@majorheading @chapheading**], page 49.

@chapter *title*

>   Begin a numbered chapter. The chapter title appears in the table of contents. In Info, the title is underlined with asterisks. See Section 5.3 [**@chapter**], page 48.

@cindex *entry*

>   Add *entry* to the index of concepts. See Section 13.1 [Defining the Entries of an Index], page 114.

@cite{*reference***}**

>   Highlight the name of a book or other reference that has no companion Info file. See Section 8.10 [**@cite**], page 77.

@clear *flag*

>   Unset *flag*, preventing the Texinfo formatting commands from formatting text between subsequent pairs of **@ifset** *flag* and **@end ifset** commands, and preventing **@value{***flag***}** from expanding to the value to which *flag* is set. See Section 18.5 [**@set @clear @value**], page 159.

@click{}   Represent a single "click" in a GUI. Used within **@clicksequence**. See Section 14.9.8 [Click Sequences], page 133.

@clicksequence{*action* **@click{}** *action***}**

>   Represent a sequence of clicks in a GUI. See Section 14.9.8 [Click Sequences], page 133.

@clickstyle @*cmd*

>   Execute **@***cmd* for each **@click**; the default is **@arrow**. The usual following empty braces on **@***cmd* are omitted. See Section 14.9.8 [Click Sequences], page 133.

@code{*sample-code***}**

>   Indicate an expression, a syntactically complete token of a program, or a program name. Unquoted in Info output. See Section 9.1.2 [**@code**], page 79.

@codequotebacktick *on-off*
@codequoteundirected *on-off*

>   Control output of ` and ' in code examples. See Section 14.2 [Inserting Quote Characters], page 121.

@comma{}   Insert a comma ',' character; only needed when a literal comma would be taken as an argument separator. See Section 14.1.3 [Inserting a Comma], page 120.

@command{*command-name***}**

>   Indicate a command name, such as **ls**. See Section 9.1.10 [**@command**], page 84.

`@comment` *comment*

> Begin a comment in Texinfo. The rest of the line does not appear in any output. A synonym for `@c`. See Section 1.10 [Comments], page 10.

`@contents`

> Print a complete table of contents. Has no effect in Info, which uses menus instead. See Section 3.5 [Generating a Table of Contents], page 38.

`@copying`   Specify copyright holders and copying conditions for the document Pair with `@end cartouche`. See Section 3.3.1 [@copying], page 33.

`@copyright{}`

> Generate the copyright symbol ©. See Section 14.8.2 [@copyright], page 128.

`@defcodeindex` *index-name*

> Define a new index and its indexing command. Print entries in an `@code` font. See Section 13.5 [Defining New Indices], page 117.

`@defcv` *category class name*
`@defcvx` *category class name*

> Format a description for a variable associated with a class in object-oriented programming. Takes three arguments: the category of thing being defined, the class to which it belongs, and its name. See Chapter 16 [Definition Commands], page 139.

`@deffn` *category name arguments...*
`@deffnx` *category name arguments...*

> Format a description for a function, interactive command, or similar entity that may take arguments. `@deffn` takes as arguments the category of entity being described, the name of this particular entity, and its arguments, if any. See Chapter 16 [Definition Commands], page 139.

`@defindex` *index-name*

> Define a new index and its indexing command. Print entries in a roman font. See Section 13.5 [Defining New Indices], page 117.

`@definfoenclose` *newcmd, before, after*

> Must be used within `@ifinfo`; create a new command `@newcmd` for Info that marks text by enclosing it in strings that precede and follow the text. See Section 19.5 [@definfoenclose], page 171.

`@defivar` *class instance-variable-name*
`@defivarx` *class instance-variable-name*

> Format a description for an instance variable in object-oriented programming. The command is equivalent to '`@defcv {Instance Variable} ...`'. See Chapter 16 [Definition Commands], page 139.

`@defmac` *macroname arguments...*
`@defmacx` *macroname arguments...*

> Format a description for a macro; equivalent to '`@deffn Macro ...`'. See Chapter 16 [Definition Commands], page 139.

`@defmethod` *class method-name arguments...*
`@defmethodx` *class method-name arguments...*

> Format a description for a method in object-oriented programming; equivalent to '`@defop Method ...`'. See Chapter 16 [Definition Commands], page 139.

`@defop` *category class name arguments...*
`@defopx` *category class name arguments...*

> Format a description for an operation in object-oriented programming. `@defop` takes as arguments the name of the category of operation, the name of the operation's class, the name of the operation, and its arguments, if any. See Chapter 16 [Definition Commands], page 139, and Section 16.5.6 [Abstract Objects], page 147.

`@defopt` *option-name*
`@defoptx` *option-name*

> Format a description for a user option; equivalent to '`@defvr {User Option} ...`'. See Chapter 16 [Definition Commands], page 139.

`@defspec` *special-form-name arguments...*
`@defspecx` *special-form-name arguments...*

> Format a description for a special form; equivalent to '`@deffn {Special Form} ...`'. See Chapter 16 [Definition Commands], page 139.

`@deftp` *category name-of-type attributes...*
`@deftpx` *category name-of-type attributes...*

> Format a description for a data type; its arguments are the category, the name of the type (e.g., '`int`') , and then the names of attributes of objects of that type. See Chapter 16 [Definition Commands], page 139, and Section 16.5.5 [Data Types], page 146.

`@deftypecv` *category class data-type name*
`@deftypecvx` *category class data-type name*

> Format a description for a typed class variable in object-oriented programming. See Chapter 16 [Definition Commands], page 139, and Section 16.5.6 [Abstract Objects], page 147.

`@deftypefn` *category data-type name arguments...*
`@deftypefnx` *category data-type name arguments...*

> Format a description for a function or similar entity that may take arguments and that is typed. `@deftypefn` takes as arguments the category of entity being described, the type, the name of the entity, and its arguments, if any. See Chapter 16 [Definition Commands], page 139.

`@deftypefnnewline` *on-off*

> Specifies whether return types for `@deftypefn` and similar are printed on lines by themselves; default is off. See Section 16.5.3 [Functions in Typed Languages], page 144.

`@deftypefun` *data-type function-name arguments...*
`@deftypefunx` *data-type function-name arguments...*

> Format a description for a function in a typed language. The command is equivalent to '`@deftypefn Function ...`'. See Chapter 16 [Definition Commands], page 139.

`@deftypeivar` *class data-type variable-name*
`@deftypeivarx` *class data-type variable-name*

> Format a description for a typed instance variable in object-oriented programming. See Chapter 16 [Definition Commands], page 139, and Section 16.5.6 [Abstract Objects], page 147.

`@deftypemethod` *class data-type method-name arguments...*
`@deftypemethodx` *class data-type method-name arguments...*

> Format a description for a typed method in object-oriented programming. See Chapter 16 [Definition Commands], page 139.

`@deftypeop` *category class data-type name arguments...*
`@deftypeopx` *category class data-type name arguments...*

> Format a description for a typed operation in object-oriented programming. See Chapter 16 [Definition Commands], page 139, and Section 16.5.6 [Abstract Objects], page 147.

`@deftypevar` *data-type variable-name*
`@deftypevarx` *data-type variable-name*

> Format a description for a variable in a typed language. The command is equivalent to '`@deftypevr Variable ...`'. See Chapter 16 [Definition Commands], page 139.

`@deftypevr` *category data-type name*
`@deftypevrx` *category data-type name*

> Format a description for something like a variable in a typed language—an entity that records a value. Takes as arguments the category of entity being described, the type, and the name of the entity. See Chapter 16 [Definition Commands], page 139.

`@defun` *function-name arguments...*
`@defunx` *function-name arguments...*

> Format a description for a function; equivalent to '`@deffn Function ...`'. See Chapter 16 [Definition Commands], page 139.

`@defvar` *variable-name*
`@defvarx` *variable-name*

> Format a description for a variable; equivalent to '`@defvr Variable ...`'. See Chapter 16 [Definition Commands], page 139.

`@defvr` *category name*
`@defvrx` *category name*

> Format a description for any kind of variable. `@defvr` takes as arguments the category of the entity and the name of the entity. See Chapter 16 [Definition Commands], page 139.

`@detailmenu`

> Mark the (optional) detailed node listing in a master menu. See Section 3.6.2 [Master Menu Parts], page 40.

`@dfn{term}`

> Indicate the introductory or defining use of a term. See Section 9.1.12 [`@dfn`], page 84.

`@DH{}`

`@dh{}`   Generate the uppercase and lowercase Icelandic letter eth, respectively: Ð, ð. See Section 14.4 [Inserting Accents], page 124.

`@dircategory dirpart`

> Specify a part of the Info directory menu where this file's entry should go. See Section 23.2.4 [Installing Dir Entries], page 218.

`@direntry`

> Begin the Info directory menu entry for this file. Pair with `@end direntry`. See Section 23.2.4 [Installing Dir Entries], page 218.

`@display`   Begin a kind of example. Like `@example` (indent text, do not fill), but do not select a new font. Pair with `@end display`. See Section 10.9 [`@display`], page 94.

`@dmn{dimension}`

> Format a unit of measure, as in 12 pt. Causes TEX to insert a thin space before *dimension*. No effect in Info. See Section 14.3.5 [`@dmn`], page 124.

`@docbook`   Enter Docbook completely. Pair with `@end docbook`. See Section 18.3 [Raw Formatter Commands], page 157.

`@documentdescription`

> Set the document description text, included in the HTML output. Pair with `@end documentdescription`. See Section 3.7.1 [`@documentdescription`], page 41.

`@documentencoding enc`

> Declare the input encoding to be *enc*. See Section 17.2 [`@documentencoding`], page 153.

`@documentlanguage CC`

> Declare the document language as the two-character ISO-639 abbreviation *CC*. See Section 17.1 [`@documentlanguage`], page 152.

`@dotaccent{c}`

> Generate a dot accent over the character *c*, as in ȯ. See Section 14.4 [Inserting Accents], page 124.

`@dotless{i-or-j}`

> Generate dotless i ('ı') and dotless j ('ȷ'). See Section 14.4 [Inserting Accents], page 124.

`@dots{}`   Generate an ellipsis, '...'. See Section 14.8.4 [`@dots`], page 128.

`@email{address[, displayed-text]}`

> Indicate an electronic mail address. See Section 9.1.16 [`@email`], page 86.

`@emph{text}`

> Emphasize *text*, by using *italics* where possible, and enclosing in asterisks in Info. See Section 9.2 [Emphasizing Text], page 86.

`@end environment`

> Ends *environment*, as in '`@end example`'. See Section 1.8 [@-commands], page 8.

`@enddots{}`

> Generate an end-of-sentence ellipsis, like this: ... See Section 14.8.4 [`@dots`], page 128.

`@enumerate [number-or-letter]`

> Begin a numbered list, using `@item` for each entry. Optionally, start list with *number-or-letter*. Pair with `@end enumerate`. See Section 11.3 [`@enumerate`], page 101.

`@env{environment-variable}`

> Indicate an environment variable name, such as PATH. See Section 9.1.8 [`@env`], page 83.

`@equiv{}`   Indicate to the reader the exact equivalence of two forms with a glyph: '≡'. See Section 14.9.6 [`@equiv`], page 132.

`@error{}`   Indicate to the reader with a glyph that the following text is an error message: ' error '. See Section 14.9.5 [`@error`], page 131.

`@errormsg{msg}`

> Report *msg* as an error to standard error, and exit unsuccessfully. Texinfo commands within *msg* are expanded to plain text. See Chapter 18 [Conditionals], page 155, and Section 19.6 [External Macro Processors], page 172.

`@euro{}`   Generate the Euro currency sign. See Section 14.8.6 [`@euro`], page 129.

`@evenfooting [left] @| [center] @| [right]`
`@evenheading [left] @| [center] @| [right]`

> Specify page footings resp. headings for even-numbered (left-hand) pages. See Section D.4 [How to Make Your Own Headings], page 271.

`@everyfooting [left] @| [center] @| [right]`
`@everyheading [left] @| [center] @| [right]`

> Specify page footings resp. headings for every page. Not relevant to Info. See Section D.4 [How to Make Your Own Headings], page 271.

`@example`   Begin an example. Indent text, do not fill, and select fixed-width font. Pair with `@end example`. See Section 10.4 [`@example`], page 91.

`@exampleindent indent`

> Indent example-like environments by *indent* number of spaces (perhaps 0). See Section 3.7.6 [`@exampleindent`], page 44.

`@exclamdown{}`

> Generate an upside-down exclamation point. See Section 14.4 [Inserting Accents], page 124.

@exdent *line-of-text*

> Remove any indentation a line might have. See Section 10.11 [**@exdent**], page 95.

@expansion{}

> Indicate the result of a macro expansion to the reader with a special glyph: '↦'. See Section 14.9.3 [**@expansion**], page 131.

@file{*filename***}**

> Highlight the name of a file, buffer, node, directory, etc. See Section 9.1.9 [**@file**], page 84.

@finalout

> Prevent TeX from printing large black warning rectangles beside over-wide lines. See Section 21.10 [Overfull hboxes], page 185.

@findex *entry*

> Add *entry* to the index of functions. See Section 13.1 [Defining the Entries of an Index], page 114.

@firstparagraphindent *word*

> Control indentation of the first paragraph after section headers according to *word*, one of 'none' or 'insert'. See Section 3.7.5 [**@firstparagraphindent**], page 44.

@float   Environment to define floating material. Pair with **@end float**. See Section 12.1 [Floats], page 107.

@flushleft
@flushright

> Do not fill text; left (right) justify every line while leaving the right (left) end ragged. Leave font as is. Pair with **@end flushleft** (**@end flushright**). See Section 10.12 [**@flushleft @flushright**], page 95.

@fonttextsize *10-11*

> Change the size of the main body font in the TeX output. See Section 9.2.3 [Fonts], page 87.

@footnote{*text-of-footnote***}**

> Enter a footnote. Footnote text is printed at the bottom of the page by TeX; Info may format in either 'End' node or 'Separate' node style. See Section 12.3 [Footnotes], page 111.

@footnotestyle *style*

> Specify an Info file's footnote style, either 'end' for the end node style or 'separate' for the separate node style. See Section 12.3 [Footnotes], page 111.

@format   Begin a kind of example. Like **@display**, but do not indent. Pair with **@end format**. See Section 10.4 [**@example**], page 91.

@frenchspacing *on-off*

> Control spacing after punctuation. See Section 14.3.4 [**@frenchspacing**], page 123.

@ftable *formatting-command*

Begin a two-column table, using @item for each entry. Automatically enter each of the items in the first column into the index of functions. Pair with @end ftable. The same as @table, except for indexing. See Section 11.4.2 [@ftable @vtable], page 104.

@geq{}   Generate a greater-than-or-equal sign, '$\geq$'. See Section 14.8.10 [@geq @leq], page 130.

@group   Disallow page breaks within following text. Pair with @end group. Ignored in Info. See Section 15.9 [@group], page 137.

@guillemetleft{}
@guillemetright{}
@guillemotleft{}
@guillemotright{}
@guilsinglleft{}
@guilsinglright{}

Double and single angle quotation marks: « » ‹ ›. @guillemotleft and @guillemotright are synonyms for @guillemetleft and @guillemetright. See Section 14.5 [Inserting Quotation Marks], page 125.

@H{c}   Generate the long Hungarian umlaut accent over *c*, as in ő.

@hashchar{}

Insert a hash '#' character; only needed when a literal hash would introduce #line directive. See Section 14.1.5 [Inserting a Hashsign], page 120, and Section 19.6 [External Macro Processors], page 172.

@heading *title*

Print an unnumbered section-like heading, but omit from the table of contents. In Info, the title is underlined with equal signs. See Section 5.7 [@unnumberedsec @appendixsec @heading], page 50.

@headings *on-off-single-double*

Turn page headings on or off, and/or specify single-sided or double-sided page headings for printing. See Section 3.7.3 [@headings], page 42.

@headitem

Begin a heading row in a multitable. See Section 11.5.2 [Multitable Rows], page 105.

@headitemfont{text}

Set *text* in the font used for multitable heading rows; mostly useful in multitable templates. See Section 11.5.2 [Multitable Rows], page 105.

@html   Enter HTML completely. Pair with @end html. See Section 18.3 [Raw Formatter Commands], page 157.

@hyphenation{hy-phen-a-ted words}

Explicitly define hyphenation points. See Section 15.3 [@- @hyphenation], page 136.

@i{text}   Set *text* in an *italic* font. No effect in Info. See Section 9.2.3 [Fonts], page 87.

`@ifclear` *txivar*

> If the Texinfo variable *txivar* is not set, format the following text. Pair with `@end ifclear`. See Section 18.5 [`@set @clear @value`], page 159.

`@ifcommanddefined` *txicmd*
`@ifcommandnotdefined` *txicmd*

> If the Texinfo code '`@txicmd`' is (not) defined, format the follow text. Pair with the corresponding `@end ifcommand....` See Section 18.6 [Testing for Texinfo Commands], page 163.

`@ifdocbook`
`@ifhtml`
`@ifinfo`   Begin text that will appear only in the given output format. `@ifinfo` output appears in both Info and (for historical compatibility) plain text output. Pair with `@end ifdocbook` resp. `@end ifhtml` resp. `@end ifinfo`. See Chapter 18 [Conditionals], page 155.

`@ifnotdocbook`
`@ifnothtml`
`@ifnotplaintext`
`@ifnottex`
`@ifnotxml`

> Begin text to be ignored in one output format but not the others. `@ifnothtml` text is omitted from HTML output, etc. Pair with the corresponding `@end` `ifnotformat`. See Chapter 18 [Conditionals], page 155.

`@ifnotinfo`

> Begin text to appear in output other than Info and (for historical compatibility) plain text. Pair with `@end ifnotinfo`. See Chapter 18 [Conditionals], page 155.

`@ifplaintext`

> Begin text that will appear only in the plain text output. Pair with `@end ifplaintext`. See Chapter 18 [Conditionals], page 155.

`@ifset` *txivar*

> If the Texinfo variable *txivar* is set, format the following text. Pair with `@end ifset`. See Section 18.5 [`@set @clear @value`], page 159.

`@iftex`   Begin text to appear only in the TeX output. Pair with `@end iftex`. See Chapter 18 [Conditionally Visible Text], page 155.

`@ifxml`   Begin text that will appear only in the XML output. Pair with `@end ifxml`. See Chapter 18 [Conditionals], page 155.

`@ignore`   Begin text that will not appear in any output. Pair with `@end ignore`. See Section 1.10 [Comments and Ignored Text], page 10.

`@image{`*filename, [width], [height], [alt], [ext]*`}`

> Include graphics image in external *filename* scaled to the given *width* and/or *height*, using *alt* text and looking for '*filename.ext*' in HTML. See Section 12.2 [Images], page 109.

`@include` *filename*

Read the contents of Texinfo source file *filename*. See Chapter 20 [Include Files], page 174.

`@indent`   Insert paragraph indentation. See Section 10.15 [`@indent`], page 97.

`@indentedblock`

Indent a block of arbitary text on the left. Pair with `@end indentedblock`. See Section 10.3 [`@indentedblock`], page 91.

`@indicateurl{`*indicateurl*`}`

Indicate text that is a uniform resource locator for the World Wide Web. See Section 9.1.15 [`@indicateurl`], page 86.

`@inforef{`*node-name, [entry-name], info-file-name*`}`

Make a cross reference to an Info file for which there is no printed manual. See Section 8.8 [`@inforef`], page 74.

`@inlinefmt{`*fmt, text*`}`

Insert *text* only if the output format is *fmt*. See Section 18.4 [Inline Conditionals], page 158.

`@inlinefmtifelse{`*fmt, text, else-text*`}`

Insert *text* if the output format is *fmt*, else *else-text*.

`@inlineifclear{`*var, text*`}`
`@inlineifset{`*var, text*`}`

Insert *text* only if the Texinfo variable *var* is (not) set.

`@inlineraw{`*fmt, raw-text*`}`

Insert *text* as in a raw conditional, only if the output format is *fmt*.

`\input` *macro-definitions-file*

Use the specified macro definitions file. This command is used only in the first line of a Texinfo file to cause TeX to make use of the `texinfo` macro definitions file. The \ in `\input` is used instead of an @ because TeX does not recognize @ until after it has read the definitions file. See Section 3.2 [Texinfo File Header], page 30.

`@insertcopying`

Insert the text previously defined with the `@copying` environment. See Section 3.3.2 [`@insertcopying`], page 34.

`@item`   Indicate the beginning of a marked paragraph for `@itemize` and `@enumerate`; indicate the beginning of the text of a first column entry for `@table`, `@ftable`, and `@vtable`. See Chapter 11 [Lists and Tables], page 99.

`@itemize` *mark-generating-character-or-command*

Begin an unordered list: indented paragraphs with a mark, such as `@bullet`, inside the left margin at the beginning of each item. Pair with `@end itemize`. See Section 11.2 [`@itemize`], page 100.

`@itemx`   Like `@item` but do not generate extra vertical space above the item text. Thus, when several items have the same description, use `@item` for the first and `@itemx` for the others. See Section 11.4.3 [`@itemx`], page 104.

`@kbd{keyboard-characters}`

Indicate characters of input to be typed by users. See Section 9.1.3 [`@kbd`], page 80.

`@kbdinputstyle style`

Specify when `@kbd` should use a font distinct from `@code` according to *style*: `code`, `distinct`, `example`. See Section 9.1.3 [`@kbd`], page 80.

`@key{key-name}`

Indicate the name of a key on a keyboard. See Section 9.1.4 [`@key`], page 81.

`@kindex entry`

Add *entry* to the index of keys. See Section 13.1 [Defining the Entries of an Index], page 114.

`@L{}`

`@l{}`   Generate the uppercase and lowercase Polish suppressed-L letters, respectively: Ł, ł.

`@LaTeX{}`   Generate the LaTeX logo. See Section 14.8.1 [`@TeX @LaTeX`], page 128.

`@leq{}`   Generate a less-than-or-equal sign, '$\leq$'. See Section 14.8.10 [`@geq @leq`], page 130.

`@lisp`   Begin an example of Lisp code. Indent text, do not fill, and select fixed-width font. Pair with `@end lisp`. See Section 10.7 [`@lisp`], page 93.

`@listoffloats`

Produce a table-of-contents-like listing of `@floats`. See Section 12.1.3 [`@listoffloats`], page 108.

`@lowersections`

Change subsequent chapters to sections, sections to subsections, and so on. See Section 5.12 [`@raisesections` and `@lowersections`], page 52.

`@macro macroname {params}`

Define a new Texinfo command `@macroname{params}`. Pair with `@end macro`. See Section 19.1 [Defining Macros], page 165.

`@majorheading title`

Print an unnumbered chapter-like heading, but omit from the table of contents. This generates more vertical whitespace before the heading than the `@chapheading` command. See Section 5.5 [`@majorheading @chapheading`], page 49.

`@math{mathematical-expression}`

Format a mathematical expression. See Section 14.7 [Inserting Math], page 127.

`@menu`   Mark the beginning of a menu of nodes. No effect in a printed manual. Pair with `@end menu`. See Chapter 7 [Menus], page 62.

`@minus{}`   Generate a minus sign, '$-$'. See Section 14.8.9 [`@minus`], page 129.

`@multitable column-width-spec`

Begin a multi-column table. Begin each row with `@item` or `@headitem`, and separate columns with `@tab`. Pair with `@end multitable`. See Section 11.5.1 [Multitable Column Widths], page 105.

@need *n*   Start a new page in a printed manual if fewer than *n* mils (thousandths of an inch) remain on the current page. See Section 15.10 [@need], page 138.

@node *name, next, previous, up*
          Begin a new node. See Section 6.1 [@node], page 54.

@noindent
          Prevent text from being indented as if it were a new paragraph. See Section 10.14 [@noindent], page 97.

@novalidate
          Suppress validation of node references and omit creation of auxiliary files with TEX. Use before @setfilename. See Section 22.4 [Pointer Validation], page 196.

@O{}
@o{}   Generate the uppercase and lowercase O-with-slash letters, respectively: Ø, ø.

@oddfooting [*left*] @| [*center*] @| [*right*]
@oddheading [*left*] @| [*center*] @| [*right*]
          Specify page footings resp. headings for odd-numbered (right-hand) pages. See Section D.4 [How to Make Your Own Headings], page 271.

@OE{}
@oe{}   Generate the uppercase and lowercase OE ligatures, respectively: Œ, œ. See Section 14.4 [Inserting Accents], page 124.

@ogonek{*c*}
          Generate an ogonek diacritic under the next character, as in ą. See Section 14.4 [Inserting Accents], page 124.

@option{*option-name*}
          Indicate a command-line option, such as -l or --help. See Section 9.1.11 [@option], page 84.

@ordf{}
@ordm{} Generate the feminine and masculine Spanish ordinals, respectively: ª, º. See Section 14.4 [Inserting Accents], page 124.

@page   Start a new page in a printed manual. No effect in Info. See Section 15.8 [@page], page 137.

@pagesizes [*width*] [, *height*]
          Change page dimensions. See [pagesizes], page 186.

@paragraphindent *indent*
          Indent paragraphs by *indent* number of spaces (perhaps 0); preserve source file indentation if *indent* is asis. See Section 3.7.4 [@paragraphindent], page 43.

@part *title*
          Begin a group of chapters or appendixes; included in the tables of contents and produces a page of its own in printed output. See Section 5.11 [@part], page 51.

@pindex *entry*
          Add *entry* to the index of programs. See Section 13.1 [Defining the Entries of an Index], page 114.

@point{}   Indicate the position of point in a buffer to the reader with a glyph: '⋆'. See
           Section 14.9.7 [@point], page 132.

@pounds{}

           Generate the pounds sterling currency sign. See Section 14.8.7 [@pounds],
           page 129.

@print{}   Indicate printed output to the reader with a glyph: '⊣'. See Section 14.9.4
           [@print], page 131.

@printindex index-name

           Generate the alphabetized index for index-name (using two columns in a printed
           manual). See Section 4.1 [Printing Indices & Menus], page 45.

@pxref{node, [entry], [node-title], [info-file], [manual]}

           Make a reference that starts with a lowercase 'see' in a printed manual. Use
           within parentheses only. Only the first argument is mandatory. See Section 8.7
           [@pxref], page 73.

@questiondown{}

           Generate an upside-down question mark. See Section 14.4 [Inserting Accents],
           page 124.

@quotation

           Narrow the margins to indicate text that is quoted from another work. Takes
           optional argument specifying prefix text, e.g., an author name. Pair with @end
           quotation. See Section 10.2 [@quotation], page 90.

@quotedblleft{}
@quotedblright{}
@quoteleft{}
@quoteright{}
@quotedblbase{}
@quotesinglbase{}

           Produce various quotation marks: " " ' ' „ ,. See Section 14.5 [Inserting Quo-
           tation Marks], page 125.

@r{text}   Set text in the regular roman font. No effect in Info. See Section 9.2.3 [Fonts],
           page 87.

@raggedright

           Fill text; left justify every line while leaving the right end ragged. Leave font
           as is. Pair with @end raggedright. No effect in Info. See Section 10.13
           [@raggedright], page 96.

@raisesections

           Change subsequent sections to chapters, subsections to sections, and so on. See
           Section 5.12 [Raise/lower sections], page 52.

@ref{node, [entry], [node-title], [info-file], [manual]}

           Make a plain reference that does not start with any special text. Follow com-
           mand with a punctuation mark. Only the first argument is mandatory. See
           Section 8.6 [@ref], page 73.

`@refill`   This command used to refill and indent the paragraph after all the other processing has been done. It is no longer needed, since all formatters now automatically refill as needed, but you may still see it in the source to some manuals, as it does no harm.

`@registeredsymbol{}`
              Generate the legal symbol ®. See Section 14.8.3 [`@registeredsymbol`], page 128.

`@result{}`
              Indicate the result of an expression to the reader with a special glyph: '⇒'. See Section 14.9.2 [`@result`], page 130.

`@ringaccent{c}`
              Generate a ring accent over the next character, as in å. See Section 14.4 [Inserting Accents], page 124.

`@samp{text}`
              Indicate a literal example of a sequence of characters, in general. Quoted in Info output. See Section 9.1.5 [`@samp`], page 82.

`@sansserif{text}`
              Set *text* in a sans serif font if possible. No effect in Info. See Section 9.2.3 [Fonts], page 87.

`@sc{text}`
              Set *text* in a small caps font in printed output, and uppercase in Info. See Section 9.2.2 [Smallcaps], page 87.

`@section title`
              Begin a section within a chapter. The section title appears in the table of contents. In Info, the title is underlined with equal signs. Within `@chapter` and `@appendix`, the section title is numbered; within `@unnumbered`, the section is unnumbered. See Section 5.6 [`@section`], page 49.

`@set txivar [string]`
              Define the Texinfo variable *txivar*, optionally to the value *string*. See Section 18.5 [`@set @clear @value`], page 159.

`@setchapternewpage on-off-odd`
              Specify whether chapters start on new pages, and if so, whether on odd-numbered (right-hand) new pages. See Section 3.7.2 [`@setchapternewpage`], page 41.

`@setcontentsaftertitlepage`
              Put the table of contents after the '`@end titlepage`' even if the `@contents` command is at the end. See Section 3.5 [Contents], page 38.

`@setfilename info-file-name`
              Provide a name to be used for the output files. This command is essential for TeX formatting as well, even though it produces no output of its own. See Section 3.2.3 [`@setfilename`], page 31.

@setshortcontentsaftertitlepage

> Place the short table of contents after the '@end titlepage' command even if the @shortcontents command is at the end. See Section 3.5 [Contents], page 38.

@settitle *title*

> Specify the title for page headers in a printed manual, and the default document title for HTML '<head>'. See Section 3.2.4 [@settitle], page 32.

@shortcaption

> Define the short caption for an @float. See Section 12.1.2 [@caption @shortcaption], page 108.

@shortcontents

> Print a short table of contents, with chapter-level entries only. Not relevant to Info, which uses menus rather than tables of contents. See Section 3.5 [Generating a Table of Contents], page 38.

@shorttitlepage *title*

> Generate a minimal title page. See Section 3.4.1 [@titlepage], page 34.

@slanted{text}

> Set *text* in a *slanted* font if possible. No effect in Info. See Section 9.2.3 [Fonts], page 87.

@smallbook

> Cause TeX to produce a printed manual in a 7 by 9.25 inch format rather than the regular 8.5 by 11 inch format. See Section 21.11 [@smallbook], page 186. Also, see Section 10.8 [@small...], page 94.

@smalldisplay

> Begin a kind of example. Like @display, but use a smaller font size where possible. Pair with @end smalldisplay. See Section 10.8 [@small...], page 94.

@smallexample

> Begin an example. Like @example, but use a smaller font size where possible. Pair with @end smallexample. See Section 10.8 [@small...], page 94.

@smallformat

> Begin a kind of example. Like @format, but use a smaller font size where possible. Pair with @end smallformat. See Section 10.8 [@small...], page 94.

@smallindentedblock

> Like @indentedblock, but use a smaller font size where possible. Pair with @end smallindentedblock. See Section 10.8 [@small...], page 94.

@smalllisp

> Begin an example of Lisp code. Same as @smallexample. Pair with @end smalllisp. See Section 10.8 [@small...], page 94.

@smallquotation

> Like @quotation, but use a smaller font size where possible. Pair with @end smallquotation. See Section 10.8 [@small...], page 94.

`@sp n`   Skip *n* blank lines. See Section 15.7 [`@sp`], page 137.

`@ss{}`   Generate the German sharp-S es-zet letter, ß. See Section 14.4 [Inserting Accents], page 124.

`@strong {text}`

Emphasize *text* more strongly than `@emph`, by using **boldface** where possible; enclosed in asterisks in Info. See [Emphasizing Text], page 87.

`@sub {text}`

Set *text* as a subscript. See Section 14.6 [Inserting Subscripts and Superscripts], page 126.

`@subheading title`

Print an unnumbered subsection-like heading, but omit from the table of contents of a printed manual. In Info, the title is underlined with hyphens. See Section 5.9 [`@unnumberedsubsec @appendixsubsec @subheading`], page 50.

`@subsection title`

Begin a subsection within a section. The subsection title appears in the table of contents. In Info, the title is underlined with hyphens. Same context-dependent numbering as `@section`. See Section 5.8 [`@subsection`], page 50.

`@subsubheading title`

Print an unnumbered subsubsection-like heading, but omit from the table of contents of a printed manual. In Info, the title is underlined with periods. See Section 5.10 [`@subsubsection`], page 51.

`@subsubsection title`

Begin a subsubsection within a subsection. The subsubsection title appears in the table of contents. In Info, the title is underlined with periods. Same context-dependent numbering as `@section`. See Section 5.10 [`@subsubsection`], page 51.

`@subtitle title`

In a printed manual, set a subtitle in a normal sized font flush to the right-hand side of the page. Not relevant to Info, which does not have title pages. See Section 3.4.3 [`@title @subtitle @author`], page 36.

`@summarycontents`

Print a short table of contents. Synonym for `@shortcontents`. See Section 3.5 [Generating a Table of Contents], page 38.

`@sup {text}`

Set *text* as a superscript. See Section 14.6 [Inserting Subscripts and Superscripts], page 126.

`@syncodeindex from-index to-index`

Merge the index named in the first argument into the index named in the second argument, formatting the entries from the first index with `@code`. See Section 13.4 [Combining Indices], page 116.

`@synindex` *from-index to-index*
> Merge the index named in the first argument into the index named in the second argument. Do not change the font of *from-index* entries. See Section 13.4 [Combining Indices], page 116.

`@t{text}` Set *text* in a `fixed-width`, typewriter-like font. No effect in Info. See Section 9.2.3 [Fonts], page 87.

`@tab` Separate columns in a row of a multitable. See Section 11.5.2 [Multitable Rows], page 105.

`@table` *formatting-command*
> Begin a two-column table (description list), using `@item` for each entry. Write each first column entry on the same line as `@item`. First column entries are printed in the font resulting from *formatting-command*. Pair with `@end table`. See Section 11.4 [Making a Two-column Table], page 102. Also see Section 11.4.2 [`@ftable @vtable`], page 104, and Section 11.4.3 [`@itemx`], page 104.

`@TeX{}` Generate the TeX logo. See Section 14.8.1 [`@TeX @LaTeX`], page 128.

`@tex` Enter TeX completely. Pair with `@end tex`. See Section 18.3 [Raw Formatter Commands], page 157.

`@textdegree{}`
> Generate the degree symbol. See Section 14.8.8 [`@textdegree`], page 129.

`@thischapter`
`@thischaptername`
`@thischapternum`
`@thisfile`
`@thispage`
`@thistitle`
> Only allowed in a heading or footing. Stands for, respectively, the number and name of the current chapter (in the format 'Chapter 1: Title'), the current chapter name only, the current chapter number only, the filename, the current page number, and the title of the document, respectively. See Section D.4 [How to Make Your Own Headings], page 271.

`@TH{}`
`@th{}` Generate the uppercase and lowercase Icelandic letter thorn, respectively: Þ, þ. See Section 14.4 [Inserting Accents], page 124.

`@tie{}` Generate a normal interword space at which a line break is not allowed. See Section 15.6 [`@tie`], page 137.

`@tieaccent{cc}`
> Generate a tie-after accent over the next two characters *cc*, as in 'o͡o'. See Section 14.4 [Inserting Accents], page 124.

`@tindex` *entry*
> Add *entry* to the index of data types. See Section 13.1 [Defining the Entries of an Index], page 114.

`@title` *title*

> In a printed manual, set a title flush to the left-hand side of the page in a larger than normal font and underline it with a black rule. Not relevant to Info, which does not have title pages. See Section 3.4.3 [`@title @subtitle @author`], page 36.

`@titlefont{text}`

> In a printed manual, print *text* in a larger than normal font. See Section 3.4.2 [`@titlefont @center @sp`], page 35.

`@titlepage`

> Begin the title page. Write the command on a line of its own, paired with `@end titlepage`. Nothing between `@titlepage` and `@end titlepage` appears in Info. See Section 3.4.1 [`@titlepage`], page 34.

`@today{}`   Insert the current date, in '1 Jan 1900' style. See Section D.4 [How to Make Your Own Headings], page 271.

`@top` *title*

> Mark the topmost `@node` in the file, which must be defined on the line immediately preceding the `@top` command. The title is formatted as a chapter-level heading. The entire top node, including the `@node` and `@top` lines, are normally enclosed with `@ifnottex ... @end ifnottex`. In TeX and `texinfo-format-buffer`, the `@top` command is merely a synonym for `@unnumbered`. See Section 6.2 [makeinfo Pointer Creation], page 58.

`@U{hex}`   Output a representation of Unicode character U+*hex*. See Section 14.10 [Inserting Unicode], page 133.

`@u{c}`
`@ubaraccent{c}`
`@udotaccent{c}`

> Generate a breve, underbar, or underdot accent, respectively, over or under the character *c*, as in ŏ, o̱, o̦. See Section 14.4 [Inserting Accents], page 124.

`@unmacro` *macroname*

> Undefine the macro `@macroname` if it has been defined. See Section 19.1 [Defining Macros], page 165.

`@unnumbered` *title*

> Begin a chapter that appears without chapter numbers of any kind. The title appears in the table of contents. In Info, the title is underlined with asterisks. See Section 5.4 [`@unnumbered @appendix`], page 49.

`@unnumberedsec` *title*

> Begin a section that appears without section numbers of any kind. The title appears in the table of contents of a printed manual. In Info, the title is underlined with equal signs. See Section 5.7 [`@unnumberedsec @appendixsec @heading`], page 50.

`@unnumberedsubsec` *title*

> Begin an unnumbered subsection. The title appears in the table of contents. In Info, the title is underlined with hyphens. See Section 5.9 [`@unnumberedsubsec` `@appendixsubsec` `@subheading`], page 50.

`@unnumberedsubsubsec` *title*

> Begin an unnumbered subsubsection. The title appears in the table of contents. In Info, the title is underlined with periods. See Section 5.10 [`@subsubsection`], page 51.

`@uref{`*url*`[, `*displayed-text*`] [, `*replacement*`}`
`@url{`*url*`[, `*displayed-text*`] [, `*replacement*`}`

> Define a cross reference to an external uniform resource locator, e.g., for the World Wide Web. See Section 8.9 [`@url`], page 75.

`@urefbreakstyle` *style*

> Specify how `@uref`/`@url` should break at special characters: `after`, `before`, `none`. See Section 8.9 [`@url`], page 75.

`@v{`*c*`}`   Generate check accent over the character *c*, as in ǒ. See Section 14.4 [Inserting Accents], page 124.

`@value{`*txivar*`}`

> Insert the value, if any, of the Texinfo variable *txivar*, previously defined by `@set`. See Section 18.5 [`@set` `@clear` `@value`], page 159.

`@var{`*metasyntactic-variable*`}`

> Highlight a metasyntactic variable, which is something that stands for another piece of text. See Section 9.1.7 [`@var`], page 83.

`@verb{`*delim literal delim*`}`

> Output *literal*, delimited by the single character *delim*, exactly as is (in the fixed-width font), including any whitespace or Texinfo special characters. See Section 9.1.6 [`@verb`], page 82.

`@verbatim`

> Output the text of the environment exactly as is (in the fixed-width font). Pair with `@end verbatim`. See Section 10.5 [`@verbatim`], page 92.

`@verbatiminclude` *filename*

> Output the contents of *filename* exactly as is (in the fixed-width font). See Section 10.6 [`@verbatiminclude`], page 93.

`@vindex` *entry*

> Add *entry* to the index of variables. See Section 13.1 [Defining the Entries of an Index], page 114.

`@vskip` *amount*

> In a printed manual, insert whitespace so as to push text on the remainder of the page towards the bottom of the page. Used in formatting the copyright page with the argument '`0pt plus 1filll`'. (Note spelling of '`filll`'.) `@vskip` may be used only in contexts ignored for Info. See Section 3.4.4 [Copyright], page 37.

`@vtable` *formatting-command*

> Begin a two-column table, using `@item` for each entry. Automatically enter each of the items in the first column into the index of variables. Pair with `@end vtable`. The same as `@table`, except for indexing. See Section 11.4.2 [`@ftable @vtable`], page 104.

`@w{`*text*`}`   Disallow line breaks within *text*. See Section 15.5 [`@w`], page 136.

`@xml`   Enter XML completely. Pair with `@end xml`. See Section 18.3 [Raw Formatter Commands], page 157.

`@xref{`*node*`, [`*entry*`], [`*node-title*`], [`*info-file*`], [`*manual*`]}`

> Make a reference that starts with 'See' in a printed manual. Follow command with a punctuation mark. Only the first argument is mandatory. See Section 8.4 [`@xref`], page 68.

`@xrefautomaticsectiontitle` *on-off*

> By default, use the section title instead of the node name in cross references. See Section 8.4.4 [Three Arguments], page 70.

A.1 @-Command Syntax

The character '@' is used to start all Texinfo commands. (It has the same meaning that '\' has in plain TeX.) Texinfo has four types of @-command:

1. Non-alphabetic commands.

   > These commands consist of an @ followed by a punctuation mark or other character that is not part of the Latin alphabet. Non-alphabetic commands are almost always part of the text within a paragraph. The non-alphabetic commands include `@@`, `@{`, `@}`, `@.`, `@SPACE`, most of the accent commands, and many more.

2. Alphabetic commands that do not require arguments.

   > These commands start with @ followed by a word followed by a left and right-brace. These commands insert special symbols in the document; they do not take arguments. Some examples: `@dots{}` ⇒ '...', `@equiv{}` ⇒ '≡', `@TeX{}` ⇒ 'TeX', and `@bullet{}` ⇒ '•'.

3. Alphabetic commands that require arguments within braces.

   > These commands start with @ followed by a letter or a word, followed by an argument within braces. For example, the command `@dfn` indicates the introductory or defining use of a term; it is used as follows: 'In Texinfo, `@@-commands are @dfn{mark-up}` commands.'

4. Alphabetic commands that occupy an entire line.

   > These commands occupy an entire line. The line starts with @, followed by the name of the command (a word); for example, `@center` or `@cindex`. If no argument is needed, the word is followed by the end of the line. If there is an argument, it is separated from the command name by a space. Braces are not used.

Whitespace following an @-command name are optional and (usually) ignored if present. The exceptions are contexts whee whitespace is significant, e.g., an `@example` environment.

Thus, the alphabetic commands fall into classes that have different argument syntaxes. You cannot tell to which class a command belongs by the appearance of its name, but you can tell by the command's meaning: if the command stands for a glyph, it is in class 2 and does not require an argument; if it makes sense to use the command among other text as part of a paragraph, the command is in class 3 and must be followed by an argument in braces; otherwise, it is in class 4 and uses the rest of the line as its argument.

The purpose of having a different syntax for commands of classes 3 and 4 is to make Texinfo files easier to read, and also to help the GNU Emacs paragraph and filling commands work properly. There is only one exception to this rule: the command `@refill`, which is always used at the end of a paragraph immediately following the final period or other punctuation character. `@refill` takes no argument and does *not* require braces. `@refill` never confuses the Emacs paragraph commands because it cannot appear at the beginning of a line. It is also no longer needed, since all formatters now refill paragraphs automatically.

A.2 @-Command Contexts

Here we describe approximately which @-commands can be used in which contexts. It merely gives the general idea and is not exhaustive or meant to be a complete reference. Discrepancies between the information here and the `makeinfo` or TEX implementations are most likely to be resolved in favor of the implementation.

By *general text* below, we mean anything except sectioning and other such outer-level document commands, such as `@section`, `@node`, and `@setfilename`.

`@c`, `@comment` and `@if ... @end if` conditional commands may appear anywhere (except the conditionals must still be on lines by themselves). `@caption` may only appear in `@float` but may contain general text. `@footnote` content likewise.

@-commands with braces marking text (such as `@strong`, `@sc`, `@asis`) may contain raw formatter commands such as `@html` but no other block commands (other commands terminated by `@end`) and may not be split across paragraphs, but may otherwise contain general text.

In addition to the block command restriction, on `@center`, `@exdent` and `@item` in `@table` lines, @-commands that makes only sense in a paragraph are not accepted, such as `@indent`.

In addition to the above, sectioning commands cannot contain `@anchor`, `@footnote` or `@verb`.

In addition to the above, remaining commands (`@node`, `@anchor`, `@printindex`, `@ref`, `@math`, `@cindex`, `@url`, `@image`, and so on) cannot contain cross reference commands (`@ref`, `@xref`, `@pxref` and `@inforef`). In one last addition, `@shortcaption` may only appear inside `@float`.

For precise and complete information, we suggest looking into the extensive test suite in the sources, which exhaustively try combinations.

Appendix B Tips and Hints

Here are some tips for writing Texinfo documentation:

- Write in the present tense, not in the past or the future.
- Write actively! For example, write "We recommend that ..." rather than "It is recommended that ...".
- Use 70 or 72 as your fill column. Longer lines are hard to read.
- Include a copyright notice and copying permissions.

Index, Index, Index!

Write many index entries, in different ways. Readers like indices; they are helpful and convenient.

Although it is easiest to write index entries as you write the body of the text, some people prefer to write entries afterwards. In either case, write an entry before the paragraph to which it applies. This way, an index entry points to the first page of a paragraph that is split across pages.

Here are more index-related hints we have found valuable:

- Write each index entry differently, so each entry refers to a different place in the document.
- Write index entries only where a topic is discussed significantly. For example, it is not useful to index "debugging information" in a chapter on reporting bugs. Someone who wants to know about debugging information will certainly not find it in that chapter.
- Consistently capitalize the first word of every concept index entry, or else consistently use lowercase. Terse entries often call for lowercase; longer entries for capitalization. Whichever case convention you use, please use one or the other consistently! Mixing the two styles looks bad.
- Always capitalize or use uppercase for those words in an index for which this is proper, such as names of countries or acronyms. Always use the appropriate case for case-sensitive names, such as those in C or Lisp.
- Write the indexing commands that refer to a whole section immediately after the section command, and write the indexing commands that refer to a paragraph before that paragraph.

In the example that follows, a blank line comes after the index entry for "Leaping":

```
@section The Dog and the Fox
@cindex Jumping, in general
@cindex Leaping

@cindex Dog, lazy, jumped over
@cindex Lazy dog jumped over
@cindex Fox, jumps over dog
@cindex Quick fox jumps over dog
The quick brown fox jumps over the lazy dog.
```

(Note that the example shows entries for the same concept that are written in different ways—'Lazy dog', and 'Dog, lazy'—so readers can look up the concept in different ways.)

Blank Lines

- Insert a blank line between a sectioning command and the first following sentence or paragraph, or between the indexing commands associated with the sectioning command and the first following sentence or paragraph, as shown in the tip on indexing. It makes the source easier to read.

- Always insert a blank line before an `@table` command and after an `@end table` command; but never insert a blank line after an `@table` command.

  For example,

  ```
  Types of fox:

  @table @samp
  @item Quick
  Jump over lazy dogs.

  @item Brown
  Also jump over lazy dogs.
  @end table

  @noindent
  On the other hand, ...
  ```

  Insert blank lines before and after `@itemize ... @end itemize` and `@enumerate ... @end enumerate` in the same way.

Complete Phrases

Complete phrases are easier to read than ...

- Write entries in an itemized list as complete sentences; or at least, as complete phrases. Incomplete expressions ... awkward ... like this.

- Write the prefatory sentence or phrase for a multi-item list or table as a complete expression. Do not write "You can set:"; instead, write "You can set these variables:". The former expression sounds cut off.

Editions, Dates and Versions

Include edition numbers, version numbers, and dates in the `@copying` text (for people reading the Texinfo file, and for the legal copyright in the output files). Then use `@insertcopying` in the `@titlepage` section for people reading the printed output (see Section 1.13 [Short Sample], page 12).

It is easiest to handle such version information using `@set` and `@value`. See Section 18.5.4 [`@value` Example], page 162, and Section C.2 [GNU Sample Texts], page 264.

Definition Commands

Definition commands are `@deffn`, `@defun`, `@defmac`, and the like, and enable you to write descriptions in a uniform format.

- Write just one definition command for each entity you define with a definition command. The automatic indexing feature creates an index entry that leads the reader to the definition.

- Use `@table ... @end table` in an appendix that contains a summary of functions, not `@deffn` or other definition commands.

Capitalization

- Capitalize "Texinfo"; it is a name. Do not write the 'x' or 'i' in uppercase.

- Capitalize "Info"; it is a name.

- Write TeX using the `@TeX{}` command. Note the uppercase 'T' and 'X'. This command causes the formatters to typeset the name according to the wishes of Donald Knuth, who wrote TeX. (Likewise `@LaTeX{}` for LaTeX.)

Spaces

Do not use spaces to format a Texinfo file, except inside of `@example ... @end example` and other literal environments and commands.

For example, TeX fills the following:

```
@kbd{C-x v}
@kbd{M-x vc-next-action}
    Perform the next logical operation
    on the version-controlled file
    corresponding to the current buffer.
```

so it looks like this:

> *C-x v M-x vc-next-action* Perform the next logical operation on the version-controlled file corresponding to the current buffer.

In this case, the text should be formatted with `@table`, `@item`, and `@itemx`, to create a table.

@code, @samp, @var, and '---'

- Use `@code` around Lisp symbols, including command names. For example,

      The main function is @code{vc-next-action}, ...

- Avoid putting letters such as 's' immediately after an '`@code`'. Such letters look bad.

- Use `@var` around meta-variables. Do not write angle brackets around them.

- Use three hyphens in a row, '---', to indicate a long dash. TeX typesets these as a long dash and the Info formatters reduce three hyphens to two.

Periods Outside of Quotes

Place periods and other punctuation marks *outside* of quotations, unless the punctuation is part of the quotation. This practice goes against some publishing conventions in the United States, but enables the reader to distinguish between the contents of the quotation and the whole passage.

For example, you should write the following sentence with the period outside the end quotation marks:

```
Evidently, 'au' is an abbreviation for ``author''.
```

since 'au' does *not* serve as an abbreviation for 'author.' (with a period following the word).

Introducing New Terms

* Introduce new terms so that a reader who does not know them can understand them from context; or write a definition for the term.

  For example, in the following, the terms "check in", "register" and "delta" are all appearing for the first time; the example sentence should be rewritten so they are understandable.

  > The major function assists you in checking in a file to your version control system and registering successive sets of changes to it as deltas.

* Use the @dfn command around a word being introduced, to indicate that the reader should not expect to know the meaning already, and should expect to learn the meaning from this passage.

Program Invocation Nodes

You can invoke programs such as Emacs, GCC, and gawk from a shell. The documentation for each program should contain a section that describes this. Unfortunately, if the node names and titles for these sections are all different, they are difficult for users to find.

So, there is a convention to name such sections with a phrase beginning with the word 'Invoking', as in 'Invoking Emacs'; this way, users can find the section easily.

ANSI C Syntax

When you use @example to describe a C function's calling conventions, use the ANSI C syntax, like this:

```
void dld_init (char *@var{path});
```

And in the subsequent discussion, refer to the argument values by writing the same argument names, again highlighted with @var.

Avoid the obsolete style that looks like this:

```
#include <dld.h>
```

```
dld_init (path)
  char *path;
```

Also, it is best to avoid writing #include above the declaration just to indicate that the function is declared in a header file. The practice may give the misimpression that the #include belongs near the declaration of the function. Either state explicitly which header file holds the declaration or, better yet, name the header file used for a group of functions at the beginning of the section that describes the functions.

Node Length

Keep nodes (sections) to a reasonable length, whatever reasonable might be in the given context. Don't hesitate break up long nodes into subnodes and have an extensive tree structure; that's what it's there for. Many times, readers will probably try to find a single specific point in the manual, using search, indexing, or just plain guessing, rather than reading the whole thing from beginning to end.

You can use the `texi-elements-by-size` utility to see a list of all nodes (or sections) in the document, sorted by size (either lines or words), to find candidates for splitting. It's in the `util/` subdirectory of the Texinfo sources.

Bad Examples

Here are several examples of bad writing to avoid:

In this example, say, " ... you must `@dfn`{check in} the new version." That flows better.

> When you are done editing the file, you must perform a `@dfn`{check in}.

In the following example, say, ". . . makes a unified interface such as VC mode possible."

> SCCS, RCS and other version-control systems all perform similar functions in broadly similar ways (it is this resemblance which makes a unified control mode like this possible).

And in this example, you should specify what 'it' refers to:

> If you are working with other people, it assists in coordinating everyone's changes so they do not step on each other.

And Finally . . .

- Pronounce TEX as if the 'X' were a Greek 'chi', as the last sound in the name 'Bach'. But pronounce Texinfo as in 'speck': "teckinfo".

- Write notes for yourself at the very end of a Texinfo file after the `@bye`. None of the formatters process text after the `@bye`; it is as if the text were within `@ignore` ... `@end ignore`.

Appendix C Sample Texinfo Files

The first example is from the first chapter (see Section 1.13 [Short Sample], page 12), given here in its entirety, without commentary. The second includes the full texts to be used in GNU manuals.

C.1 Short Sample

Here is a complete, short sample Texinfo file, without any commentary. You can see this file, with comments, in the first chapter. See Section 1.13 [Short Sample], page 12.

In a nutshell: The `makeinfo` program transforms a Texinfo source file such as this into an Info file or HTML; and TeX typesets it for a printed manual.

```
\input texinfo   @c -*-texinfo-*-
@c %**start of header
@setfilename sample.info
@settitle Sample Manual 1.0
@c %**end of header


@copying
This is a short example of a complete Texinfo file.

Copyright @copyright{} 2015 Free Software Foundation, Inc.
@end copying


@titlepage
@title Sample Title
@page
@vskip 0pt plus 1filll
@insertcopying
@end titlepage


@c Output the table of the contents at the beginning.
@contents


@ifnottex
@node Top
@top GNU Sample

This manual is for GNU Sample
(version @value{VERSION}, @value{UPDATED}).
@end ifnottex


@menu
* First Chapter::    The first chapter is the
                     only chapter in this sample.
* Index::            Complete index.
```

```
@end menu


@node First Chapter
@chapter First Chapter

@cindex chapter, first

This is the first chapter.
@cindex index entry, another

Here is a numbered list.

@enumerate
@item
This is the first item.

@item
This is the second item.
@end enumerate


@node Index
@unnumbered Index

@printindex cp

@bye
```

C.2 GNU Sample Texts

Following is a sample Texinfo document with the full texts that should be used (adapted as necessary) in GNU manuals.

As well as the legal texts, it also serves as a practical example of how many elements in a GNU system can affect the manual. If you're not familiar with all these different elements, don't worry. They're not required and a perfectly good manual can be written without them. They're included here nonetheless because many manuals do (or could) benefit from them.

See Section 1.13 [Short Sample], page 12, for a minimal example of a Texinfo file. See Chapter 3 [Beginning a File], page 29, for a full explanation of that minimal example.

Here are some notes on the example:

- The '`$Id:`' comment is for the CVS (`http://www.nongnu.org/cvs/`), RCS (see *Revision Control System*) and other version control systems, which expand it into a string such as:

  ```
  $Id: texinfo.texi 6362 2015-06-25 22:48:32Z gavin $
  ```

(This is potentially useful in all sources that use version control, not just manuals.) You may wish to include the '$Id:' comment in the @copying text, if you want a completely unambiguous reference to the documentation source version.

If you want to literally write Id, use @w: @w{$}Id$. Unfortunately, this technique does not work in plain text output, where it's not clear what should be done.

- The version.texi in the @include command is maintained automatically by Automake (see *GNU Automake*). It sets the 'VERSION' and 'UPDATED' values used elsewhere. If your distribution doesn't use Automake, but you do use Emacs, you may find the time-stamp.el package helpful (see Section "Time Stamps" in *The GNU Emacs Manual*).

- The @syncodeindex command reflects the recommendation to use only one index where possible, to make it easier for readers to look up index entries.

- The @dircategory is for constructing the Info directory. See Section 23.2.4 [Installing Dir Entries], page 218, which includes a variety of recommended category names.

- The 'Invoking' node is a GNU standard to help users find the basic information about command-line usage of a given program. See Section "Manual Structure Details" in *GNU Coding Standards*.

- It is best to include the entire GNU Free Documentation License in a GNU manual, unless the manual is only a few pages long. Of course this sample is even shorter than that, but it includes the FDL anyway in order to show one conventional way to do so. The fdl.texi file is available on the GNU machines and in the Texinfo and other GNU source distributions.

  The FDL provides for omitting itself under certain conditions, but in that case the sample texts given here have to be modified. See Appendix G [GNU Free Documentation License], page 287.

- If the FSF is not the copyright holder, then use the appropriate name.

- If your manual is published on paper by the FSF or is longer than 400 pages, you should include the standard FSF cover texts (see Section "License Notices for Documentation" in *GNU Maintainer Information*).

- For documents that express your personal views, feelings or experiences, it is more appropriate to use a license permitting only verbatim copying, rather than the FDL. See Section C.3 [Verbatim Copying License], page 267.

Here is the sample document:

```
\input texinfo    @c -*-texinfo-*-
@comment $Id@w{$}
@comment %**start of header
@setfilename sample.info

@finalout
@include version.texi
@settitle GNU Sample @value{VERSION}
@syncodeindex pg cp
@comment %**end of header
@copying
```

This manual is for GNU Sample (version @value{VERSION}, @value{UPDATED}),
which is an example in the Texinfo documentation.

Copyright @copyright{} 2015 Free Software Foundation, Inc.

@quotation
Permission is granted to copy, distribute and/or modify this document
under the terms of the GNU Free Documentation License, Version 1.3 or
any later version published by the Free Software Foundation; with no
Invariant Sections, with no Front-Cover Texts, and with no Back-Cover
Texts. A copy of the license is included in the section entitled
``GNU Free Documentation License''.
@end quotation
@end copying

@dircategory Texinfo documentation system
@direntry
* sample: (sample)Invoking sample.
@end direntry

@titlepage
@title GNU Sample
@subtitle for version @value{VERSION}, @value{UPDATED}
@author A.U. Thor (@email{bug-sample@@gnu.org})
@page
@vskip 0pt plus 1filll
@insertcopying
@end titlepage

@contents

@ifnottex
@node Top
@top GNU Sample

This manual is for GNU Sample (version @value{VERSION}, @value{UPDATED}).
@end ifnottex

@menu
* Invoking sample::
* GNU Free Documentation License::
* Index::
@end menu

@node Invoking sample
@chapter Invoking sample

```
@pindex sample
@cindex invoking @command{sample}

This is a sample manual.  There is no sample program to
invoke, but if there were, you could see its basic usage
and command line options here.


@node GNU Free Documentation License
@appendix GNU Free Documentation License

@include fdl.texi


@node Index
@unnumbered Index

@printindex cp

@bye
```

C.3 Verbatim Copying License

For software manuals and other documentation, it is critical to use a license permitting free redistribution and updating, so that when a free program is changed, the documentation can be updated as well.

On the other hand, for documents that express your personal views, feelings or experiences, it is more appropriate to use a license permitting only verbatim copying.

Here is sample text for such a license permitting verbatim copying only. This is just the license text itself. For a complete sample document, see the previous sections.

```
@copying
This document is a sample for allowing verbatim copying only.

Copyright @copyright{} 2015 Free Software Foundation, Inc.

@quotation
Permission is granted to make and distribute verbatim copies
of this entire document without royalty provided the
copyright notice and this permission notice are preserved.
@end quotation
@end copying
```

C.4 All-permissive Copying License

For software manuals and other documentation, it is important to use a license permitting free redistribution and updating, so that when a free program is changed, the documentation can be updated as well.

On the other hand, for small supporting files, short manuals (under 300 lines long) and rough documentation (README files, INSTALL files, etc.), the full FDL would be overkill. They can use a simple all-permissive license.

Here is sample text for such an all-permissive license. This is just the license text itself. For a complete sample document, see the previous sections.

```
Copyright @copyright{} 2015 Free Software Foundation, Inc.

Copying and distribution of this file, with or without modification,
are permitted in any medium without royalty provided the copyright
notice and this notice are preserved.
```

Appendix D Page Headings

Most printed manuals contain headings along the top of every page except the title and copyright pages. Some manuals also contain footings. Headings and footings have no meaning in Info or the other output formats.

D.1 Headings Introduced

Texinfo provides standard page heading formats for manuals that are printed on one side of each sheet of paper and for manuals that are printed on both sides of the paper. Typically, you will use these formats, but you can specify your own format if you wish.

In addition, you can specify whether chapters should begin on a new page, or merely continue the same page as the previous chapter; and if chapters begin on new pages, you can specify whether they must be odd-numbered pages.

By convention, a book is printed on both sides of each sheet of paper. When you open a book, the right-hand page is odd-numbered, and chapters begin on right-hand pages—a preceding left-hand page is left blank if necessary. Reports, however, are often printed on just one side of paper, and chapters begin on a fresh page immediately following the end of the preceding chapter. In short or informal reports, chapters often do not begin on a new page at all, but are separated from the preceding text by a small amount of whitespace.

The `@setchapternewpage` command controls whether chapters begin on new pages, and whether one of the standard heading formats is used. In addition, Texinfo has several heading and footing commands that you can use to generate your own heading and footing formats.

In Texinfo, headings and footings are single lines at the tops and bottoms of pages; you cannot create multiline headings or footings. Each header or footer line is divided into three parts: a left part, a middle part, and a right part. Any part, or a whole line, may be left blank. Text for the left part of a header or footer line is set flushleft; text for the middle part is centered; and, text for the right part is set flushright.

D.2 Standard Heading Formats

Texinfo provides two standard heading formats, one for manuals printed on one side of each sheet of paper, and the other for manuals printed on both sides of the paper.

By default, nothing is specified for the footing of a Texinfo file, so the footing remains blank.

The standard format for single-sided printing consists of a header line in which the left-hand part contains the name of the chapter, the central part is blank, and the right-hand part contains the page number.

A single-sided page looks like this:

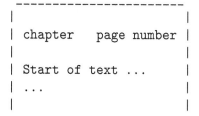

```
 ----------------------
|                      |
| chapter   page number |
|                      |
| Start of text ...    |
| ...                  |
|                      |
```

The standard format for two-sided printing depends on whether the page number is even or odd. By convention, even-numbered pages are on the left- and odd-numbered pages are on the right. (TeX will adjust the widths of the left- and right-hand margins. Usually, widths are correct, but during double-sided printing, it is wise to check that pages will bind properly—sometimes a printer will produce output in which the even-numbered pages have a larger right-hand margin than the odd-numbered pages.)

In the standard double-sided format, the left part of the left-hand (even-numbered) page contains the page number, the central part is blank, and the right part contains the title (specified by the @settitle command). The left part of the right-hand (odd-numbered) page contains the name of the chapter, the central part is blank, and the right part contains the page number.

Two pages, side by side as in an open book, look like this:

```
---------------------------          ----------------------------
|                         |  |        |                          |
| page number      title  |  |        | chapter    page number   |
|                         |  |        |                          |
| Start of text ...       |  |        | More  text ...           |
| ...                     |  |        | ...                      |
|                         |  |        |                          |
```

The chapter name is preceded by the word "Chapter", the chapter number and a colon. This makes it easier to keep track of where you are in the manual.

D.3 Specifying the Type of Heading

TeX does not begin to generate page headings for a standard Texinfo file until it reaches the @end titlepage command. Thus, the title and copyright pages are not numbered. The @end titlepage command causes TeX to begin to generate page headings according to a standard format specified by the @setchapternewpage command that precedes the @titlepage section.

There are four possibilities:

No @setchapternewpage command
> Cause TeX to specify the single-sided heading format, with chapters on new pages. This is the same as @setchapternewpage on.

@setchapternewpage on
> Specify the single-sided heading format, with chapters on new pages.

@setchapternewpage off
> Cause TeX to start a new chapter on the same page as the last page of the preceding chapter, after skipping some vertical whitespace. Also cause TeX to typeset for single-sided printing. (You can override the headers format with the @headings double command; see Section 3.7.3 [@headings], page 42.)

@setchapternewpage odd
> Specify the double-sided heading format, with chapters on new pages.

Texinfo lacks an @setchapternewpage even command.

D.4 How to Make Your Own Headings

You can use the standard headings provided with Texinfo or specify your own. By default, Texinfo has no footers, so if you specify them, the available page size for the main text will be slightly reduced.

Texinfo provides six commands for specifying headings and footings:

- `@everyheading` and `@everyfooting` generate page headers and footers that are the same for both even- and odd-numbered pages.
- `@evenheading` and `@evenfooting` command generate headers and footers for even-numbered (left-hand) pages.
- `@oddheading` and `@oddfooting` generate headers and footers for odd-numbered (right-hand) pages.

Write custom heading specifications in the Texinfo file immediately after the `@end titlepage` command. You must cancel the predefined heading commands with the `@headings off` command before defining your own specifications.

Here is how to tell TeX to place the chapter name at the left, the page number in the center, and the date at the right of every header for both even- and odd-numbered pages:

```
@headings off
@everyheading @thischapter @| @thispage @| @today{}
```

You need to divide the left part from the central part and the central part from the right part by inserting '`@|`' between parts. Otherwise, the specification command will not be able to tell where the text for one part ends and the next part begins.

Each part can contain text or @-commands. The text is printed as if the part were within an ordinary paragraph in the body of the page. The @-commands replace themselves with the page number, date, chapter name, or whatever.

Here are the six heading and footing commands:

`@everyheading` *left* `@|` *center* `@|` *right*
`@everyfooting` *left* `@|` *center* `@|` *right*

> The 'every' commands specify the format for both even- and odd-numbered pages. These commands are for documents that are printed on one side of each sheet of paper, or for documents in which you want symmetrical headers or footers.

`@evenheading` *left* `@|` *center* `@|` *right*
`@oddheading` *left* `@|` *center* `@|` *right*
`@evenfooting` *left* `@|` *center* `@|` *right*
`@oddfooting` *left* `@|` *center* `@|` *right*

> The 'even' and 'odd' commands specify the format for even-numbered pages and odd-numbered pages. These commands are for books and manuals that are printed on both sides of each sheet of paper.

Use the '`@this...`' series of @-commands to provide the names of chapters and sections and the page number. You can use the '`@this...`' commands in the left, center, or right portions of headers and footers, or anywhere else in a Texinfo file so long as they are between `@iftex` and `@end iftex` commands.

Here are the '`@this...`' commands:

`@thispage`

> Expands to the current page number.

`@thissectionname`

> Expands to the name of the current section.

`@thissectionnum`

> Expands to the number of the current section.

`@thissection`

> Expands to the number and name of the current section, in the format 'Section 1: Title'.

`@thischaptername`

> Expands to the name of the current chapter.

`@thischapternum`

> Expands to the number of the current chapter, or letter of the current appendix.

`@thischapter`

> Expands to the number and name of the current chapter, in the format 'Chapter 1: Title'.

`@thistitle`

> Expands to the name of the document, as specified by the `@settitle` command.

`@thisfile`

> For `@include` files only: expands to the name of the current `@include` file. If the current Texinfo source file is not an `@include` file, this command has no effect. This command does *not* provide the name of the current Texinfo source file unless it is an `@include` file. (See Chapter 20 [Include Files], page 174, for more information about `@include` files.)

You can also use the `@today{}` command, which expands to the current date, in '1 Jan 1900' format.

Other @-commands and text are printed in a header or footer just as if they were in the body of a page. It is useful to incorporate text, particularly when you are writing drafts:

```
@headings off
@everyheading @emph{Draft!} @| @thispage @| @thischapter
@everyfooting @| @| Version: 0.27: @today{}
```

Beware of overlong titles: they may overlap another part of the header or footer and blot it out.

If you have very short chapters and/or sections, several of them can appear on a single page. You can specify which chapters and sections you want `@thischapter`, `@thissection` and other such macros to refer to on such pages as follows:

`@everyheadingmarks` *ref*
`@everyfootingmarks` *ref*

> The *ref* argument can be either `top` (the `@this...` commands will refer to the chapter/section at the top of a page) or `bottom` (the commands will reflect the

situation at the bottom of a page). These '@every...' commands specify what to do on both even- and odd-numbered pages.

`@evenheadingmarks` *ref*
`@oddheadingmarks` *ref*
`@evenfootingmarks` *ref*
`@oddfootingmarks` *ref*

These '@even...' and '@odd...' commands specify what to do on only even- or odd-numbered pages, respectively. The *ref* argument is the same as with the '@every...' commands.

Write these commands immediately after the `@...contents` commands, or after the `@end titlepage` command if you don't have a table of contents or if it is printed at the end of your manual.

By default the `@this...` commands reflect the situation at the bottom of a page both in headings and in footings.

Appendix E Catching Mistakes

Besides mistakes in the content of your documentation, there are two kinds of mistake you can make with Texinfo: you can make mistakes with @-commands, and you can make mistakes with the structure of the nodes and chapters.

Emacs has two tools for catching the @-command mistakes and two for catching structuring mistakes.

For finding problems with @-commands, you can run TeX or a region formatting command on the region that has a problem; indeed, you can run these commands on each region as you write it.

For finding problems with the structure of nodes and chapters, you can use *C-c C-s* (`texinfo-show-structure`) and the related `occur` command and you can use the *M-x Info-validate* command.

E.1 `makeinfo` Preferred

The `makeinfo` program does an excellent job of catching errors and reporting them—far better than `texinfo-format-region` or `texinfo-format-buffer`. In addition, the various functions for automatically creating and updating node pointers and menus remove many opportunities for human error.

If you can, use the updating commands to create and insert pointers and menus. These prevent many errors. Then use `makeinfo` (or its Texinfo mode manifestations, `makeinfo-region` and `makeinfo-buffer`) to format your file and check for other errors. This is the best way to work with Texinfo. But if you cannot use `makeinfo`, or your problem is very puzzling, then you may want to use the tools described in this appendix.

E.2 Catching Errors with Info Formatting

After you have written part of a Texinfo file, you can use the `texinfo-format-region` or the `makeinfo-region` command to see whether the region formats properly.

Most likely, however, you are reading this section because for some reason you cannot use the `makeinfo-region` command; therefore, the rest of this section presumes that you are using `texinfo-format-region`.

If you have made a mistake with an @-command, `texinfo-format-region` will stop processing at or after the error and display an error message. To see where in the buffer the error occurred, switch to the '*Info Region*' buffer; the cursor will be in a position that is after the location of the error. Also, the text will not be formatted after the place where the error occurred (or more precisely, where it was detected).

For example, if you accidentally end a menu with the command @end menus with an 's' on the end, instead of with @end menu, you will see an error message that says:

```
@end menus is not handled by texinfo
```

The cursor will stop at the point in the buffer where the error occurs, or not long after it. The buffer will look like this:

```
---------- Buffer: *Info Region* ----------
* Menu:

* Using texinfo-show-structure::  How to use
                                  `texinfo-show-structure'
                                  to catch mistakes.
* Running Info-validate::          How to check for
                                  unreferenced nodes.
@end menus
*
---------- Buffer: *Info Region* ----------
```

The `texinfo-format-region` command sometimes provides slightly odd error messages. For example, the following cross reference fails to format:

    (@xref{Catching Mistakes, for more info.)

In this case, `texinfo-format-region` detects the missing closing brace but displays a message that says 'Unbalanced parentheses' rather than 'Unbalanced braces'. This is because the formatting command looks for mismatches between braces as if they were parentheses.

Sometimes `texinfo-format-region` fails to detect mistakes. For example, in the following, the closing brace is swapped with the closing parenthesis:

    (@xref{Catching Mistakes), for more info.}

Formatting produces:

    (*Note for more info.: Catching Mistakes)

The only way for you to detect this error is to realize that the reference should have looked like this:

    (*Note Catching Mistakes::, for more info.)

Incidentally, if you are reading this node in Info and type *f RET* (Info-follow-reference), you will generate an error message that says:

    No such node: "Catching Mistakes) The only way ...

This is because Info perceives the example of the error as the first cross reference in this node and if you type a RET immediately after typing the Info *f* command, Info will attempt to go to the referenced node. If you type *f catch TAB RET*, Info will complete the node name of the correctly written example and take you to the 'Catching Mistakes' node. (If you try this, you can return from the 'Catching Mistakes' node by typing *l* (Info-last).)

E.3 Debugging with TEX

You can also catch mistakes when you format a file with TEX.

Usually, you will want to do this after you have run `texinfo-format-buffer` (or, better, `makeinfo-buffer`) on the same file, because `texinfo-format-buffer` sometimes displays error messages that make more sense than TEX. (See Section E.2 [Debugging with Info], page 274, for more information.)

For example, TEX was run on a Texinfo file, part of which is shown here:

```
---------- Buffer: texinfo.texi ----------
name of the Texinfo file as an extension.  The
@samp{??} are `wildcards' that cause the shell to
substitute all the raw index files.  (@xref{sorting
indices, for more information about sorting
indices.)@refill
---------- Buffer: texinfo.texi ----------
```

(The cross reference lacks a closing brace.) TeX produced the following output, after which it stopped:

```
---------- Buffer: *tex-shell* ----------
Runaway argument?
{sorting indices, for more information about sorting
indices.) @refill @ETC.
! Paragraph ended before @xref was complete.
<to be read again>
                    @par
l.27

?
---------- Buffer: *tex-shell* ----------
```

In this case, TeX produced an accurate and understandable error message:

```
Paragraph ended before @xref was complete.
```

'@par' is an internal TeX command of no relevance to Texinfo. '1.27' means that TeX detected the problem on line 27 of the Texinfo file. The '?' is the prompt TeX uses in this circumstance.

Unfortunately, TeX is not always so helpful, and sometimes you must truly be a Sherlock Holmes to discover what went wrong.

In any case, if you run into a problem like this, you can do one of three things.

1. You can tell TeX to continue running and ignore just this error by typing RET at the '?' prompt.

2. You can tell TeX to continue running and to ignore all errors as best it can by typing *r RET* at the '?' prompt.

   This is often the best thing to do. However, beware: the one error may produce a cascade of additional error messages as its consequences are felt through the rest of the file. To stop TeX when it is producing such an avalanche of error messages, type *C-c* (or *C-c C-c*, if you are running a shell inside Emacs).

3. You can tell TeX to stop this run by typing *x RET* at the '?' prompt.

If you are running TeX inside Emacs, you need to switch to the shell buffer and line at which TeX offers the '?' prompt.

Sometimes TeX will format a file without producing error messages even though there is a problem. This usually occurs if a command is not ended but TeX is able to continue processing anyhow. For example, if you fail to end an itemized list with the @end itemize command, TeX will write a DVI file that you can print out. The only error message that TeX will give you is the somewhat mysterious comment:

```
(@end occurred inside a group at level 1)
```

However, if you print the DVI file, you will find that the text of the file that follows the itemized list is entirely indented as if it were part of the last item in the itemized list. The error message is the way TEX says that it expected to find an **@end** command somewhere in the file; but that it could not determine where it was needed.

Another source of notoriously hard-to-find errors is a missing **@end group** command. If you ever are stumped by incomprehensible errors, look for a missing **@end group** command first.

If the Texinfo file lacks header lines, TEX may stop in the beginning of its run and display output that looks like the following. The '*' indicates that TEX is waiting for input.

```
This is TeX, Version 3.14159 (Web2c 7.0)
(test.texinfo [1])
*
```

In this case, simply type *\end RET* after the asterisk. Then write the header lines in the Texinfo file and run the TEX command again. (Note the use of the backslash, '\'. TEX uses '\' instead of '@'; and in this circumstance, you are working directly with TEX, not with Texinfo.)

E.4 Using `texinfo-show-structure`

It is not always easy to keep track of the nodes, chapters, sections, and subsections of a Texinfo file. This is especially true if you are revising or adding to a Texinfo file that someone else has written.

In GNU Emacs, in Texinfo mode, the `texinfo-show-structure` command lists all the lines that begin with the @-commands that specify the structure: **@chapter**, **@section**, **@appendix**, and so on. With an argument (*C-u* as prefix argument, if interactive), the command also shows the **@node** lines. The `texinfo-show-structure` command is bound to *C-c C-s* in Texinfo mode, by default.

The lines are displayed in a buffer called the '*Occur*' buffer, indented by hierarchical level. For example, here is a part of what was produced by running `texinfo-show-structure` on this manual:

```
Lines matching "^@\\(chapter \\|sect\\|subs\\|subh\\|
unnum\\|major\\|chapheading \\|heading \\|appendix\\)"
in buffer texinfo.texi.
...
4177:@chapter Nodes
4198:    @heading Two Paths
4231:    @section Node and Menu Illustration
4337:    @section The @code{@@node} Command
4393:        @subheading Choosing Node and Pointer Names
4417:        @subsection How to Write an @code{@@node} Line
4469:        @subsection @code{@@node} Line Tips
...
```

This says that lines 4337, 4393, and 4417 of `texinfo.texi` begin with the **@section**, **@subheading**, and **@subsection** commands respectively. If you move your cursor into the

'*Occur*' window, you can position the cursor over one of the lines and use the `C-c C-c` command (`occur-mode-goto-occurrence`), to jump to the corresponding spot in the Texinfo file. See Section "Using Occur" in *The GNU Emacs Manual*, for more information about `occur-mode-goto-occurrence`.

The first line in the '*Occur*' window describes the *regular expression* specified by *texinfo-heading-pattern*. This regular expression is the pattern that `texinfo-show-structure` looks for. See Section "Using Regular Expressions" in *The GNU Emacs Manual*, for more information.

When you invoke the `texinfo-show-structure` command, Emacs will display the structure of the whole buffer. If you want to see the structure of just a part of the buffer, of one chapter, for example, use the `C-x n n` (`narrow-to-region`) command to mark the region. (See Section "Narrowing" in *The GNU Emacs Manual*.) This is how the example used above was generated. (To see the whole buffer again, use `C-x n w` (`widen`).)

If you call `texinfo-show-structure` with a prefix argument by typing `C-u C-c C-s`, it will list lines beginning with `@node` as well as the lines beginning with the @-sign commands for `@chapter`, `@section`, and the like.

You can remind yourself of the structure of a Texinfo file by looking at the list in the '*Occur*' window; and if you have mis-named a node or left out a section, you can correct the mistake.

E.5 Using `occur`

Sometimes the `texinfo-show-structure` command produces too much information. Perhaps you want to remind yourself of the overall structure of a Texinfo file, and are overwhelmed by the detailed list produced by `texinfo-show-structure`. In this case, you can use the `occur` command directly. To do this, type:

    M-x occur

and then, when prompted, type a *regexp*, a regular expression for the pattern you want to match. (See Section "Regular Expressions" in *The GNU Emacs Manual*.) The `occur` command works from the current location of the cursor in the buffer to the end of the buffer. If you want to run `occur` on the whole buffer, place the cursor at the beginning of the buffer.

For example, to see all the lines that contain the word '`@chapter`' in them, just type '`@chapter`'. This will produce a list of the chapters. It will also list all the sentences with '`@chapter`' in the middle of the line.

If you want to see only those lines that start with the word '`@chapter`', type '`^@chapter`' when prompted by `occur`. If you want to see all the lines that end with a word or phrase, end the last word with a '`$`'; for example, '`catching mistakes$`'. This can be helpful when you want to see all the nodes that are part of the same chapter or section and therefore have the same 'Up' pointer.

See Section "Using Occur" in *The GNU Emacs Manual*, for more information.

E.6 Finding Badly Referenced Nodes

You can use the `Info-validate` command to check whether any of the 'Next', 'Previous', 'Up' or other node pointers fail to point to a node. This command checks that every node pointer points to an existing node. The `Info-validate` command works only on Info files, not on Texinfo files.

The `makeinfo` program validates pointers automatically, so you do not need to use the `Info-validate` command if you are using `makeinfo`. You only may need to use `Info-validate` if you are unable to run `makeinfo` and instead must create an Info file using `texinfo-format-region` or `texinfo-format-buffer`, or if you write an Info file from scratch.

E.6.1 Using `Info-validate`

To use `Info-validate`, visit the Info file you wish to check and type:

    M-x Info-validate

Note that the `Info-validate` command requires an uppercase 'I'. You may also need to create a tag table before running `Info-validate`. See Section E.6.3 [Tagifying], page 280.

If your file is valid, you will receive a message that says "File appears valid". However, if you have a pointer that does not point to a node, error messages will be displayed in a buffer called '*problems in info file*'.

For example, `Info-validate` was run on a test file that contained only the first node of this manual. One of the messages said:

    In node "Overview", invalid Next: Texinfo Mode

This meant that the node called 'Overview' had a 'Next' pointer that did not point to anything (which was true in this case, since the test file had only one node in it).

Now suppose we add a node named 'Texinfo Mode' to our test case but we do not specify a 'Previous' for this node. Then we will get the following error message:

    In node "Texinfo Mode", should have Previous: Overview

This is because every 'Next' pointer should be matched by a 'Previous' (in the node where the 'Next' points) which points back.

`Info-validate` also checks that all menu entries and cross references point to actual nodes.

`Info-validate` requires a tag table and does not work with files that have been split. (The `texinfo-format-buffer` command automatically splits large files.) In order to use `Info-validate` on a large file, you must run `texinfo-format-buffer` with an argument so that it does not split the Info file; and you must create a tag table for the unsplit file.

E.6.2 Creating an Unsplit File

You can run `Info-validate` only on a single Info file that has a tag table. The command will not work on the indirect subfiles that are generated when a master file is split. If you have a large file (longer than 300,000 bytes or so), you need to run the `texinfo-format-buffer` or `makeinfo-buffer` command in such a way that it does not create indirect subfiles. You will also need to create a tag table for the Info file. After you have done this, you can run `Info-validate` and look for badly referenced nodes.

The first step is to create an unsplit Info file. To prevent `texinfo-format-buffer` from splitting a Texinfo file into smaller Info files, give a prefix to the *M-x texinfo-format-buffer* command:

```
    C-u M-x texinfo-format-buffer
```
or else
```
    C-u C-c C-e C-b
```
When you do this, Texinfo will not split the file and will not create a tag table for it.

E.6.3 Tagifying a File

After creating an unsplit Info file, you must create a tag table for it. Visit the Info file you wish to tagify and type:
```
    M-x Info-tagify
```
(Note the uppercase 'I' in `Info-tagify`.) This creates an Info file with a tag table that you can validate.

The third step is to validate the Info file:
```
    M-x Info-validate
```
(Note the uppercase 'I' in `Info-validate`.) In brief, the steps are:
```
    C-u M-x texinfo-format-buffer
    M-x Info-tagify
    M-x Info-validate
```
After you have validated the node structure, you can rerun `texinfo-format-buffer` in the normal way so it will construct a tag table and split the file automatically, or you can make the tag table and split the file manually.

E.6.4 Splitting a File Manually

You should split a large file or else let the `texinfo-format-buffer` or `makeinfo-buffer` command do it for you automatically. (Generally you will let one of the formatting commands do this job for you. See Section 23.1 [Creating an Info File], page 213.)

The split-off files are called the indirect subfiles.

Info files are split to save memory. With smaller files, Emacs does not have make such a large buffer to hold the information.

If an Info file has more than 30 nodes, you should also make a tag table for it. See Section E.6.1 [Using `Info-validate`], page 279, for information about creating a tag table. (Again, tag tables are usually created automatically by the formatting command; you only need to create a tag table yourself if you are doing the job manually. Most likely, you will do this for a large, unsplit file on which you have run `Info-validate`.)

Visit the Info file you wish to tagify and split and type the two commands:
```
    M-x Info-tagify
    M-x Info-split
```
(Note that the 'I' in 'Info' is uppercase.)

When you use the `Info-split` command, the buffer is modified into a (small) Info file which lists the indirect subfiles. This file should be saved in place of the original visited file. The indirect subfiles are written in the same directory the original file is in, with names generated by appending '-' and a number to the original file name.

The primary file still functions as an Info file, but it contains just the tag table and a directory of subfiles.

Appendix F Info Format Specification

Here we describe the technical details of the Info format.

This format definition was written some 25 years after the Info format was first devised. So in the event of conflicts between this definition and actual practice, practice wins. It also assumes some general knowledge of Texinfo; it is meant to be a guide for implementors rather than a rigid technical standard. We often refer back to other parts of this manual for examples and definitions, rather than redundantly spelling out every detail.

In this formal description, the characters `<>*()|=#` are used for the language of the description itself. Other characters are literal. The formal constructs used are typical: `<...>` indicates a metavariable name, '`=`' means definition, '`*`' repetition, '`?`' optional, '`()`' grouping, '`|`' alternation, '`#`' comment. Exception: '`*`' at the beginning of a line is literal.

The sections in an Info file (such as nodes or tag tables) are separated with a sequence:

```
(^L)?^_(^L)?^J
```

That is, a '`CTRL-_`' character followed by a newline, with optional formfeed characters. We refer to such sequences as `<separator>`.

We specify literal parentheses (those that are part of the Info format) with `<lparen>` and `<rparen>`, meaning the single characters '`(`' and '`)`' respectively. The two-character sequence '`^x`' means the single character '`CTRL-x`', for any x.

F.1 Info Format General Layout

This section describes the overall layout of Info manuals.

Info Format: A Whole Manual

To begin, an Info manual is either *nonsplit* (contained wholly within a single file) or *split* (across several files).

The syntax for a nonsplit manual is:

```
    <nonsplit info file> =
<preamble>
<node>*
<tag table>?
<local variables>?
```

When split, there is a *main file*, which contains only pointers to the nodes given in other *subfiles*. The main file looks like this:

```
    <split info main file> =
<preamble>
<indirect table>
<tag table>
<local variables>?
```

The subfiles in a split manual have the following syntax:

```
    <split info subfile> =
<preamble>
<node>*
```

Note that the tag table is not optional for split files, as it is used with the indirect table to deduce which subfile a particular node is in.

Info Format: Preamble

The `<preamble>` is text at the beginning of all output files. It is not intended to be visible by default in an Info viewer, but may be displayed upon user request.

```
          <preamble> =
<identification>        # "This is FILENAME, produced by ..."
<copying text>          # Expansion of @copying text.
<dir entries>           # Derived from @dircategory and @direntry.
```

These pieces are:

`<identification line>`

An arbitrary string beginning the output file, followed by a blank line.

`<copying text>`

The expansion of an `@copying` environment, if the manual has one (see Section 3.3.1 [@copying], page 33).

`<dir entries>`

The result of any `@dircategory` and `@direntry` commands present in the manual (see Section 23.2.4 [Installing Dir Entries], page 218).

Info Format: Indirect Table

```
          <indirect table> =
<separator>
Indirect:
(<filename>: <bytepos>)*
```

The indirect table is written to the main file in the case of split output only. It specifies, as a decimal integer, the starting byte position (zero-based) that the first node of each subfile would have if the subfiles were concatenated together in order, not including the top-level file. The first node of actual content is pointed to by the first entry.

As an example, suppose split output is generated for the GDB manual. The top-level file `gdb.info` will contain something like this:

```
<separator>
Indirect:
gdb.info-1: 1878
gdb.info-2: 295733

...
```

This tells Info viewers that the first node of the manual occurs at byte 1878 of the file `gdb.info-1` (which would be after that file's preamble.) The first node in the `gdb.info-2` subfile would start at byte 295733 if `gdb.info-2` were appended to `gdb.info-1`, including any preamble sections in both files.

Unfortunately, Info-creating programs such as `makeinfo` have not always implemented these rules perfectly, due to various bugs and oversights. Therefore, robust Info viewers should fall back to searching "nearby" the given position for a node, instead of giving up immediately if the position is not exactly at a node beginning.

Info Format: Tag Table

```
      <tag table> =
<separator>
Tag Table:
(<lparen>Indirect<rparen>)?
(Node|Ref): <nodeid>^?<bytepos>
<separator>
End Tag Table
```

The '(Indirect)' line appears in the case of split output only.

The tag table specifies the starting byte position of each node and anchor in the file. In the case of split output, it is only written in the main output file.

Each line defines an identifier as either an anchor or a node, as specified. For example, 'Node: Top^?1647' says that the node named 'Top' starts at byte 1647 while 'Ref: Overview-Footnote-1^?30045' says that the anchor named 'Overview-Footnote-1' starts at byte 30045. It is an error to define the same identifier both ways.

In the case of nonsplit output, the byte positions simply refer to the location in the output file. In the case of split output, the byte positions refer to an imaginary file created by concatenating all the split files (but not the top-level file). See the previous section.

Here is an example:

```
^_
Tag Table:
Node: Top^?89
Node: Ch1^?292
^_
End Tag Table
```

This specifies a manual with two nodes, 'Top' and 'Ch1', at byte positions 89 and 292 respectively. Because the '(Indirect)' line is not present, the manual is not split.

Preamble sections or other non-node sections of files do not have a tag table entry.

Info Format: Local Variables

The local variables section is optional and is currently used to give the encoding information. It may be augmented in the future.

```
      <local variables> =
<separator>
Local Variables:
coding: <encoding>
End:
```

See Section 17.2 [@documentencoding], page 153.

Info Format: Regular Nodes

Regular nodes look like this:

```
      <node> =
<separator>
File: <fn>, Node: <id1>, (Next: <id2>, )? (Prev: <id3>, )? Up: <id4>
```

```
<general text, until the next ^_ or end-of-file>
```

At least one space or tab must be present after each colon and comma, but any number of spaces are ignored. The `<id>` node identifiers have following format:

```
<id> = (<lparen><infofile><rparen>)?(<nodename>)?
```

This `<node>` defines `<id1>` in file `<fn>`, which is typically either 'manualname' or 'manualname.info'. No parenthesized `<infofile>` component may appear within `<id1>`.

Each of the identifiers after `Next`, `Prev` and `Up` refer to nodes or anchors within a file. These pointers normally refer within the same file, but '(dir)' is often used to point to the top-level dir file. If an `<infofile>` component is used then the node name may be omitted, in which case the node identifier refers to the 'Top' node within the referenced file.

The `Next` and `Prev` pointers are optional. The `Up` pointer is technically also optional, although most likely this indicates a mistake in the node structuring. Conventionally, the nodes are arranged to form a tree, but this is not a requirement of the format.

Node names containing periods, commas, colons or parentheses (including @-commands which produce any of these) can confuse Info readers. See Section 6.1.3 [Node Line Requirements], page 56.

The use of non-ASCII characters in the names of nodes is permitted, but can cause problems in cross-references between nodes in Info files with different character encodings, and also when node names from many different files are listed (for example, with the `--apropos` option to the standalone Info browser), so we recommend avoiding them whenever feasible. For example, prefer the use of the ASCII apostrophe character (') to Unicode directional quotes.

The `<general text>` of the node can include the special constructs described next.

F.2 Info Format Text Constructs

These special Info constructs can appear within the text of a node.

F.2.1 Info Format: Menu

Conventionally menus appear at the end of nodes, but the Info format places no restrictions on their location.

```
<menu> =
* Menu:
(<menu entry> | <menu comment>)*
```

The parts of a `<menu entry>` are also described in Section 7.3 [Menu Parts], page 63. They have the same syntax as cross-references (see Section F.2.4 [Info Format Cross Reference], page 286). Indices extend the menu format to specify the destination line; see Section F.2.3 [Info Format Printindex], page 285.

A `<menu comment>` is any line not beginning with '*' that appears either at the beginning of the menu or is separated from a menu entry by one or more blank lines. These comments are intended to be displayed as part of the menu, as-is (see Section 7.2 [Writing a Menu], page 62).

F.2.2 Info Format: Image

The `@image` command results in the following special directive within the Info file (see Section 12.2 [Images], page 109):

```
        <image> =
 ^@^H[image src="<image file>"
             (text="<txt file contents>")?
             (alt="<alt text>")?
 ^@^H]
```

The line breaks and indentation in this description are editorial; the whitespace between the different parts of the directive in Info files is arbitrary.

In the strings `<image file>`, `<txt file contents>` and `<alt text>`, '"' is quoted as '\"' and '\' is quoted as '\\'. The txt and alt specifications are optional.

The `alt` value serves the same purpose as in HTML: A prose description of the image. In text-only displays or speech systems, for example, the `alt` value may be used instead of displaying the (typically graphical) `<image file>`.

The `<txt file contents>`, if present, should be taken as an ASCII representation of the image, for possible use on a text-only display.

The format does not prescribe the choice between displaying the `<image file>`, the `<alt text>` or the `<txt file contents>`.

F.2.3 Info Format: Printindex

Indices in Info format are generally written as a menu (see Chapter 13 [Indices], page 114), but with an additional directive at the beginning marking this as an index node:

```
        <printindex> =
 ^@^H[index^@^H]
 * Menu:


 <index entry>*
```

The `<index entry>` items are similar to normal menu entries, but the free-format description is replaced by the line number of where the entries occurs in the text:

```
        <index entry> =
 * <entry text>: <entry node>. <lparen>line <lineno><rparen>
```

The `<entry text>` is the index term. The `<lineno>` is an unsigned integer, given relative to the start of the `<entry node>`. There may be arbitrary whitespace after the colon and period, as usual in menus, and may be broken across lines. Here is an example:

```
 ^@^H[index^@^H]
 * Menu:


 * thunder:           Weather Phenomena.          (line 5)
```

This means that an index entry for 'thunder' appears at line 5 of the node 'Weather Phenomena'.

F.2.4 Info Format: Cross Reference

A general cross reference in Info format has one of the following two forms:

```
    <cross-reference> =
  * (N|n)ote <id>::
| * (N|n)ote <label>:<id>(.|,)


    <id> = (<lparen><infofile><rparen>)?(<nodename>)?
    <label> = <del>?<label text><del>?
```

No space should occur between the '*' character and the following 'N' or 'n'. '*Note' should be used at the start of a sentence, otherwise '*note' should be used. (Some Info readers, such as the one in Emacs, can display '*Note' and '*note' as 'See' and 'see' respectively.) In both cases, <label text> is descriptive text.

In both forms the <id> refers to a node or anchor, in the same way as a reference in the node information line does (see [Info Format Regular Nodes], page 283). The optional parenthesized '<infofile>' is the filename of the manual being referenced, and the <nodename> is the node or anchor within that manual,

The second form has a descriptive label. A cross-reference in this form should be terminated with a comma or period, to make it feasible to find the end of the <id>.

The format does not prescribe how to find other manuals to resolve such references.

Here are some examples:

```
 *note GNU Free Documentation License::
 *note Tag table: Info Format Tag Table, for details.
 *Note Overview: (make)Top.
```

The first shows a reference to a node in the current manual using the short form.

The second also refers to a node in the current manual, namely 'Info Format Tag Table'; the 'Tag table' before the ':' is only a label on this particular reference, and the 'for details.' is text belonging to the sentence, not part of the reference.

The third example refers to the node 'Top' in another manual, namely 'make', with 'Overview' being the label for this cross reference.

See Chapter 8 [Cross References], page 66.

Appendix G GNU Free Documentation License

Version 1.3, 3 November 2008

Copyright © 2000, 2001, 2002, 2007, 2008 Free Software Foundation, Inc.
`http://fsf.org/`

Everyone is permitted to copy and distribute verbatim copies
of this license document, but changing it is not allowed.

0. PREAMBLE

The purpose of this License is to make a manual, textbook, or other functional and useful document *free* in the sense of freedom: to assure everyone the effective freedom to copy and redistribute it, with or without modifying it, either commercially or non-commercially. Secondarily, this License preserves for the author and publisher a way to get credit for their work, while not being considered responsible for modifications made by others.

This License is a kind of "copyleft", which means that derivative works of the document must themselves be free in the same sense. It complements the GNU General Public License, which is a copyleft license designed for free software.

We have designed this License in order to use it for manuals for free software, because free software needs free documentation: a free program should come with manuals providing the same freedoms that the software does. But this License is not limited to software manuals; it can be used for any textual work, regardless of subject matter or whether it is published as a printed book. We recommend this License principally for works whose purpose is instruction or reference.

1. APPLICABILITY AND DEFINITIONS

This License applies to any manual or other work, in any medium, that contains a notice placed by the copyright holder saying it can be distributed under the terms of this License. Such a notice grants a world-wide, royalty-free license, unlimited in duration, to use that work under the conditions stated herein. The "Document", below, refers to any such manual or work. Any member of the public is a licensee, and is addressed as "you". You accept the license if you copy, modify or distribute the work in a way requiring permission under copyright law.

A "Modified Version" of the Document means any work containing the Document or a portion of it, either copied verbatim, or with modifications and/or translated into another language.

A "Secondary Section" is a named appendix or a front-matter section of the Document that deals exclusively with the relationship of the publishers or authors of the Document to the Document's overall subject (or to related matters) and contains nothing that could fall directly within that overall subject. (Thus, if the Document is in part a textbook of mathematics, a Secondary Section may not explain any mathematics.) The relationship could be a matter of historical connection with the subject or with related matters, or of legal, commercial, philosophical, ethical or political position regarding them.

The "Invariant Sections" are certain Secondary Sections whose titles are designated, as being those of Invariant Sections, in the notice that says that the Document is released under this License. If a section does not fit the above definition of Secondary then it is not allowed to be designated as Invariant. The Document may contain zero Invariant Sections. If the Document does not identify any Invariant Sections then there are none.

The "Cover Texts" are certain short passages of text that are listed, as Front-Cover Texts or Back-Cover Texts, in the notice that says that the Document is released under this License. A Front-Cover Text may be at most 5 words, and a Back-Cover Text may be at most 25 words.

A "Transparent" copy of the Document means a machine-readable copy, represented in a format whose specification is available to the general public, that is suitable for revising the document straightforwardly with generic text editors or (for images composed of pixels) generic paint programs or (for drawings) some widely available drawing editor, and that is suitable for input to text formatters or for automatic translation to a variety of formats suitable for input to text formatters. A copy made in an otherwise Transparent file format whose markup, or absence of markup, has been arranged to thwart or discourage subsequent modification by readers is not Transparent. An image format is not Transparent if used for any substantial amount of text. A copy that is not "Transparent" is called "Opaque".

Examples of suitable formats for Transparent copies include plain ASCII without markup, Texinfo input format, LaTeX input format, SGML or XML using a publicly available DTD, and standard-conforming simple HTML, PostScript or PDF designed for human modification. Examples of transparent image formats include PNG, XCF and JPG. Opaque formats include proprietary formats that can be read and edited only by proprietary word processors, SGML or XML for which the DTD and/or processing tools are not generally available, and the machine-generated HTML, PostScript or PDF produced by some word processors for output purposes only.

The "Title Page" means, for a printed book, the title page itself, plus such following pages as are needed to hold, legibly, the material this License requires to appear in the title page. For works in formats which do not have any title page as such, "Title Page" means the text near the most prominent appearance of the work's title, preceding the beginning of the body of the text.

The "publisher" means any person or entity that distributes copies of the Document to the public.

A section "Entitled XYZ" means a named subunit of the Document whose title either is precisely XYZ or contains XYZ in parentheses following text that translates XYZ in another language. (Here XYZ stands for a specific section name mentioned below, such as "Acknowledgements", "Dedications", "Endorsements", or "History".) To "Preserve the Title" of such a section when you modify the Document means that it remains a section "Entitled XYZ" according to this definition.

The Document may include Warranty Disclaimers next to the notice which states that this License applies to the Document. These Warranty Disclaimers are considered to be included by reference in this License, but only as regards disclaiming warranties: any other implication that these Warranty Disclaimers may have is void and has no effect on the meaning of this License.

2. VERBATIM COPYING

You may copy and distribute the Document in any medium, either commercially or noncommercially, provided that this License, the copyright notices, and the license notice saying this License applies to the Document are reproduced in all copies, and that you add no other conditions whatsoever to those of this License. You may not use technical measures to obstruct or control the reading or further copying of the copies you make or distribute. However, you may accept compensation in exchange for copies. If you distribute a large enough number of copies you must also follow the conditions in section 3.

You may also lend copies, under the same conditions stated above, and you may publicly display copies.

3. COPYING IN QUANTITY

If you publish printed copies (or copies in media that commonly have printed covers) of the Document, numbering more than 100, and the Document's license notice requires Cover Texts, you must enclose the copies in covers that carry, clearly and legibly, all these Cover Texts: Front-Cover Texts on the front cover, and Back-Cover Texts on the back cover. Both covers must also clearly and legibly identify you as the publisher of these copies. The front cover must present the full title with all words of the title equally prominent and visible. You may add other material on the covers in addition. Copying with changes limited to the covers, as long as they preserve the title of the Document and satisfy these conditions, can be treated as verbatim copying in other respects.

If the required texts for either cover are too voluminous to fit legibly, you should put the first ones listed (as many as fit reasonably) on the actual cover, and continue the rest onto adjacent pages.

If you publish or distribute Opaque copies of the Document numbering more than 100, you must either include a machine-readable Transparent copy along with each Opaque copy, or state in or with each Opaque copy a computer-network location from which the general network-using public has access to download using public-standard network protocols a complete Transparent copy of the Document, free of added material. If you use the latter option, you must take reasonably prudent steps, when you begin distribution of Opaque copies in quantity, to ensure that this Transparent copy will remain thus accessible at the stated location until at least one year after the last time you distribute an Opaque copy (directly or through your agents or retailers) of that edition to the public.

It is requested, but not required, that you contact the authors of the Document well before redistributing any large number of copies, to give them a chance to provide you with an updated version of the Document.

4. MODIFICATIONS

You may copy and distribute a Modified Version of the Document under the conditions of sections 2 and 3 above, provided that you release the Modified Version under precisely this License, with the Modified Version filling the role of the Document, thus licensing distribution and modification of the Modified Version to whoever possesses a copy of it. In addition, you must do these things in the Modified Version:

A. Use in the Title Page (and on the covers, if any) a title distinct from that of the Document, and from those of previous versions (which should, if there were any, be listed in the History section of the Document). You may use the same title as a previous version if the original publisher of that version gives permission.

B. List on the Title Page, as authors, one or more persons or entities responsible for authorship of the modifications in the Modified Version, together with at least five of the principal authors of the Document (all of its principal authors, if it has fewer than five), unless they release you from this requirement.

C. State on the Title page the name of the publisher of the Modified Version, as the publisher.

D. Preserve all the copyright notices of the Document.

E. Add an appropriate copyright notice for your modifications adjacent to the other copyright notices.

F. Include, immediately after the copyright notices, a license notice giving the public permission to use the Modified Version under the terms of this License, in the form shown in the Addendum below.

G. Preserve in that license notice the full lists of Invariant Sections and required Cover Texts given in the Document's license notice.

H. Include an unaltered copy of this License.

I. Preserve the section Entitled "History", Preserve its Title, and add to it an item stating at least the title, year, new authors, and publisher of the Modified Version as given on the Title Page. If there is no section Entitled "History" in the Document, create one stating the title, year, authors, and publisher of the Document as given on its Title Page, then add an item describing the Modified Version as stated in the previous sentence.

J. Preserve the network location, if any, given in the Document for public access to a Transparent copy of the Document, and likewise the network locations given in the Document for previous versions it was based on. These may be placed in the "History" section. You may omit a network location for a work that was published at least four years before the Document itself, or if the original publisher of the version it refers to gives permission.

K. For any section Entitled "Acknowledgements" or "Dedications", Preserve the Title of the section, and preserve in the section all the substance and tone of each of the contributor acknowledgements and/or dedications given therein.

L. Preserve all the Invariant Sections of the Document, unaltered in their text and in their titles. Section numbers or the equivalent are not considered part of the section titles.

M. Delete any section Entitled "Endorsements". Such a section may not be included in the Modified Version.

N. Do not retitle any existing section to be Entitled "Endorsements" or to conflict in title with any Invariant Section.

O. Preserve any Warranty Disclaimers.

If the Modified Version includes new front-matter sections or appendices that qualify as Secondary Sections and contain no material copied from the Document, you may at your option designate some or all of these sections as invariant. To do this, add their titles to the list of Invariant Sections in the Modified Version's license notice. These titles must be distinct from any other section titles.

You may add a section Entitled "Endorsements", provided it contains nothing but endorsements of your Modified Version by various parties—for example, statements of peer review or that the text has been approved by an organization as the authoritative definition of a standard.

You may add a passage of up to five words as a Front-Cover Text, and a passage of up to 25 words as a Back-Cover Text, to the end of the list of Cover Texts in the Modified Version. Only one passage of Front-Cover Text and one of Back-Cover Text may be added by (or through arrangements made by) any one entity. If the Document already includes a cover text for the same cover, previously added by you or by arrangement made by the same entity you are acting on behalf of, you may not add another; but you may replace the old one, on explicit permission from the previous publisher that added the old one.

The author(s) and publisher(s) of the Document do not by this License give permission to use their names for publicity for or to assert or imply endorsement of any Modified Version.

5. COMBINING DOCUMENTS

You may combine the Document with other documents released under this License, under the terms defined in section 4 above for modified versions, provided that you include in the combination all of the Invariant Sections of all of the original documents, unmodified, and list them all as Invariant Sections of your combined work in its license notice, and that you preserve all their Warranty Disclaimers.

The combined work need only contain one copy of this License, and multiple identical Invariant Sections may be replaced with a single copy. If there are multiple Invariant Sections with the same name but different contents, make the title of each such section unique by adding at the end of it, in parentheses, the name of the original author or publisher of that section if known, or else a unique number. Make the same adjustment to the section titles in the list of Invariant Sections in the license notice of the combined work.

In the combination, you must combine any sections Entitled "History" in the various original documents, forming one section Entitled "History"; likewise combine any sections Entitled "Acknowledgements", and any sections Entitled "Dedications". You must delete all sections Entitled "Endorsements."

6. COLLECTIONS OF DOCUMENTS

You may make a collection consisting of the Document and other documents released under this License, and replace the individual copies of this License in the various documents with a single copy that is included in the collection, provided that you follow the rules of this License for verbatim copying of each of the documents in all other respects.

You may extract a single document from such a collection, and distribute it individually under this License, provided you insert a copy of this License into the extracted document, and follow this License in all other respects regarding verbatim copying of that document.

7. AGGREGATION WITH INDEPENDENT WORKS

A compilation of the Document or its derivatives with other separate and independent documents or works, in or on a volume of a storage or distribution medium, is called an "aggregate" if the copyright resulting from the compilation is not used to limit the legal rights of the compilation's users beyond what the individual works permit. When the Document is included in an aggregate, this License does not apply to the other works in the aggregate which are not themselves derivative works of the Document.

If the Cover Text requirement of section 3 is applicable to these copies of the Document, then if the Document is less than one half of the entire aggregate, the Document's Cover Texts may be placed on covers that bracket the Document within the aggregate, or the electronic equivalent of covers if the Document is in electronic form. Otherwise they must appear on printed covers that bracket the whole aggregate.

8. TRANSLATION

Translation is considered a kind of modification, so you may distribute translations of the Document under the terms of section 4. Replacing Invariant Sections with translations requires special permission from their copyright holders, but you may include translations of some or all Invariant Sections in addition to the original versions of these Invariant Sections. You may include a translation of this License, and all the license notices in the Document, and any Warranty Disclaimers, provided that you also include the original English version of this License and the original versions of those notices and disclaimers. In case of a disagreement between the translation and the original version of this License or a notice or disclaimer, the original version will prevail.

If a section in the Document is Entitled "Acknowledgements", "Dedications", or "History", the requirement (section 4) to Preserve its Title (section 1) will typically require changing the actual title.

9. TERMINATION

You may not copy, modify, sublicense, or distribute the Document except as expressly provided under this License. Any attempt otherwise to copy, modify, sublicense, or distribute it is void, and will automatically terminate your rights under this License.

However, if you cease all violation of this License, then your license from a particular copyright holder is reinstated (a) provisionally, unless and until the copyright holder explicitly and finally terminates your license, and (b) permanently, if the copyright holder fails to notify you of the violation by some reasonable means prior to 60 days after the cessation.

Moreover, your license from a particular copyright holder is reinstated permanently if the copyright holder notifies you of the violation by some reasonable means, this is the first time you have received notice of violation of this License (for any work) from that copyright holder, and you cure the violation prior to 30 days after your receipt of the notice.

Termination of your rights under this section does not terminate the licenses of parties who have received copies or rights from you under this License. If your rights have been terminated and not permanently reinstated, receipt of a copy of some or all of the same material does not give you any rights to use it.

10. FUTURE REVISIONS OF THIS LICENSE

The Free Software Foundation may publish new, revised versions of the GNU Free Documentation License from time to time. Such new versions will be similar in spirit to the present version, but may differ in detail to address new problems or concerns. See `http://www.gnu.org/copyleft/`.

Each version of the License is given a distinguishing version number. If the Document specifies that a particular numbered version of this License "or any later version" applies to it, you have the option of following the terms and conditions either of that specified version or of any later version that has been published (not as a draft) by the Free Software Foundation. If the Document does not specify a version number of this License, you may choose any version ever published (not as a draft) by the Free Software Foundation. If the Document specifies that a proxy can decide which future versions of this License can be used, that proxy's public statement of acceptance of a version permanently authorizes you to choose that version for the Document.

11. RELICENSING

"Massive Multiauthor Collaboration Site" (or "MMC Site") means any World Wide Web server that publishes copyrightable works and also provides prominent facilities for anybody to edit those works. A public wiki that anybody can edit is an example of such a server. A "Massive Multiauthor Collaboration" (or "MMC") contained in the site means any set of copyrightable works thus published on the MMC site.

"CC-BY-SA" means the Creative Commons Attribution-Share Alike 3.0 license published by Creative Commons Corporation, a not-for-profit corporation with a principal place of business in San Francisco, California, as well as future copyleft versions of that license published by that same organization.

"Incorporate" means to publish or republish a Document, in whole or in part, as part of another Document.

An MMC is "eligible for relicensing" if it is licensed under this License, and if all works that were first published under this License somewhere other than this MMC, and subsequently incorporated in whole or in part into the MMC, (1) had no cover texts or invariant sections, and (2) were thus incorporated prior to November 1, 2008.

The operator of an MMC Site may republish an MMC contained in the site under CC-BY-SA on the same site at any time before August 1, 2009, provided the MMC is eligible for relicensing.

ADDENDUM: How to use this License for your documents

To use this License in a document you have written, include a copy of the License in the document and put the following copyright and license notices just after the title page:

```
Copyright (C)  year  your name.
Permission is granted to copy, distribute and/or modify this document
under the terms of the GNU Free Documentation License, Version 1.3
or any later version published by the Free Software Foundation;
with no Invariant Sections, no Front-Cover Texts, and no Back-Cover
Texts.  A copy of the license is included in the section entitled ``GNU
Free Documentation License''.
```

If you have Invariant Sections, Front-Cover Texts and Back-Cover Texts, replace the "with...Texts." line with this:

```
with the Invariant Sections being list their titles, with
the Front-Cover Texts being list, and with the Back-Cover Texts
being list.
```

If you have Invariant Sections without Cover Texts, or some other combination of the three, merge those two alternatives to suit the situation.

If your document contains nontrivial examples of program code, we recommend releasing these examples in parallel under your choice of free software license, such as the GNU General Public License, to permit their use in free software.

Command and Variable Index

This is an alphabetical list of all the @-commands, assorted Emacs Lisp functions, and several variables. To make the list easier to use, the commands are listed without their preceding '@'.

key.. 81
kindex..................................... 114

L

l.. 125
LaTeX 128
lbracechar{} (literal '{')................... 119
leq 130
lisp 93
listoffloats............................... 108
lowersections 52
L.. 125

M

macro 165
majorheading 49
makeinfo-buffer........................... 213
makeinfo-kill-job 214
makeinfo-recenter-output-buffer 214
makeinfo-region........................... 213
math 127
menu 62
minus 129
move_index_entries_after_items 209
multitable................................ 104

N

need 138
next-error 213
node 54
noindent 97
novalidate 179

O

o... 125
occur 278
occur-mode-goto-occurrence................ 20
oddfooting 271
oddfootingmarks........................... 273
oddheading 271
oddheadingmarks 273
oe.. 125
OE.. 125
ogonek 124
option 84
ordf 125
ordm 125
O... 125

P

page 137
page, within @titlepage................... 35
pagesizes.................................. 186

paragraphindent 43
parse 199
part 51
pdf 199
phoo 171
pindex 114
plaintexinfo 199
plaintext 199
point 132
pounds 129
print 131
printindex................................. 45
ps.. 199
pxref 73

Q

questiondown 125
quotation 90
quotedblbase 126
quotedblleft 126
quotedblright 126
quoteleft.................................. 126
quoteright 126
quotesinglbase............................. 126

R

r (roman font)............................. 88
raggedright 96
raisesections 52
rawtext.................................... 199
rbracechar{} (literal '}').................. 119
ref... 73
refill...................................... 250
regenerate_master_menu.................... 209
registeredsymbol.......................... 128
result 130
ringaccent 124
rmacro 166

S

samp 82
sansserif (sans serif font)................ 88
sc (small caps font) 87
section.................................... 49
set 159
setchapternewpage 41
setcontentsaftertitlepage 39
setfilename 31
setshortcontentsaftertitlepage............ 39
settitle................................... 32
shortcaption 108
shortcontents 38
shorttitlepage 35
simple_menu 209
slanted (slanted font) 88

X

General Index

D

J

K

L

P

Q

R

W

X

Y

Z

www.ingramcontent.com/pod-product-compliance
Lightning Source LLC
LaVergne TN
LVHW060135070326

832902LV00018B/2813